Bulk Sales

Que Publishing offers excellent discounts on this book when ordered in quantity for bulk purchases or special sales. For more information, please contact

U.S. Corporate and Government Sales
1-800-382-3419
corpsales@pearsontechgroup.com

For sales outside of the U.S., please contact

International Sales
international@pearson.com

This Book Is Safari Enabled

The Safari® Enabled icon on the cover of your favorite technology book means the book is available through Safari Bookshelf. When you buy this book, you get free access to the online edition for 45 days.

Safari Bookshelf is an electronic reference library that lets you easily search thousands of technical books, find code samples, download chapters, and access technical information whenever and wherever you need it.

To gain 45-day Safari Enabled access to this book:

- Go to http://www.informit.com/onlineedition
- Complete the brief registration form
- Enter the coupon code T5AV-BXDC-JT7G-IVCD-GKAH

If you have difficulty registering on Safari Bookshelf or accessing the online edition, please email customer-service@safaribooksonline.com.

Contents at a Glance

Windows
LOCKDOWN!

Your XP and Vista Guide Against Hacks, Attacks, and Other Internet Mayhem

Andy Walker

800 East 96th Street,
Indianapolis, Indiana 46240

Windows Lockdown! Your XP and Vista Guide Against Hacks, Attacks, and Other Internet Mayhem

Copyright © 2009 by Pearson Education, Inc.

ISBN-13: 978-0-7897-3672-7
ISBN-10: 0-7897-3672-1

Library of Congress Cataloging-in-Publication data is on file.

Printed in the United States of America

First Printing: July 2008

Trademarks

Associate Publisher
Greg Wiegand

Acquisitions Editor
Rick Kughen

Development Editor
Rick Kughen

Managing Editor
Patrick Kanouse

Project Editor
Mandie Frank

Copy Editor
Margaret Berson

Indexer
Ken Johnson

Proofreader
Matt Purcell

Technical Editor
Mark Reddin

Publishing Coordinator
Cindy Teeters

Designer
Ann Jones

Composition
Mark Shirar

Table of Contents

About the Author

Andy Walker is one of North America's top technology journalists and is the author of three books published by Que including *Microsoft Windows Vista Help Desk*. Since 1995, he has written about personal technology for dozens of newspapers, magazines, and websites. His personal technology advice column was syndicated across Canada and today the body of work is published at Cyberwalker.com where more than 5 million unique visitors read the advice annually. Andy has appeared as a tech expert on hundreds of TV and radio broadcasts and he also co-hosted the internationally syndicated TV show "Call for Help" with Leo Laporte.

Andy hosts and produces the acclaimed Internet video show "Lab Rats" at www.labrats.tv and appears weekly on the TV show "HomePage" on the Canadian news channel CP24. He also stars in his own technology teaching DVD called "Getting Started with Windows Vista." You can get more info at www.gettingstartedvideo.com.

Andy was born in the United Kingdom, educated and raised in Canada, and now lives in Toronto with two cats and a really secure personal computer.

Dedication

This book is fondly dedicated to my niece Asia Ramesh and my nephew Oliver Jessup Walker-Kim.

Acknowledgments

This book was made possible by the hard work and support of some amazing people. I want to take a moment of your time to acknowledge them:

To my development editor Rick Kughen at Pearson. You continue to show remarkable patience and understanding with me. Thank you for being a champion of my projects at Que.

To the team at Pearson who developed this book. Thanks for your dedication and talent in making this book as great as it is.

To my agent Sam Hiyate at The Rights Factory. Thank you for your tireless promotion of my work and championing my career and my bestselling future.

To Ted Gallardo, my assistant on this book, who provided superb background research and commentary for this book and is one of the hardest-working geeks I know.

To the team at Cyberwalker.com: Craig, Pedro, Peter, Jason, Ted, Gary, and Mike for keeping the site running ever so smoothly when I am off writing yet another book.

To Sean Carruthers, my co-host on Lab Rats, who is a depthless resource and lets me shamelessly promote my books on the show, always with good humor.

To Darren Weir, my producer at CP24, a remarkable television professional who keeps me and my books in front of a TV audience week in and week out.

To Gregory and Dorothy Walker, my parents, and my ever-expanding family, for their love and unwavering support.

And to you, my dear readers, who bought this book and are always hungry for more.

We Want to Hear from You!

As the reader of this book, *you* are our most important critic and commentator. We value your opinion and want to know what we're doing right, what we could do better, what areas you'd like to see us publish in, and any other words of wisdom you're willing to pass our way.

As an associate publisher for Que Publishing, I welcome your comments. You can email or write me directly to let me know what you did or didn't like about this book—as well as what we can do to make our books better.

Please note that I cannot help you with technical problems related to the topic of this book. We do have a User Services group, however, where I will forward specific technical questions related to the book.

When you write, please be sure to include this book's title and author as well as your name, email address, and phone number. I will carefully review your comments and share them with the author and editors who worked on the book.

Email: feedback@quepublishing.com

Mail: Greg Wiegand
Associate Publisher
Que Publishing
800 East 96th Street
Indianapolis, IN 46240 USA

Reader Services

Visit our website and register this book at informit.com/register for convenient access to any updates, downloads, or errata that might be available for this book.

Introduction: Ignore This Book at Your Own Peril!

As I started to write this introduction, a disturbing statistic arrived in my inbox. Security software maker F-Secure reported that the total number of viruses and Trojans will hit one million by 2009.

One million viruses! That's astounding. Now for the good news: The reason so many are being written is that it's become more difficult for these infections to succeed in infecting systems. That's because security practices have been improved. Computer owners are more educated. Security software is increasingly effective. We are simply more savvy about computer security. And that's great!

In response, the bad guys are shifting their strategies and using new tools to make their malware more effective against us. So while much has changed since I wrote the first edition of this book, much is still the same. The hacks, attacks, and scams keep coming.

So sitting back smugly is not the thing to do now. It's clear to me that we have to always be one step ahead in this game. And that's why I wrote this book.

The first version of this book was first released in 2005 as the *Absolute Beginner's Guide to Security, Spam, Spyware, and Viruses*. Back then it had become clear that malware had shifted from being an ego trip for its authors to a source of revenue. Viruses and spyware and other electronic trickery, like phishing and spam, made money for their authors.

This book builds on the original book, expanding on what has changed since 2005—like the arrival of Windows Vista—and adding lots more useful information.

In this book, I'll show you how to cleanse your computer, halt further infections, sidestep scams, do major damage control, plan for the future, and lock down Windows XP and Vista nice and tight.

To that end, I've updated and added new content to every chapter and written two new ones, including Chapter 3 on rootkits, and Chapter 8 on how to remove infections.

By the time you get through the whole book, you'll not only be able to protect yourself and your family from the threats out there on the Internet, but you'll be well equipped to help your grandma, your friends, your co-workers, and anyone who owns a computer and is not properly protected.

So congratulations on picking up this book, because it shows a commitment to the malware writer that you will not be defeated. There may be one million malware programs out there, but they'll have to write even more to keep up with us.

I say bring on the next million!

How This Book Is Organized

Chapter 1—Viruses: Attack of the Malicious Programs

In this first and vividly exciting chapter, I tell you what viruses are, why they are a problem, and how to get rid of them. Plus, you will learn secrets, such as the real reason people write viruses in the first place.

Chapter 2—Spyware: Overrun by Advertisers, Hijackers, and Opportunists

Spyware is a modern-day computer pandemic. Your computer is probably rife with this malware. Bad companies are making money with it learning what you do on your computer. At the same time, spyware is also slowing your computer down. Most people experience a 30%–50% performance boost when they get rid of spyware for the first time. How's that for an upsell?

Chapter 3—Rootkits: Sneaky, Stealthy Toolboxes

Root kits were made famous by Sony's blundering move to sneak them onto computers using their music CDs. But the problem is much bigger than that. Learn why rootkits, when used by malware writers, make it difficult to remove infections.

Chapter 4—Hackers: There's a Man in My Machine

Who are the hackers? And why do they want to get into your computer? I tell you why and then show you how to shut them out. And I make a good joke about cheese in this chapter.

Chapter 5—Identity Thieves and Phishers: Protect Your Good Name and Bank Account

These people are going to suck your bank account dry. And they trick you into helping them do it. I show you how to stop them.

Chapter 6—Spam: Unwanted Email from Hell

Junk mail is a deluge, but like a Shop Vac on spilled ketchup, it's easy to clean up. I'll show you how in only a few pages.

Chapter 7—Wireless Network Snoops: Lock Down Your Wi-Fi Network

Let's pretend you're free of all the other nasties in this book, but I bet if you have a wireless home network, your neighbors are using your Internet connection and maybe even snooping in places they shouldn't be inside your computer. I help you stop them.

Chapter 8—Damage Control: How to Remove Viruses and Spyware

This is the chapter you go to after shrieking: "Oh no! I have a virus!" Most people will buy this book for this chapter alone because I show you how to get rid of an infection here.

Chapter 9—Ground Up Security: Wipe Your Hard Drive and Build a Secure Windows PC from the Ground Up

When all else fails, you can always wipe your system clean and start fresh. This chapter shows you how to scrub your system and rebuild it so it really is locked down!

Chapter 10—Ongoing Maintenance: Fend Off Future Threats!

Learn what you need to do to keep your system running infection-free for the rest of your days. Lots of cool strategies that are easy to learn.

Chapter 11—Selecting Software: Steals, Deals, and Software Duds

Next, I'll go over what the story is with lots of different security software. Do you have to buy it or can you get it all free?

Chapter 12—Tools of the Trade: Security Products You Should Own

And in the final chapter I'll tell you what software is really good and where to get it.

Glossary: Computer Threat Lingo

Also, my talented assistant, Ted Gallardo has written the best and most exciting glossary you have ever read. It's really scintillating and has been nominated for glossary of the year.

Special Elements Used in this Book

You'll also see a lot of help in the margins of this book. Here's how it looks and what it means.

note **Notes**—This is stuff that I figured I should tell you when it popped into my head. Notes aren't essential reading, but I urge you not to skip them as you'll learn a lot of extra stuff here that you might not find elsewhere.

tip **Tips**—These succulent bits of info should help you with odd problems or give you insight into issues that are confusing. Don't skip these! Here, you'll find faster ways to accomplish tasks, insider tidbits, and expert tips I've accumulated along the way.

caution **Cautions**—These blurbs keep you out of trouble. I hope. If you don't read these, you're asking for trouble. Security is risky business. I've done my best to point out common pitfalls, gotchas, and other assorted nasties.

SIDEBARS

Occasionally, I've added some additional information that's ancillary to the main topic, but still worth reading. Think of these as important stuff that didn't fit anywhere within the confines of the chapter you're reading, but is too important to skip.

Reader Competition...of Sorts

If you are one of the first 10 people to tell me the name of the guy that wrote the HijackThis program and what page he is mentioned on, I'll send you a copy of my fun and informative DVD, "Getting Started with Windows Vista." Learn more about this blockbuster DVD at www.gettingstartedvideo.com.

When you email me at lockdown@cyberwalker.com, include the answer and your full name, and put "Windows Lockdown Contest" in the subject line.

Finally, if you want to contact me and say nice things, tell me about how you saved your grandma with advice from this book, or send me chocolate cake (which I also love), email me at andy@cyberwalker.com.

PART

I

Security Basics:
Some Very Real Threats

Viruses: Attack of the Malicious Programs

We all know computer viruses are bad. This chapter explains what they are, what they do, and where they come from. It examines all the types that can potentially infect your computer and make your life a living hell. It also covers specialty viruses called worms and Trojan horses. And it looks at how viruses exploit programming bugs in your computer and what to do about it. Of course, the best part is that it shows you how to use the computer equivalent of a sledgehammer to squish them before they leap into your computer and delete your prom photos, steal the contents of your savings account, or turn your computer into a spam factory or a corporate computer killer.

1

What Is a Computer Virus?

Fifteen years ago, viruses were pretty simple. They got into a system and infected a file or two. It was as basic as ordering coffee when coffee was easy to order. "One coffee please—black."

Today, the catalog of viruses you have to defend yourself against is frighteningly complex. In fact, it's become as complex as, well, ordering coffee.

"Looks like you've been infected by a dropper that's put a Trojan on your system, which deployed a multi-partite that opened a backdoor and also infected the master boot record."

Sounds like an order at Starbucks, don't you think?

These days a discussion about a virus can actually occur without using the word *virus* because sometimes viruses are worms or Trojan horses, which are virus-like nasties that act a little different than their infectious cousins.

Don't let all this frighten you, though. It's not that hard to figure out, and defending your computer against viruses is pretty straightforward. Still, if the idea makes you queasy, skip ahead to the part of the chapter about how to easily protect yourself from viruses. But I hope you stick around because the more you know, the geekier you will be. Okay, not really. But understanding them makes them much less scary.

Viruses were one of the first real security threats people had to deal with when personal computers started appearing in homes a couple of decades ago. The first computer viruses were written in the 1980s; however, they really didn't become a big threat until the late 1990s when everyone who owned a personal computer started connecting to the Internet.

note Why are they called computer *viruses*? Because they have similar characteristics to biological viruses that infect humans—in at least one way. The computer variety jumps from computer to computer much like a cold virus jumps from your kids to you, and from you to your spouse.

note Interestingly, viruses were first conceived in 1949, when computer pioneer John von Neumann wrote a paper theorizing that programs could become self-replicating. Von Neumann's theories came to life in the 1950s at Bell Labs where programmers created a game called "Core Wars" in which two players could unleash software "organisms" into the mainframe computer and watch as they competed for control of the machine. It would take more than 30 years for computer viruses to become a threat, but when PCs started becoming commonplace in homes and schools in the early 1980s, computer viruses could replicate and move from computer to computer—first by infected floppies, and later via networked PCs.

Now you know…

Originally, viruses spread via floppy disks or CDs. They would ride on the back of files stored on a disk or in the boot area of the floppy and replicate when the disk was inserted into the computer.

The Internet's popularity has become the chief reason that security on personal computers has become such a hot topic. A Net connection is the off-ramp from the Internet into your computer for all data. And guess what? For viruses it's an express lane.

Before we go any further, let's define what a computer virus is because it's important to understand that before we start smacking them with a hammer. Here's a basic definition:

> A *computer virus* is a malicious computer program that, when executed by an unsuspecting human, performs tasks that primarily include replicating itself and deploying a payload.

Not so hard, right? Let's break it down into easy-to-chew pieces.

What Is It?

> A computer virus is a malicious computer program...

A virus is just a program, but it's written by a person of questionable character who wants to do harm, or more likely these days, earn its author a living through surreptitious means. It's made up of lines of programming instructions and runs like any other program.

Who Triggers a Computer Virus?

> ...that, when executed by an unsuspecting human...

For a virus to be successful, it has to be executed on a computer by a human. That means a file has to be opened, a program has to be run, or a computer has to be booted. In other words, programming code has to be run by a human action. That could be you, me, friends, or family—anyone who uses a computer. This is not to say that anyone executes a virus on purpose. Usually we're tricked into it. But a virus requires a human's help to proliferate. Remembering this fact goes a long way toward preventing viruses from ever running amuck on your computer.

note In 1984, University of New Haven professor Fred Cohen first used the term *computer virus* in a research paper "Experiments with Computer Viruses." Although Cohen is sometimes credited with coining the term, he credits theoretical computer scientist Leonard Adleman with inventing the term.

How Does It Spread?

(It) performs tasks that primarily include replicating itself...

To steal a little lingo from Star Trek, replicating is a virus's prime directive. For a computer virus to be successful by any definition, it must clone itself, make its way into other computers, and repeat the replication cycle. This is how it spreads. Of course, it uses many tricks to do this, including riding on other programs' backs, moving in email as a file attachment, and even downloading from a web page. Virus writers use many methods to move a virus between computers, but you can categorize them into two types:

> **note** There's an exception to this rule—computer worms. They are a type of virus that self-executes and can spread without human intervention. Worms are discussed in more detail later in "Worms: Network-Savvy Viruses," **p. 14.**

> **tip** One worm that gained a fair amount of notoriety a few years ago was called the KakWorm. The Kakworm embedded itself in an HTML email (an email that works like a web page to display pictures and layout). All you need to do to execute it is to preview the email in either Microsoft Outlook or Microsoft Outlook Express. The security hole that allowed this has long since been patched, so it's not much of a threat any more. If you have all your Windows security patches installed you won't get Kakked.

- **External media**—Any storage device that can contain a computer file, such as a floppy disk, USB key, DVD, or CD, and can be connected or inserted into a computer. External media is an antique distribution approach rarely used by virus writers any more.

- **A network connection**—A network is a group of computers connected so they can exchange data. The Internet, which is the most common source of viruses these days, is a large network. Viruses use the connection to arrive via chat programs, as an email attachment, or via the Web. These days, if your computer is not connected to the Internet, you are mostly (but not completely) safe from viruses. It's not a realistic defense strategy, however.

DON'T SNEEZE ON MY PC AND GIVE IT A VIRUS!

In the early 1990s, when people started buying personal computers for the home, a very concerned woman stopped me in the hall at work one day in a bit of a tizzy. Her home computer had been infected by a virus and her husband was blaming her. But she couldn't understand how that might have happened. "I didn't sneeze on the computer," she said, puzzled. "I had a cold, but I was very careful. How did it jump from me and get into the computer?"

Of course, a computer virus and a human virus are not the same thing. The virus that gives you the sniffles is a tiny living organism that gets inside your body and makes you sick.

A computer virus, on the other hand, is a program. It's designed to find its way inside a computer, often without your permission or knowledge, using a very specific set of instructions.

I explained that to her, and, calmer, she went home to tell her husband, who refused to believe the explanation and continued to keep sick people away from his precious virus-free computer.

What Damage Can It Do?

...and deploys a payload.

This last piece of the definition is the scariest part. A virus can be (and usually is) programmed to do bad things. This part of the virus is called a *payload*, or sometimes referred to as a *bomb*.

Here are the most common payloads:

- **Jokes or vandalism**—Sometimes virus writers just want you to know they have succeeded in getting a virus into your computer. So they post messages or alerts to your computer. It's the equivalent of writing "Andy has a cute bum" on a bus shelter. It might not be true, but it's slightly amusing (at least to its author).

note The Melissa virus had a curious payload that executed every hour. When the day of the month equaled the minute value, the following text appeared at the computer's cursor: "Twenty-two points, plus triple-word score, plus fifty points for using all my letters. Game's over. I'm outta here." The quote, which refers to the game of Scrabble, is taken from a Simpsons episode.

1

- **Data destruction or corruption**—Viruses can infect files and damage them or make them unusable. They can also wipe out entire hard drives.

- **Spam distribution**—One of the most common payloads in viruses today are infections that send spam from your computer. This takes the heat off the perpetrator when angry spam recipients trace unwanted email back to its source. Spam gets sent from *your* computer and *you* get the blame. Or a virus can also open up a door so someone can come along later to take control of your computer and use it remotely for their purposes. The mass-mailing worm known as Sober.P sends an email enticing people to open an email attachment. The worm then steals email addresses from the victim and blasts spam at the victim's contacts.

> **note** In late July 2007, the largest virus attack security experts had seen in two years started. Over a period of a week, two million spam e-mails laden with the Storm worm started arriving in inboxes across the Internet (during the attack 42 million emails were detected in one day). They contained attachments that purported to be an electronic greeting card but contained a malware infection that added the target computer to a botnet. A *botnet* is a remote-controlled network of infected computers that can be used by malware writers for nefarious purposes.

- **Data or information theft**—Viruses can deploy payloads that monitor and steal data or personal information from your computer.

- **Hijacking**—Your computer can be infected with a program that can be called from the Internet to achieve a task by the malware writer (or a client he has sold it to). Tasks include sending spam, bombarding another computer with nonsense data, or mining personal data. Malware writers can command a network of bots. When your system is infected with a bot, it is a soldier in an army of bots called a botnet. The botnet can be commanded like an army by the malware creator or the person he sells it to.

- **Ransomware**—A fairly new and rather nasty payload has been detected that can hold your data ransom. It encrypts (scrambles) part of your hard drive so you can't get at it without typing in a password. The virus leaves a ransom note for

> **note** A botnet is a powerful tool. If directed at one particular web server, it can crash the computer by bombarding it with packets of data. Victims of an attack from a botnet include CNN, Yahoo!, and Amazon.com. This strategy is called a *Distributed Denial of Service (DDoS) attack*.

you that says the data will be unlocked if you pay a ransom. So far, ransomware attacks have been rare. The first was discovered in May 2005. In the summer of 2007, the FBI reported that attacks were on the rise. They could become widespread as virus writers figure out how to perfect the extortion and cover their tracks (so the ransom payment can't be tracked to them).

> **note** In one ransomware attack, an employee of a targeted company visited a website that had been hacked. The site dropped a Trojan horse on the victim's network through vulnerability in the Internet Explorer web browser. The malware searched all of the system directories and mapped drives and then encrypted its files, left the ransom note, and deleted itself.

■ **Virus and spyware distribution**—Your computer can be harnessed to redistribute viruses and spyware to your friends, family, and business contacts.

> **note** Some people will tell you that viruses can purportedly overheat and damage computer hardware by turning off cooling systems. If this has been done, its success has been limited. I think this is a myth.

Viruses: As Many Kinds As Sniffles in Kindergarten

So far I've been using the word *virus* fairly liberally. And for sheer practicality, it's handy to have a catch-all word that more or less covers what we're talking about. Some self-righteous sticklers, however, will poke you with a pointy stick if you use the term *virus* too broadly.

If you start ranting across your corn flakes about how viruses spread on their own, inevitably a stickler will pipe up: "Actually, that's not a virus."

"Yes, it is," you might say indignantly.

"No, it's not," he'll say as he spoons his cereal. "That's a worm."

A worm?

Yeah, bad news here. Not all viruses are viruses.

I know that's confusing, but so is a man in a clingy dress. Bear with me a sec—we'll get to the bottom of this.

To say "I have a *virus*" is sort of like saying "I am having *meat* for dinner" as opposed to "I am having quail with a tasty pistachio butter." The word *virus* is often used as a generic term to describe all malicious computer files that do bad stuff to your computer, but note that the word *virus* is specific to malicious programs that need human intervention to run.

So let's talk about the different types and all their trimmings, and then I'll cover viruses' evil cousins: worms, Trojan Horses, and virus hoaxes.

Macro Viruses

A *macro language* is computer programming built into a larger program. It's used to automate tasks. For example, a Microsoft Word macro can be written to format an entire document or share the contents of a Word file with other Microsoft Office programs (meaning that instead of performing multiple steps to format and share a Word file, you simply run a macro and it automates the entire process). Windows has a few built-in macro languages (sometimes called scripting languages) as do Microsoft Office, Corel WordPerfect Office, and other productivity software programs

A macro can be as short as a few lines of programming code, or it can be a massive program that contains zillions of instructions. And it can be designed to run as soon as a file is opened. It's not surprising that virus writers saw this technology as a great opportunity to deploy their malicious software. And sure enough, they have been exploiting this feature feverishly in the last half decade or so.

The basic strategy has been to generate a virus in a macro and then send a file with a macro embedded as an email attachment. The secret to making this work is, once again, people. A virus writer has to also convince someone to start the macro so the virus can execute and proliferate.

I DON'T LOVE YOU, BUT MY VIRUS DOES

The best viruses are ones that convince people to help spread them. This is a form of what security experts call *social engineering*. It's a term used to describe a technique of tricking people into revealing information or compromising computer security voluntarily. Social engineering is used by virus writers to convince people to deploy viruses. If I sent you an email that said "I love you," you'd open it, if only to satisfy your curiosity. Or maybe you are secretly in love with me. (Okay, maybe not—you only bought my book. What was I thinking?) Anyway, that's what the I Love You worm (dubbed the Love Bug) did back in 2000. And many love-starved people opened the "love letter" attached to the email only to infect their computers. They had been socially engineered.

1

One of the most famous macro viruses is called Melissa, purportedly named after an exotic dancer the virus writer was rather taken with. The virus became famous because of the speed with which it spread. Within three days of its release, Melissa (the virus, not the woman) had infected 100,000 computers.

Melissa spread by arriving as an email with an infected Word document attached with the message "Here's the document you asked for…don't show it to anyone else ;->." When it was opened the virus code executed and sent an email to the first 50 entries in a victim's Outlook email address book.

The Scary Stuff

Unlike other viruses, macro viruses infect documents or document templates. Still, they can do substantial damage to a system by turning off security programs, including antivirus applications. A macro virus can generate unusual system behavior including random beeping and sending rude or cryptic messages. It can also modify the Windows Registry or destroy data.

The Windows Registry is a filing cabinet in Windows that keeps track of a zillion settings that makes Windows what it is. It's so important that in case it gets damaged or deleted, Windows keeps a backup. However, if both get corrupted, Windows will not start.

Perhaps the worst impact of a macro virus is the annoyance factor. It wastes your time and, in widespread outbreaks, can force companies to shut down their systems and networks until the problem is dealt with.

Webopedia.com suggests that 75% of the world's active viruses are macro viruses. It's the virus you are most likely to come into contact with because macro viruses spread as attachments to email.

> **caution** In Windows XP, you can look in your system's Registry by clicking Start, Run, typing **regedit**, and clicking OK. In Vista, click the Windows button, type **regedit** in the Search bar and press Enter, and then click Continue in the UAC dialog box. This opens a registry editor. I'll warn you now: Do not mess with it unless you know exactly what you are doing. This cautionary tip is brought to you by the slogan "Look, but don't touch."

1

MANAGING MACROS IN MICROSOFT OFFICE

One good way to defend against macro viruses is to turn off the capability to open them by default and have a document warn you if a macro is present and give you the option to turn it on. It's annoying to get bugged like that, but it's a good and easy way to defend against macro viruses.

To change the macro security level in Office 2003 programs, click Tools, Options, and then the Security tab. Under Macro Security, click the Macro Security button. Click the Security Level tab, and then select the security level you want to use. The medium setting is a good choice.

In Office 2007, click the Office button in the top-left corner and choose The *Product Name* Options button at the bottom of the menu, where *Product Name* is the name of the Office program you are in. So in Word this is called Word Options; in Excel it's called Excel Options; and so on. Next, click Trust Center on the left of the menu that opens and then click the Trust Center Settings button. Choose the macro setting from the list by selecting its radio button and click OK. My preferred option is Disable All Macros with Notification.

This results in an alert when an Office document contains a macro, which gives you the opportunity to enable, a step you'd take if you knew it was safe.

Memory-Resident Viruses

A *memory-resident virus* gets into a computer's random access memory (RAM). This is where files and programs are loaded when a computer runs them. For example, when you edit a photo or document, it is loaded into the RAM. From its privileged perch in the RAM, the virus gets access to all key operations carried out on the computer, and it can corrupt files and programs with great ease when they are accessed, modified, or manipulated. When the computer is turned off, all data in the memory is purged, including the virus. However, when it infects a system, it ensures it is activated in memory every time a computer turns on.

The Scary Stuff

Memory-resident viruses can slow down your computer by stealing system resources. They can damage data and system files that could stop your computer from running correctly.

File Infector Viruses

There are many types of files on a computer, but the files that do the heavy lifting are program files. Document files have file extensions such as .TXT or .DOC. A letter to Grandma might be called grandma.TXT or letter to grandma.DOC. Program files, however, are identified with the extensions .EXE and .COM. A program like this appears as MyProgam.EXE or time wasting game.COM. It's these program files that are vulnerable to *file infector viruses*. They attach themselves to the file, making them slightly bigger, and execute when the file is run.

The Scary Stuff

File infector viruses can damage program or data files. Your files can be disinfected or replaced from original installation disks, but there's a possibility the viruses can damage your crucial files and either cripple your computer or eat your data.

Boot Viruses

A *boot virus* affects the boot sector of a floppy or hard disk. The boot sector is an area on a disk that contains a program that starts the computer up when it is first switched on. A boot virus swaps itself for the program that boots the computer and spreads to other disks when it is active. You can get a boot virus from a floppy disk, which, in turn, infects your hard drive.

The Scary Stuff

This kind of virus infects any disk with which it comes in contact. It can render a computer unbootable. That means that if you turn the computer on, Windows won't start.

Multi-Partite Viruses

These complex viruses are cleverly designed. They can infect a computer several times using a whole toolbox of techniques. The idea is to attack a computer at several vulnerable spots including files, programs, disk drives, and macros. For example, the multi-partite virus called Tequilla infected the master boot record of a hard disk and then tried to infect program files that have the .EXE file extension.

The Scary Stuff

Multi-partites can do all the usual kinds of nasty things that viruses do, including making computers unbootable and files unusable. The tough part is that they are good at hiding, and just as you think you've cleaned one infection up, you discover another.

Worms: Network-Savvy Viruses

A *computer worm*, quite simply, is a virus that moves from computer to computer across a network. It's a traveling virus. Many worms email themselves to email addresses found on the infected computer. They arrive as attachments—often with tantalizing subject lines—and when the attachment is opened by a human, the replication cycle starts all over again (see Figure 1.1).

FIGURE 1.1

A variant of the Bagle worm arrives via email pretending to be a come-on from a pretty girl.

Some are designed with no need for human intervention to execute. They worm their way from computer to computer over a network connection, employing techniques that are normally used to move files or information between computers.

During a bad worm outbreak, you might notice the Internet or your company network responding very slowly. Two famous examples are Sasser and Blaster. In 2004, Sasser hit hundreds of thousands of Windows XP and Windows 2000 computers globally, including computer systems at American Express and Delta Airlines. The slower-moving Blaster worm hit a year earlier than Sasser and crawled across the Internet infecting computers with Windows XP, Window NT, Windows 2000, and Windows Server 2003. It caused infected systems to either freeze or reboot repeatedly every few minutes. It also initiated a denial of service (DoS) attack against the Windows Update server at Microsoft. A *denial of service attack* is an effort to overwhelm a server by flooding it with data requests across the Internet.

The Scary Stuff

The most famous threat worms pose is network congestion. They clog the Internet as they proliferate. However, they are now the primary tools that deploy payloads that allow bad guys to earn money by using your computer for illicit purposes (see Table 1.1).

note Viruses and worms are seed bots—software that can seek out vulnerable computers and infect them. They then work quietly in the background without the owner of the system knowing they are there. They wait for commands from a remote attacker through chat servers and peer-to-peer networks.

Table 1.1   Top 10 Nastiest Viruses in the Wild, Sept. 2006 to Sept. 2007

Virus Name	Type	Payload
MyDoom	Worm	Sends spam from infected computers. Twenty-five percent of infections attacked the web site of SCO Group, a Unix software company.
LoveSan/Blaster	Worm	Attacks the Microsoft Windows Update web site. Causes system reboots.
Storm Worm	Worm	Makes victim computer part of a botnet, so it can be controlled remotely.
Padobot/Korgo	Worm	Makes victim computer part of a botnet, so it can be controlled remotely.
Rbot	Worm	Makes victim computer part of a botnet, so it can be controlled remotely.
Bagle	Worm	Makes victim computer part of a botnet, so it can be controlled remotely.
Sasser	Worm	Shuts down the computer on a timer. Clogged networks are the result.
Netsky	Worm	Various payloads, including deployment of denial of service attacks. Provides remote access to the victim's computer or in one variant, triggers a series of beeps in the middle of the night.
Mytob	Worm	Sends itself to email addresses in victim's address book. Provides remote access to the victim's computer.
Nyxem/Mywife	Worm	Corrupts document files on the third day of every month.

Source: Paul Piccard, Director of Threat Research, Webroot Software, Inc.

Trojan Horses: Hey Helen, the Achaeans Left Us a Present!

You have probably heard of the story of how the Achaeans (also known as the Greeks) rolled up a great big wooden horse to the gates of Troy (see Figure 1.2). When the delighted Trojans found it, they figured it was a peace offering from their sworn enemies and brought it inside the city. But in the middle of the night, a bunch of sneaky Achaeans hopped out of the horse's hollow belly, let their friends through the gates of Troy, and then attacked the somewhat dim Trojans and burnt and ransacked their city.

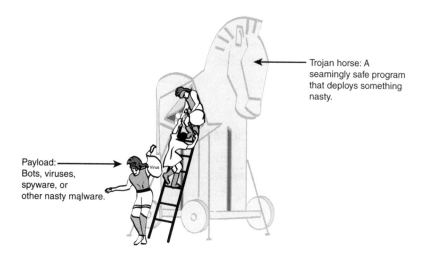

Trojan horse: A
seamingly safe program
that deploys something
nasty.

Payload:
Bots, viruses,
spyware, or
other nasty malware.

FIGURE 1.2

Trojan horses appear to be fun, useful, or harmless programs. After you have been tricked into installing them on your computer, they do bad things such as deploy viruses.

Guess what? A computer virus called a *Trojan horse* works in a similar way. You find (or are sent) a fun, maybe useful computer program and install it on your computer, or it may be a file that looks harmless and installs as part of a larger application. After the file is installed, bad stuff comes out of the file's belly and sets up camp to send spam, install a virus, or open the door to import other bad programming from the Internet.

A Trojan horse is sometimes deployed by a *dropper*. That's a file that conceals a Trojan horse (or a virus) so it evades antivirus programs (see Figure 1.3).

FIGURE 1.3

This dropper is detected by Norton AntiVirus as it tries to dump a virus or Trojan horse into a Windows XP computer.

The Scary Stuff

It's common for a Trojan to create what's known as a *backdoor*, which gives bad guys on the Internet an easy way in to hijack your computer or snoop around. Trojan horses can also deploy viruses, ransack a computer, or deploy bots that send spam or that can attack another computer.

Virus Hoaxes: Fake Viruses That Scare the Heck Out of You

Virus hoaxes are almost as annoying as the actual thing. They arrive as emails from a well-meaning friend who thinks he is doing you a favor by forwarding on an email he thinks is a virus alert (see Figure 1.4). The email comes in various forms, but typically contains details about a rampant virus that is wiping out hard drives or doing similarly awful things to people's computers. Of course it's all fiction, but it's written in a convincing way, urging recipients to send the warning to all their friends. The irony is that the act of forwarding a hoax is the key to the hoax's success. It's how it replicates.

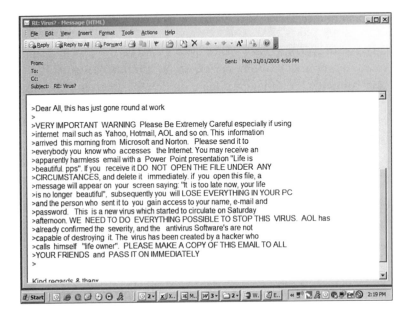

FIGURE 1.4
The "Life Is Beautiful" hoax was first circulated in Portuguese and later in English, French, German, and Chinese.

The Scary Stuff

A virus hoax is scary to those who don't know better because they think there's a nasty out-of-control virus that is about to eat their computer. It's not a real threat, though. It's also a big annoyance to those who know they are hoaxes but receive them on a regular basis. Mostly it results in embarrassment for the naïve sender when they are outed as fools by their angry, in-the-know buddies.

How to Spot a Virus Hoax

The email message goes something like this: "If you receive email titled Win A Holiday—Do Not Open It. It will erase everything on your hard drive."

These types of email chain letters are a plague to email users because they waste time and cause unnecessary panic. The truth is that they are hoaxes. But how do you know for sure? By applying a little bit of knowledge and common sense. Here are some telltale signs of an email hoax.

- They all reference a technology authority. Sometimes it's IBM or Microsoft or the FBI. Sometimes the author claims that several sources have verified the threat.

- The author also promises that the catastrophic virus will arrive as email and wipe out a computer's hard drive or do some other awful damage.

- They also encourage the recipient to spread the word about the impending evil that's about to descend by forwarding the message to all their friends. That line is the giveaway to the hoax. It is the reason for the email's existence and the mechanism by which the hoax is spread. Sometimes the request to forward the message is urged more than once in the hoax.

- The best way to see if an email warning is a virus hoax is to copy a sentence or two from it and search for it on Google.com or your favorite search engine. For example, the first line of the Win a Holiday virus hoax says:

  If you receive an email titled Win a Holiday—Do Not Open It. It will erase everything on your hard drive.

  If you cut and paste this into Google.com, you see dozens of websites that tell you it's a hoax. You can also look up viruses hoaxes at www.f-secure.com/virus-info/hoax/. Another good site to look up hoaxes is www.snopes.com.

1

Who Creates Computer Viruses?

Computer viruses are written by a variety of perpetrators.

They can be smart programmers who want to fiddle with a virus-writing kit they got from the Internet. They can be groups of loosely related people who are working to make money. They can be companies that exist in countries where laws around malware creation are lax. Sometimes they are organized crime rings that use freelancers to harvest personal data used for identity theft.

Historically, virus writers have been brilliant teenage kids or desperate people in search of attention. They are typically male and in their teens (see Figure 1.5) or early 20s. However, David L. Smith, author of the famous Melissa virus, was 30 when the FBI caught up with him.

Once upon a time virus writers were 14-year-old kids who couldn't get a date, had incredible talent, and were looking for a challenge to bring millions of computers down just to get a little notoriety. Today, those same kids, now several years older, are writing virus code for money.

In one variant of the MyDoom worm, there was a message to the antivirus software industry that said, "We [sic] searching 4 work in AV industry."

It's an ill-conceived strategy, of course. No one in the antivirus industry will go near them. Graham Cluley, senior technology consultant for Sophos, an antivirus company, said in a posting to the company website, "It's hard to tell if the creators of these new versions of the MyDoom worm are being serious, but there is no

caution Some virus hoaxes tell you to search for and delete specific files on your system that it claims are viruses. When you look for the specified file to see if it's on your system, you always find it. That's because it's part of Windows! Deleting the file can damage your system.

tip Your best bet when it comes to emails you receive about viruses is to consider the source. If the email comes from a friend or co-worker and has been forwarded like a chain letter, chances are that it's a hoax. That's not to say that your friend or co-worker is in on the sham. Rather, that person—like all the others in the email trail—has been duped into believing the virus is real. If you receive an email regarding a virus *directly from* your Internet Service provider, *directly from* your system administrator at work, or some other extremely reliable source, you should consider the threat real. A hoax often refers to the source of the hoax as a reliable source, but it never comes straight from one of those sources. In any case, forwarding virus warning emails doesn't help anyone and only serves to clog inboxes and create unnecessary panic.

way that anybody in the antivirus industry would touch them with a barge-pole," adding, "It's very simple—if you write a virus, we will never ever employ you. Not only is it unethical to write malicious code, but it raises issues as to whether you could ever be trusted to develop the software which protects millions of users around the world from attack every day." So the people who employ them are well-organized crime syndicates that are profiting from spam, identity theft, or outright online bank account rip-offs. Some use them as tools of extortion.

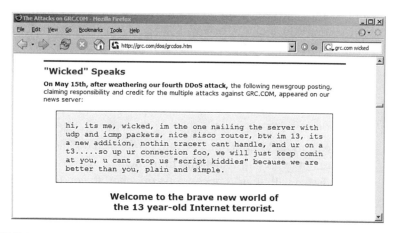

FIGURE 1.5

An excerpt from an email communication with a 13-year-old who had attacked GRC.com, a website run by famed security expert Steve Gibson, using zombie computers in a DDoS attack.

Not all virus writers are geniuses, however. You don't need much programming savvy to write a decent virus these days. The writers just modify existing viruses, creating what are called *variants*. The programming code is widely available on the Internet. Virus writers, hiding behind pseudonyms, even meet anonymously in chat rooms and swap tips, tricks, and bragging rights.

Ultimately, motivations behind virus writing these days are financial. The virus drops a bot that turns your computer into a zombie, which is a computer that can be controlled remotely by a hacker or virus writer. After it takes control of your computer, the virus secretly executes malicious tasks such as sending spam or attacking another computer by sending a flood of data at it across the Internet. These are called *distributed denial of service (DDoS)* attacks.

Spam makes money for the virus writer by distributing massive volumes of junk email. DDoS attacks work via extortion. A wealthy corporation receives an email that demands a lump sum payment in return for protection. If the

1

demand isn't paid, the perpetrator remotely commands all the zombies to attack and crash the company's server. Gambling web sites are often targets of these schemes.

What Not to Do!

When it comes to computer security, it's often as important to learn what not to do as it is to learn what you should do to protect yourself. If you have a family computer used by children, your spouse, or other family members, this is the section you should review with them. Good computer security habits are as critical as good security software.

Here's what not to do:

- A large volume of viruses come via email attachments these days, so don't open attachments you are not expecting, especially if they arrive from someone you don't know.

- Be cautious of attachments from people you do know, especially if you are not expecting something from them. If your friend's computer is infected with a virus, it can send an email to you that looks like it's from your friend. Your virus scanner should scan all inbound attachments, but if it doesn't, right-click suspicious attachments and save them to your Windows desktop. Then use the file scanner feature in your antivirus program to scan the attachment before opening it. Or better yet, call your friend and ask him if he sent you a file via email.

- Don't use peer-to-peer (P2P) programs for downloading music, software, or other files. Teens like to download files from P2P services such as Kazaa. The company says it scans for viruses on its P2P network and has built-in antivirus protection in its software, but suggests you should use an antivirus program on your computer as well.

- Never turn off your antivirus protection for any length of time. You will be instantly vulnerable. If you need to turn it off to service the computer, consider disconnecting it from the Internet first.

- Although less common these days, infections from floppy disks and home-burned CDs and DVDs can still contain infected files. Don't copy files from disks, CDs, DVDs, and other external sources without your antivirus program running on your computer.

- Make sure your computer is protected with a software or hardware firewall. It will help protect you against worms.

- Don't accept unsolicited files from people you don't know when using Internet chat programs such as MSN Messenger, AOL Instant Messenger, and Yahoo! Messenger. Infected files can also be transmitted via Internet Relay Chat (IRC), an open type of chat service on the Internet.

When Viruses Attack!

When you're hit by a bad virus attack, it probably won't be obvious. Once upon a time you'd notice a problem pretty fast. Your computer would start to behave oddly.

Nowadays, viruses are profit-making machines, so they are designed to conceal themselves and do their work without causing any undue damage to a computer. That said, they will have an impact, depending on how well they are designed.

Here are a few symptoms you might see individually or in combination:

- Crashes or system restarts
- Slow or erratic performance
- Broken or erratic Internet connection
- An active Internet connection when you're not using your computer
- Email in Sent Items folder of your email program that you personally didn't send
- Missing or corrupt data or system files
- If infected by a poorly written virus, your computer might fail to start and may display errors

As soon as you think you might be infected with a virus, immediately use your antivirus program to update its virus signatures—these are snapshots of viruses used by the program to identify an infection (see Figure 1.6). All antivirus programs have this feature built in. You click an update button in the software and the updates are fetched from the Internet.

The bad news is that some well-designed viruses are designed to disable or modify security features and administration tools to stop you from getting rid of them. They may also turn off security defenses such as:

- Antivirus and anti-spyware program(s)
- Access to your Windows registry through the `regedit` utility

- Access to the Windows System Configuration utility called `msconfig`
- Windows Firewall or third-party firewall
- In Windows Vista, the User Account Control feature
- The Data Execution Prevention (DEP) mechanism in XP or Vista

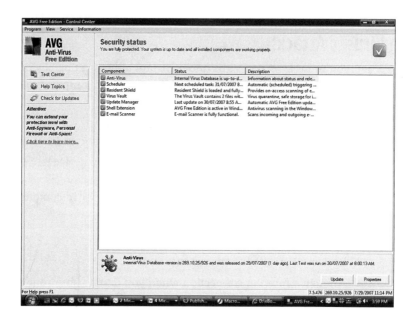

FIGURE 1.6

Is your antivirus program's signature file up to date like this copy of AVG Anti-Virus Free Edition?

Then use the antivirus program to run a system scan (see Figure 1.7). Choose to run a deep or thorough scan, if possible, as opposed to a quick scan.

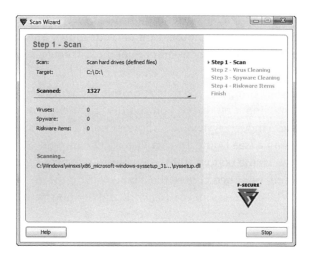

FIGURE 1.7

Use your antivirus program (like F-Secure Internet Security, shown here) to scan your computer for infections.

Disconnect As Soon As Possible

One of the first things most viruses (and spyware) do when a machine is infected is to make contact with the outside world. So one of the first things you should do after detecting an infection (after updating your virus and spyware signatures via the Internet) is to disconnect your computer from your home network, if you have one, and get off the Internet.

- If you are one of the dwindling number of people who use a dial-up account (where your computer dials a number using the phone line), unplug the phone line from the computer.

- If you use a high-speed Internet service such as cable, DSL or satellite, or wireless broadband, turn off your high-speed modem.

tip If you don't have an up-to-date antivirus program, go out right now—leave the book open on the table and I'll wait—and download one. I recommend the free AVG Free Edition program from http://free.grisoft.com (don't get it from www.grisoft.com, as that's only a 30-day trial version). It's as good as any commercial program and it's free for personal use. After you get it, install it and run it. AVG runs on Windows 98, Me, NT, 2000, XP, and Vista.

1

- If your computer shares a high-speed Internet connection with other computers in the house, turn off your router. This is the little box (usually with one or more antennae) that's connected to your high-speed modem.

- If your computer is wireless, disable the Wi-Fi adapter by physically switching it off. In XP, you can also right-click the connection icon in the Windows system tray (bottom right of your screen) and choose Disable (see Figure 1.8). In Vista, you can right-click the connection icon in the bottom right, roll your mouse over the option Disconnect From, and then choose the connection you want to drop. You can also click Disconnect in the Network and Sharing Center.

FIGURE 1.8

Right-click the wireless icon in your Windows XP system tray in the bottom right and choose Disable to turn off your Wi-Fi connection. It works similarly in Vista.

Virus Infection Found! How to Clean Your System

When your antivirus program finds a virus, it will alert you immediately and ask for a decision. Make a note of the virus's name and then have the antivirus program remove it automatically.

If your antivirus program fails to remove the virus, all is not lost. It could be that infected files are running and so they can't be deleted by Windows. Try scanning the computer in Windows Safe Mode. This is a special emergency mode in which Windows starts up in a raw state and loads only the bare necessities into memory.

To get into Safe Mode, shut down and restart the computer. When the screen is black (and before the Windows logo appears), hit the F8 key. You might have to tap the F8 key a few times like a woodpecker to trigger it. A menu appears. Use the arrow key to choose Safe Mode, and press Enter.

If you are presented with a choice of Windows logins (one for you, your spouse, and your hairy little children, perhaps), choose the administrator login. If it's your computer, chances are that you are the administrator.

When the Windows desktop appears in Safe Mode, run your antivirus program and scan the system for viruses. Because Safe Mode loads only the necessary processes in memory, the virus is not loaded unless it has infected one of the system files that is part of Windows. In Safe Mode, you should be able to easily kill the virus.

tip While in Safe Mode, you are not able to connect to the Internet. If you need to, restart the system and press F8 again, but this time choose Safe Mode with Networking.

The other tip I can give you can also be found on shampoo bottles: Rinse and repeat. Or in computer-speak, rescan and reboot continuously until your antivirus program no longer detects any vestige of the infection.

"In the first sweep, it might find and disable the root kit, then in the next scan it'll disable another mechanism and so on until the system is clean," Paul Piccard told me in a helpful chat we had when I was researching new material for this book. He is Director of Threat Research at Webroot Software, a company that makes anti-malware programs.

On detection, your antivirus program might ask you if it should quarantine the virus or delete it. If you quarantine the files, they are put in the computer equivalent of jail, an electronically walled-off area where they can't cause any further damage.

From the quarantine area, they can be submitted to the antivirus maker for analysis, if you choose to do this. If you choose to delete the snared virus, it is wiped from your computer.

tip The big antivirus software publishers offer free virus removal programs for specific virus threats. These tools can be downloaded from the company's websites. Here's a list:

Symantec: http://www.sarc.com/avcenter/tools.list.html

McAfee: http://us.mcafee.com/virusInfo/default.asp?id=vrt.

Kaspersky: http://www.kaspersky.com/removaltools

Bit Defender: http://www.bitdefender.com/site/Download/browseFreeRemovalTool/

F-Secure: http://www.f-secure.com/download-pur-chase/tools.shtml

Microsoft: http://www.microsoft.com/security/malwareremove/

My Antivirus Program Won't Update!

If your antivirus program fails to fetch the latest virus signatures, a virus might have stomped on your Internet connection. Some viruses modify the Windows HOSTS file, a holdover from the early days of computer networking that helps a system find other computers on the Internet. The

1

HOSTS file on your computer is normally found in the following folders:

- In Windows Vista, it's in `C:\WINDOWS\SYSTEM32\DRIVERS\ETC`.

- In Windows XP, it's in `C:\WINDOWS\SYSTEM32\DRIVERS\ETC`.

- In Windows 2000, it's in `C:\WINNT\SYSTEM32\DRIVERS\ETC`.

- In Win 98\Me, it's in `C:\WINDOWS`.

The file can be opened with Notepad or another text editor. It contains comments that begin with the character #—these can be left alone (see Figure 1.9).

The HOSTS file should contain only one other line:

`127.0.0.1 localhost`

In Vista, you will also see this line at the bottom:

`::1          localhost`

Any other lines of text can be removed. After editing it, save the file and close it. Now try to update your antivirus program. You should have no problem.

tip Editing the HOSTS file in Windows Vista can be a bit tricky because of all the new-fangled security features. Here's how to steer around it:

1. Click the Windows button and type **Notepad** in the Search box.

2. When it appears in the Start menu, right-click Notepad and select Run as Administrator.

3. When you see the UAC prompt, click Continue.

4. In Notepad, click the File menu, then Open.

5. Browse to C:\Windows\System32\Drivers\etc.

6. Change the selection in the File Filter drop-down box from "Text Documents (*.txt)" to "All Files (*.*)".

7. Select hosts when it appears in the file list and click Open.

8. Make the needed edits and click Save, then close Notepad.

Lines beginning with # should be left alone

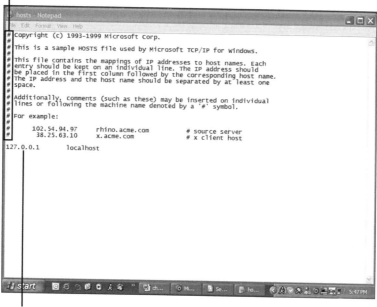

This is the only other entry that
should be in your HOSTS file

FIGURE 1.9

*The HOSTS file can be modified by malware to block access to websites. Pictured is a healthy
HOSTS file.*

Now That I Have Your Attention...

Let's say I have made you a little worried (a little fear can be a good thing,
right?) and you want to ensure your computer never gets infected with a virus.
To help with this, I've divided the virus protection help into easy tasks you can
follow.

Some are easy-to-do defense strategies that thwart most virus attacks in both
Windows XP and Windows Vista. These steps should only take about 10 minutes each.

That's not all you'll have to do, however. The quick strategies are like putting
a screen door on a castle. It'll keep the local peasants out, but if you really
want to fortify your keep against the angry pointy-helmeted hordes, you'll

1

need to spend a little more time. That's where the more in-depth tips come in. They require more time, perhaps a couple of hours in an afternoon.

Because XP and Vista are not identical in how they work, I've broken the steps you need to take into two checklists, one for XP and one for Vista. After that I outline:

- How to achieve each task
- How long it will take
- Which operating system it applies to

tip Here's an easy way to tell which operating system is on your computer. Look at the button in the bottom-left side of your computer screen. If it is square and has the word Start on it, you have Windows XP. If it is round and has the Windows logo on it, your system has Windows Vista installed.

To make this section easy to scan, look for a notation at the start of each task to see this information.

Here's the Windows XP to-do list:

- Update your virus signatures if you have an antivirus program installed.
- Install an antivirus program, or upgrade if your program is old.
- Run Windows Update to get the latest security patches from Microsoft.
- Install Service Pack 2 if you have an older copy of Windows XP and turn on key SP2 features, including the firewall. See Chapter 9 for this procedure. Microsoft will also issue Service Pack 3 for Windows XP in 2008 so install that as well.
- Review and tweak Data Execution Prevention settings in XP.

Here's the Windows Vista to-do list:

- Update your virus signatures if you have an antivirus program installed.
- Install an antivirus program, or upgrade if your program is old.
- Run Windows Update to get the latest security patches on Vista Service Pack 1 from Microsoft.
- Review and understand User Account Control.
- Review and set up administrator and standard user accounts.
- Review and tweak Data Execution Prevention settings.

As you can see, there's lots of work to do, so let's get to it.

Antivirus Defense: Tactics for XP and Vista

Here are your 10-minute virus protection strategies that quickly make your Vista and XP computer safer from viruses, if you only have a few minutes.

Install Windows Security Updates and Service Packs

Operating system: Windows XP and Windows Vista

Time requirement: 10 to 15 minutes (Service packs can take 30-60 minutes)

At the click of a button you can be almost instantly safer from viruses by installing security updates issued by Microsoft. These can be downloaded from the Internet and installed to your computer in a matter of minutes.

Virus writers exploit software bugs (mistakes made by programmers) in programs and operating systems such as Windows. When these are discovered, patches or fixes are issued by the maker of the software that can be downloaded free from the Internet. If you can imagine an operating system as if it were a house, think of a software patch as a toolbox that is used to fix a loose window, a wonky door lock, or a hole in a wall.

To take advantage of these fixes all you need to do is run the Windows Update feature, a service that has been around since Windows 95 was released.

In Windows XP: Click the Start button, All Programs, and look for Windows Update.

You can also open the Internet Explorer web browser and go to the Windows Update site directly by typing `http://windowsupdate.microsoft.com`. Choose the Express Install option to get all the latest critical updates. You can go back later and get the noncritical optional updates when you have more time.

Later versions of XP shipped with a security update called Service Pack 2 (SP2). SP2 was issued in the Fall of 2004, so if your computer is newer than that, SP2 is preinstalled. Be sure to install XP Service Pack as well as it is due out in 2008.

If you don't have it installed because you have reinstalled Windows with a copy of XP that predates SP2 or SP3, then Windows Update will download and install a copy of SP2 when you run it the first time.

> **caution** If Windows Update wants to download and install SP2 and SP3 for Windows XP, then you should be aware that this is not a quickie task. It can take a while, so you should make sure you have an hour or so to babysit the process.

1

In Windows Vista: Click the round Windows button on the bottom-left side of your screen. Then type **Update** in the Search box. Click Windows Update when it appears in the Start menu.

When the Windows Update window opens, click Check for Updates (see Figure 1.10) at the top left or if it shows that updates are available, click the Download Updates button in the main window. Note that Service Pack 1 for Windows Vista will be installed automatically.

> **caution** For noncritical updates, Microsoft makes you download a program called genuinecheck.exe to validate your Windows XP or Vista system to ensure it's not a pirated copy before you can get at the updates. This slows you down by about five minutes, so leave the noncritical updates for another time. To learn more about the Windows validation process, see Chapter 9, "Ground Up Security: Wipe Your Hard Drive and Build a Secure Windows PC from the Ground Up."

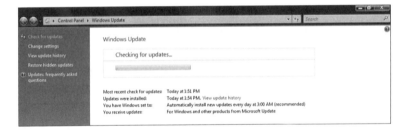

FIGURE 1.10

The Microsoft Windows Update feature on XP and Vista (shown here) downloads updates, including security fixes, for your operating system.

Update Your Virus Signatures

Operating system: Windows XP and Windows Vista

Time requirement: 5 minutes

Another critical step you can do in a few minutes is to update the virus signatures in your antivirus program on your computer. (You do have one installed, don't you? If not, immediately see the next section on how to install a free antivirus program called AVG Free Edition.)

Virus signatures are, in effect, digital mugshots of what each virus looks like. Imagine if a security guard had pictures and descriptions of all the known bad guys that could possibly come into the building he guards. As people arrived, he'd compare the profiles to each person and if they turned out to be a crook, he'd stop them. That's what an antivirus program uses virus signatures for. The antivirus software publishers issue signatures for download as new viruses are discovered, often within hours of their very first infection.

To update your virus signatures, take the following steps:

- Open your antivirus program and look for a feature either under the Tools menu or a configuration menu of some sort. There is likely to be a feature called Automatic Updates, Update Signatures, Internet Update, or some other variation.

- Ensure that your computer is connected to the Internet and run this option. The program looks for virus signature updates on the website run by the antivirus software maker and downloads and installs them. You should do this daily if you have time and weekly at a minimum. It only takes a few minutes.

- Most programs these days, from the commercial security companies such as McAfee, Symantec (aka Norton) and F-Secure, automatically look for updates and install them as they become available (see Figure 1.11). If your program has an automatic signature update feature like this, it is probably turned on, but you should double-check, by looking

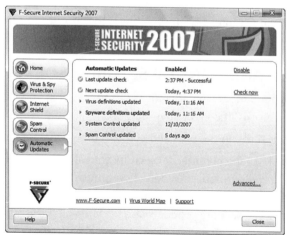

through the signature update options.

FIGURE 1.11

F-Secure Internet Security checks for new malware signatures several times per day.

Install or Upgrade an Antivirus Program

Operating system: Windows XP and Windows Vista

Time requirement: 10 to 20 minutes

Most people have heard of an antivirus program, but amazingly many don't even have one installed on their computer.

An antivirus program watches what comes into your computer and checks it against a library of known viruses. Some antivirus programs also look for virus-like behavior and stop it before it starts.

> **tip** Many computers come with a free 30-day starter antivirus program that continues to run after the trial period expires. It does not continue to download virus signatures, however. Don't rely on a program like this to protect you. If you haven't updated your virus signatures in years, you are extremely vulnerable to new infections. Dump the program and replace it with an up-to-date antivirus program.

There are many antivirus programs to choose from. The two you have probably heard about are Symantec's Norton AntiVirus and McAfee's VirusScan. Both companies also market these programs as part of security suites.

Although no antivirus package is completely foolproof, having an up-to-date antivirus program installed drastically reduces the risk of a virus infection.

So how do you get one? Well, you can run out to the store and buy a boxed antivirus product from your local software dealer. Or you can download one from the Internet. For a list of antivirus programs and where to find them, flip to **p. 379** in Chapter 12, "Tool of the Trade." for tips on what to buy and an overview of some key titles.

PROS AND CONS OF SECURITY SOFTWARE YOU BUY

Why spend money on an antivirus product when you can get one free from free.grisoft.com or www.avast.com?

Let's go through the pros and cons of commercial security software.

Pros: Big-brand commercial security software companies have well-staffed, well-funded, virus detection groups that research new infections and write antivirus signatures to defend against them. Commercial security products also update your virus signatures automatically when new signatures are available, so updates occur more often than once a day. You also get telephone support. In a crisis, it can be valuable to have someone helpful at the other end of the phone when a virus is gorging on your data.

Cons: Commercial security programs cost money and you have to renew them annually. They can be overly dominant on your system. The big-brand security suites can take over your system and slow it down. They also can interrupt with dialog box alerts too frequently.

Symantec in particular, which makes Norton AntiVirus and a related security suite, suffers from bloat-itis. The program is enormous, uses lots of memory, and slows down any system it is installed on significantly. It also can strangle the Internet connection on some programs. They just won't connect because Norton blocks them without warning. McAfee's AV product was a bit better on XP, but the company stumbled with their Vista version, so steer clear there as well.

Recommended payware: If you want a security solution to take advantage of their good features, look at products from these companies, which offer good solutions without the performance issues:

- F-Secure: www.fsecure.com
- Trend Micro: www.trendmicro.com
- Panda: www.pandasecuritysoftware.com
- Grisoft: www.grisoft.com

See more about these and other payware security options in Chapter 12.

If you don't already have an antivirus program installed, let me show you how to install a very good free antivirus program called Grisoft AVG Anti-Virus Free Edition.

Okay, let's get started. Here is what you need to do to install AVG Free Edition (see Figure 1.12) :

1. Connect to the Internet and open your web browser.

2. Browse to the web page http://free.grisoft.com.

tip Note that AVG's license allows for private individuals to use it free. If you use it for business purposes, the company asks you to pay for its commercial product.

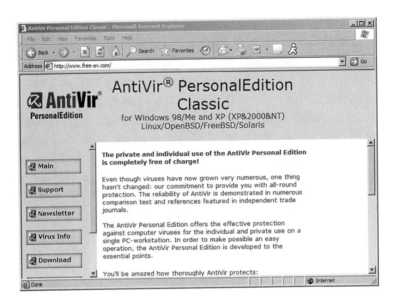

FIGURE 1.12
AVG Free Edition is a great antivirus program for XP and Vista that's free to download.

3. Look for the Download button, click on it, and on the ensuing page look for a Download link to AVG Anti-Virus Free. This is where Grisoft tries to upsell you to its paid version. Go for it if you are inspired and want better protection, tech support, and other features for Windows 98/Me & NT/2000/XP/Vista.

4. There may be two more upsell pages before you get to the actual download hosted when I last checked on Download.com. If your web browser is Microsoft Internet Explorer, click on the download link on that page and when prompted, click Save in the File Download box and save it to a place you can find it later. I like to drop downloaded files onto my desktop.

5. When it is downloaded, close all programs on your system that don't need to be open and double-click on the AVG installation file and follow the installation steps.

6. Note that in Windows Vista, a User Account Warning (UAC) will pop open when you start the installation process. Click Continue to allow the program to install.

> **tip** The direct route to the actual download page is: http://www.download.com/3000-2239_4-10703202.html. However, by the time you read this, it may have changed to a different address.

7. The program will ask you whether it should do an Express or Custom installation. Choose Custom if you want to tweak AVG settings; otherwise, Express is the easiest way to go.

Once the program is installed, there are a few optional steps that it walks you through:

1. It'll ask to update its virus signatures via the Internet. Let it update the virus signatures now, or do it right after you finish the installation (see Figure 1.13) .

2. You are also asked to pick between either High Priority or Low Priority Scanning. High Priority finishes faster but will slow your system during the scan. The Low Priority Scan takes longer but doesn't hog system memory during the scan so it won't annoy you as much if you're working on the computer at the same time. Be sure to also check the box on this screen to enable a scheduled daily scan.

3. You can also opt to do an initial system scan. If you have time this is a good idea.

4. You'll also be asked to register your product. If you do you'll get access to the AVG discussion forum in case you need tech support. The free version doesn't entitle you to access tech support directly from Grisoft.

After the program is installed, you're much more protected from viruses than you were 10 minutes ago!

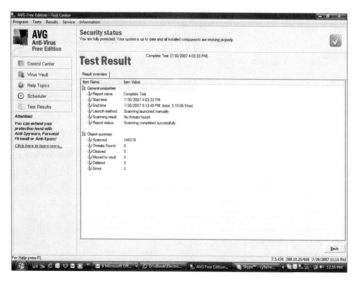

FIGURE 1.13

During installation AVG does an initial scan of your hard drive to look for viruses.

Scan Your Computer for Viruses

1

Operating system: Windows XP and Windows Vista

Time requirement: A few minutes to get started. Up to an hour or more to complete (unattended).

> **tip** Some antivirus programs have a quick scan feature, which checks the likely places on your computer where viruses like to hide. A quick scan is handy if you want to scan more than once a week.

All antivirus programs have the ability to scan your computer for viruses in case a clever piece of malware has slipped past your defenses.

I recommend that you a scan once a week.

All antivirus programs have an intensive scan that looks at every file on the system and in every nook and cranny. Run the intensive scan once a week. Usually this can be scheduled to run automatically. If you leave your computer on, it's a good idea to schedule the intensive scan overnight; maybe on a Friday night so you can deal with any results Saturday morning, if your schedule permits.

Here's how to do a scan with Grisoft AVG Free Edition:

1. Start the AVG Test Center by locating it in the Start menu under All Programs.

2. In Vista you can also type `AVG Test Centre` in the Start menu Search box to easily locate the program.

3. Alternatively, in both XP and Vista, double-click the AVG Control Center icon in the System Tray (bottom-right corner of your screen) and when the program opens, click the Test Center button on the left side of the AVG window.

4. Once the AVG Test Center window is open, click the Check for Updates button to see if there are any new virus signatures. If there are, download and install them. If there are several available updates, repeat this process to install them all until no more are detected.

5. Then click Scan Computer. A window will open so you can track the scan's progress and respond to any alerts that are triggered.

Install Service Packs on Windows XP

Operating system: Windows XP

Time requirement: 15 minutes to more than an hour to download depending on the speed of your Internet connection. Installation can take up to 15 to 30 minutes. Factor in time to back up critical data and programs beforehand.

As I mentioned earlier, Microsoft issued a major security update called Service Pack 2 (SP2) for Windows XP in the Fall of 2004 and Service Pack 3 was slated for release in 2008.

COMMENTARY:

DO I HAVE SP2 OR SP3?

Not sure if you have Windows XP service packs installed? To figure it out, click your Start button, and then click Run. In the Run dialog box, type **winver** and click OK. A box displays the Windows version you are running and any service packs that are installed. If you are running Windows XP, look for a notation that says Service Pack 2 or Service Pack 3.

There's always more than one way to do stuff in Windows, so if you don't like that trick because it's too geeky, try this alternate method: Open any folder on your hard drive (My Documents is an easy choice), click on the Help menu, and then select About Windows. A dialog box appears showing the version of Windows running on your PC, as well as any Service Pack updates.

If you have been religious about using Windows Update, you probably have already installed them. If not, please visit (and I am begging you!) http://windowsupdate.microsoft.com right now and download and install any available service packs now.

Monitor and Tweak Windows Security Center

Operating system: Windows XP and Windows Vista

Time requirement: A few minutes.

Microsoft introduced a new feature called Security Center (see Figure 1.14) when it released Service Pack 2 for Windows XP. It further refined it for Windows Vista, which was launched in early 2007.

It's a dashboard that gives you the status of key security features on the operating system and their status.

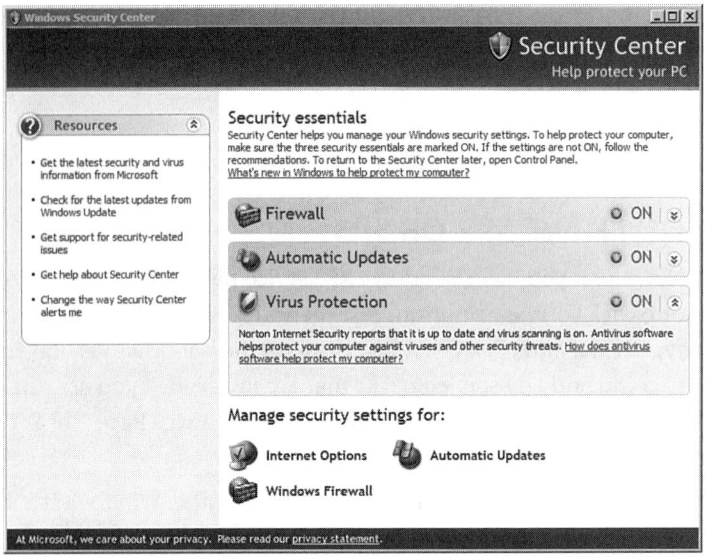

FIGURE 1.14

Windows Security Center shows the status of key security features on XP (shown) and Vista.

In Windows XP, check it by clicking Start, Control Panel, and double-clicking on the Security Center icon. It's also represented by a little colored shield in the Windows XP System Tray, which is the row of icons at the bottom right of your screen.

In Windows Vista, access Security Center by clicking the Windows button at the bottom-left side of the screen and then typing `Security Center` in the search box and clicking it when it appears in the Start menu.

The Security Center in XP has three key areas. In Vista, it has four.

Firewall (XP and Vista)

I talk more about firewalls in Chapter 4, "Hackers: There's a Man in My Machine," but for now all you need to know is that you should ensure the Windows Firewall is on because it gives you added protection against worms and other intrusions from the Internet.

There are two scenarios in which you would turn it off:

- If you were running a third-party software firewall, such as ZoneAlarm or PC Tools Firewall Plus or the firewall built into your security suite. Windows XP and Vista can detect some third-party firewalls. If it does,

1

it will show that Windows Firewall is turned off and that the third-party firewall is protecting the computer instead.

> **tip** Not all third-party firewalls are detected by Security Center; however, that doesn't mean that your system is not protected. Check the third-party firewall separately to ensure it's active.

- If you have a home network and use a router that shares the Internet connection among several computers. Home Internet routers (sometimes called *gateways*) have a built-in firewall mechanism called Network Address Translation (NAT) that acts as a firewall. (I will teach you how NAT works in Chapter 4.) If this is the case, you could turn the Windows Firewall off; however, it doesn't hurt to leave it on. It doesn't impair system performance and it adds an extra layer of security.

Automatic Updates (Automatic Updating in Vista)

When this feature is turned on, it automatically seeks the latest Windows updates and downloads and offers to install them. This should be turned on unless you have a really good reason to deactivate it.

Virus Protection (XP Only)

This Security Center feature monitors your antivirus program and alerts you when it is out of date so you can download the latest virus signatures. It also monitors the built-in Windows Defender anti-spyware program that comes preinstalled in Windows Vista.

Malware Protection (Vista Only)

This feature replaces the "Virus Protection" heading found in the Security Center in XP. This feature monitors your antivirus program and alerts you when it is out of date so you can download the latest virus signatures.

> **tip** Note that in Vista you can toggle the various security features on or off using items listed on the left side of the center. Also note the setting that says Change the Way the Security Center Alerts Me. This can be used to suppress the Security Center if it keeps bugging you about security alerts that you're already aware of or dealing with.

Other Security Settings (Vista Only)

This Vista-only setting shows you the status of the Internet options in Internet Explorer and if the new User Account Control setting is turned on.

Understanding User Account Control

Operating system: Windows Vista

Time requirement: Less than 5 minutes

Microsoft's not-so-secret weapon in its Vista security strategy is a new feature called User Account Control or UAC.

It's a permission-based mechanism that pops up an alert when a change is initiated to a Vista computer. When it's triggered, the screen dims and you see a challenge to Continue or Cancel (see Figure 1.15).

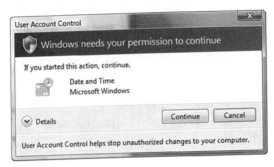

FIGURE 1.15

Get used to these. User Account Control alerts pop onto a dimmed secure desktop whenever a system setting change is initiated.

If you initiated the system change, you would of course click Continue. If you didn't, another process is at work, likely malware, that's trying to make an unauthorized change.

If a UAC alert occurs and you didn't initiate a change, you'd want to click Cancel to stop the illicit activity. Then go on a virus hunt. Be sure to scan your system with an antivirus program (and antispyware applications as I explain in Chapter 2).

tip Learn more about UAC and its implementation at http://tinyurl.com/33glen.

UAC TRIGGERS

UAC is triggered under the following conditions:

- Changes that impact the Windows registry, where Vista tracks system settings and configurations
- Changes to the startup routine
- Software installations, uninstallations, or changes to installed programs, drivers, or Windows components
- Changes to network/Internet mechanisms

I Hate UAC

Now the downside of UAC is that it is very annoying. Most people get used to it, but after a while you may suffer dialog fatigue and be tempted to turn it off.

I recommend strongly that you don't. Let me say that again. I recommend strongly that you don't turn off UAC.

If you do turn it off, it will be deactivated for you and everyone else with an account (like your children) on the computer.

I have some good news though. There's a compromise: If you want to better manage UAC and reduce its irritation factor without losing its effectiveness, download and install a copy of TweakUAC, a free program you can get from www.tweakuac.com.

TweakUAC is useful because it lets you turn UAC on and off easily, but it also has a feature called "quiet mode." This turns UAC off when you are logged in as an administrator, but leaves UAC on for those with standard user accounts, like your spouse or children.

tip I talk about UAC in depth in my book *Windows Vista Help Desk*, so if you want to become a Vista master and a UAC expert tweaker, pick up a copy. You'll find it in fine bookstores everywhere and on the Web at all the well-known online book sellers.

That said, let me also show you how to turn off UAC manually:

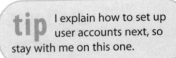

tip I explain how to set up user accounts next, so stay with me on this one.

1. Click the Windows button, type **msconfig**, and press Enter.

2. Click Continue on the UAC warning for the last time.

tip Note that there is also an Enable UAC option here to turn it back on.

3. In the System Configuration dialog click the Tools tab.

4. Scroll down to Disable UAC and select it.

5. Click Launch.

6. A command window will open and run a script. Click it afterwards to close it.

7. UAC will be turned off.

Review and Set Up Administrator and Standard User Accounts.

Operating system: Windows Vista

Time requirement: 15 to 30 minutes

When you first got your computer, you were asked to create an account to log in the first time. You likely still use that account today.

That account is called an administrator account and it lets you make maintenance changes, install software, and generally "administer" the system, even if you are the sole user.

In previous versions of Windows, Microsoft provided an option to create alternate accounts for your family members or other users of the computer. These provided users with their own personal desktop and settings. However this "standard" user account was a pain to use because it limited the user's freedom without curtailing their ability to damage the system (even by accident).

Review and Tweak Data Execution Prevention Settings.

Operating system: Windows XP and Windows Vista

Time requirement: 5 minutes

One of the tricks malware uses to take control of your computer is to access protected memory illicitly to execute malicious code.

Vista includes a defense mechanism against this tactic called Data Execution Prevention (see Figure 1.16).

DEP stops a tactic called a buffer overrun. It's one of the most common tricks malware uses to break into your computer and infect its guts.

The problem with DEP is that it can also trip up older software and throw false positives. So you'll be tootling along with a program when suddenly DEP appears like Dick Cheney in the woods, and without warning, takes the application out, shutting it down.

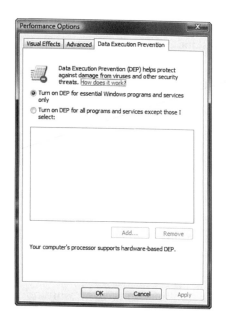

FIGURE 1.16

Vista's Data Execution Protection guards against buffer overruns.

I recommend that you keep DEP on in both Windows XP and Vista for optimal protection. You may find that it plays nice with your system and leave it at that, confident in the knowledge that another layer of protection is in place to lock down Windows.

Here's how to adjust DEP so your system is protected:

Windows XP:

1. Click the Start button, then Run.

2. Type `sysdm.cpl` and click OK.

3. On the Advanced tab, under Performance, click the Settings button.

1

4. That will take you to the Data Execution Prevention tab.

5. Click Turn on DEP for Essential Windows Programs and Services Only if you want basic DEP protection.

6. If you want to be more aggressive, choose Turn on DEP for All Programs and Services Except Those I Select.

7. If DEP starts to bug you like crazy using the latter settings, then click the Add button and browse to the program that appears to be causing the problem. You will want to locate the program's executable file, which ends in the file extension .EXE and add it to the exceptions list. This may take a bit of digging.

> **tip** To find the location of a program's executable file, right-click on the menu item or icon you use to start the program and choose Properties, then click the Shortcut tab and then look for the box that says Target. It contains the folder path to the executable. You can also open the folder that contains the executable file by clicking the Find Target button at the bottom of the Shortcut tab.

Windows Vista: To get to DEP settings you have to dig deep into Vista.

1. Click the Windows button and then type `system` into the Start menu and click on System when it appears in the Start menu.

2. Then click Advanced System Settings on the left side of the System dialog.

3. Next click Continue on the UAC warning.

4. Then on the Advanced tab under the Performance section, click the Settings button.

5. Finally, click the Data Execution Prevention tab on the Performance Options window to open the DEP settings.

You will find two DEP options to choose from.

■ Turn on DEP for essential Windows programs and services only.

■ Turn on DEP for all programs and services except those I select.

The simplest approach is to choose DEP for only essential Windows programs and services. This will give you minimal headaches and very few DEP false positive alerts.

However, if you want to be more aggressive you can choose the second option. The problem with this is it may throw a lot of false positives. To be honest this drives me a bit bonkers, so as cautious as I am around security and Windows,

I kind of hate DEP when it's on this aggressive setting. It's like a gassy baby—it produces sudden and unpleasant alerts.

That said you can leave the more aggressive DEP setting on and exclude the programs that are causing the false positives as follows:

Click the Add button and browse to the program that is causing the problem. You will want to locate the program's executable file, which ends in the file extension .EXE, and add it to the exceptions list. This may take a bit of digging. When you find it, click Add. That should sort it out.

> **tip** You can also find the System icon in the Control Panel. Click the Window button, then Control Panel, then click Classic View on the left side of Control Panel and find the icon alphabetically or type **System** in the search box at the top of the Control Panel.

HOW TO (TEMPORARILY) DISABLE DEP ON VISTA

If DEP gets in the way of the installation of a program and you want to temporarily disable it, try this:

1. Open a command prompt by typing cmd in the search bar on the Start menu.

2. Right-click it when it appears in the Start menu and choose Run As Administrator. A command-prompt window will open.

3. Type the following command to disable DEP:

   ```
   bcdedit.exe /set {current} nx AlwaysOff
   ```

4. Leave the command-prompt window open and run the installation that DEP was shutting down.

5. When it is done go back to the command-prompt window and turn DEP back on again by typing:

   ```
   bcdedit.exe /set {current} nx AlwaysOn
   ```

Now you may be tempted to leave DEP off. I don't recommend it as it provides a vital service in defending your computer against the most common trick a virus uses to infect your system. If I sound like your mother here, then good—she's a nice lady and she's right most of the time.

No Worm in My Apple?

If you own an Apple Macintosh computer, should you worry about viruses, worms, and Trojan horses? Yes, but not to the same extent as on a PC. Viruses have been written for Apple computers, but they haven't proliferated to epidemic proportions in the same way they have on Windows-based PCs.

tip More detailed information about DEP for XP can be found at http://support.microsoft.com/kb/875352. For Vista, have a look at: http://tinyurl.com/2ytwf5

So why not? Well, for one, Apple has designed its operating systems really well, especially the latest one called Mac OS X.

Before the operating system came along, there were about 60–80 Mac viruses in the wild that threatened Mac computers. Since, then there has only been a handful designed to infect Macs running OS X. Those had little impact because they were design to demonstrate vulnerabilities, not assault the system. But as a result, Apple had to fix security holes in the operating system and issue patches.

By comparison, McAfee reports there are more than 100,000 viruses that can attack PCs.

Arguably, contrarians would say there are far fewer Macs in the world than there are Windows-based PCs. The impact of a Mac virus wouldn't have the same earning potential for a virus writer looking to exploit the platform, so they don't bother. Since viruses are a revenue-generating tool for criminals these days, it hasn't made financial sense to develop viruses for the Mac so far because it has fewer users relative to Windows. That, however, is changing. Mac's market share is growing relative to PCs since Apple adapted them to use faster Intel chips and they have the ability to run Windows now.

The reality is that viruses are not currently a problem on Mac computers, but be aware that that may change moving forward.

There are two exceptions Mac users should be aware of.

1. A PC virus can still live inside a file stored on a Mac. If an unsuspecting Mac user sent an infected file to a PC-using friend, she might not be a friend for much longer.

2. Apple also switched the microprocessors inside Macs to Intel-based CPUs. This allows Mac owners to install Windows XP or Vista on their Macs. So of course they are now vulnerable to all the Windows viruses when running Windows mode.

caution In October of 2007, a series of Trojans were released for Mac OS X suggesting that malware writers were starting to pay more attention to the Mac platform as they rise in popularity.

Antivirus programs are available for the Mac OS. Symantec, Sophos, and McAfee all make them. And there's a free Mac antivirus program called ClamXav that can also be downloaded from http://www.clamxav.com (see Figure 1.17).

Macs that run Windows should have a Windows-based antivirus product installed on the Windows portion of the computer.

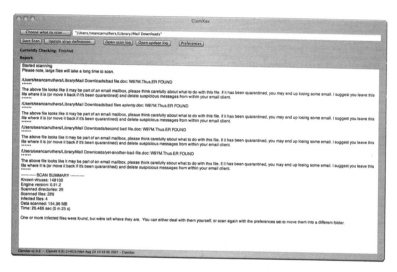

FIGURE 1.17

ClamXav is a free antivirus program for Apple computers.

Is That a Virus in Your Pocket?

Mobile gadgets, such as smart phones and personal digital assistants (PDAs), are vulnerable to viruses written for them, but the threat is still relatively small. No mobile gadget virus has run rampant through the world's pockets in any notable way—yet.

The current crop of mobile viruses attack the Symbian operating system, which is the world's most dominant mobile operating system. It has tens of millions of users across the planet. That may seem like a lot; however, it is installed on only 2%–3% of mobile phones worldwide. To put that into perspective, 1 billion mobile phones shipped worldwide in 2006.

The first mobile virus, which appeared in 2004, was called Cabir. It jumps between devices using Bluetooth, a short-range wireless technology designed for gadget-to-gadget data transfer. The virus Commwarrior uses multimedia messaging service (MMS) to transfer the virus. Normally MMS is used to send pictures and audio between phones. And the Skulls virus spreads into a Symbian smartphone inside another program.

Antivirus companies now have substantial numbers of Trojans and worms designed for mobile phones in their labs. New malicious programs aimed at the Symbian operating system continue to appear since their first appearance in 2004.

However, the upshot is that you really have to work hard to infect your gadgets with a virus. That might change as gadgets evolve and get more powerful, like computers, but for the time being your devices are mostly safe from viruses.

Absolute Minimum

- Computer viruses are programs written by malcontents that do bad things to your computer. These days most new viruses are written to earn their authors money through sending spam or extortion rackets.

- Viruses are triggered by an action you take. You have to execute a virus for it to infect your computer.

- Specialty viruses, known as worms, can deploy without your intervention. Worms travel across networks.

- Viruses can destroy data, vandalize your computer, take control of it, or use it as a spam sender.

- Your best defense is to run an up-to-date antivirus program and scan your computer with it once a week.

- You should download Windows security updates as they become available.

- The most important security updates for Windows XP is Service Pack 2 (SP2) and Service Pack 3 (available sometime in 2008). For Windows Vista, it's Service Pack 1.

Spyware: Overrun by Advertisers, Hijackers, and Opportunists

Spyware and adware, its rude sister, are two of the most prolific threats to the privacy and the security of your computer today. This chapter explains what they are, how they spy on you, and what methods they use to sneak onto your computer. It also covers the many flavors of spyware and a snoop profile for each type. Of course, no chapter on spyware would be complete without tips on how to remove infections and defend against future threats. By the end of the chapter you will have a license to kill (spyware, that is). Just don't drop your gun in your breakfast milk, okay?

2

What Is Spyware?

Cue the spy theme music. Pulse-pound music plays over the scene of a Cold War–era suburb. Outside a row of cookie-cutter houses, a devastatingly handsome man and his mysterious and shapely cohort (who has a Luger in her fishnets) sneak up on a lit window. Inside, the room is warm, cozy, and full of minivan dads. And wait, there *you* are, mousing away on a computer.

That's what spyware is all about, right? International intrigue!

Sadly, it's not that exciting. No one is interested in the soccer-league spreadsheet on your Dell or whose turn it is to bring the orange slices to next Sunday's game.

Spyware is software. And it's not written and distributed to pursue some fancy spy agency agenda, such as finding out the color of Fidel Castro's shower curtain. It's mostly written so its authors can find out about you, where you live, what you like to do on your computer, and where you go on the Web. Why do they care? Because they can make money from that information.

Now there's nothing wrong with earning a living, but spyware makers do it in a nasty underhanded way that is generally immoral, sometimes illegal, and definitely annoying. I like the way that my friend (and famed security guru) Steve Gibson, president of Gibson Research Corp. and owner of www.grc.com, once described spyware:

> Spyware is "uninvited, unwanted, stealthful, invasive, annoying, exploitive, and potentially privacy-compromising PC add-on software whose ongoing presence in millions of PCs worldwide benefits not the computer's owner and operator, but the interests of the publishers of this troubling new class of software."

Steve is the guy who coined the term *spyware* when he first caught a program chattering from his computer back to a server on the Internet. He's a notorious James Bond character in the geek world. And while Steve's spy wear is jeans and a T-shirt most days, he probably would look great in a tux.

What Does Spyware Do and Why Is It Bad?

Spyware is considered *malware* (malicious software) because it installs itself on your computer without your knowledge. Then it watches your computer habits, compromising your privacy. Spyware is also annoying because it pushes unwanted advertising at you. Pop-up ads appear out of nowhere on your desktop. And because spyware is spying on you, it pushes ads at you that it thinks you'll click on.

If that's not enough, spyware can clog your system's memory and use space on your hard drive, causing performance slowdowns. It can get so cloggy that it'll make your computer unusable.

Some spyware programs can even capture your keystrokes and send them to a third party. This can potentially expose your user IDs and passwords to thieves. It can also allow installation of an electronic backdoor that allows bad people to log in to your computer remotely and use it for their own purposes, such as sending spam or launching malicious attacks on other computers on the Internet. Spyware can change settings and hijack your web browser so that a rogue home page is loaded every time you surf the Web.

On top of all this, some spyware embeds itself so cleverly and deeply into your system that removing it requires a lot of computer expertise. You almost have to be as computer-savvy as a nine-year-old.

How Does Spyware Sneak onto My Computer?

Spyware gets onto your computer through a variety of sneaky techniques:

- It arrives as an automatic download from a website you are surfing. This is called *drive-by downloading*. If you visit naughty websites, those sites are probably your chief source of spyware.

- You can be tricked into clicking on a link that downloads spyware from a website. Those browser windows that pop up telling you that you've won a prize are a prime example.

- Spyware can be embedded in the installation process of a free or pirated piece of software you download. File-sharing programs, such as Kazaa, are known for including a variety of spyware programs with their installers.

- Spyware can also get on your computer via an email attachment you shouldn't have opened. It often comes as an attachment to commercial email, also called *spam*.

INTERNET DOWNLOADS THAT MIGHT CONTAIN SPYWARE

Here are the kinds of files that you can download from the Internet that might contain spyware:

- Toolbars for your desktop or web browser

- Free games, puzzles, or other interactive entertainment

- Free screensavers or animated characters (see Figure 2.1) for your computer's desktop

- Free pop-up blocker programs

- Files downloaded from file-sharing services

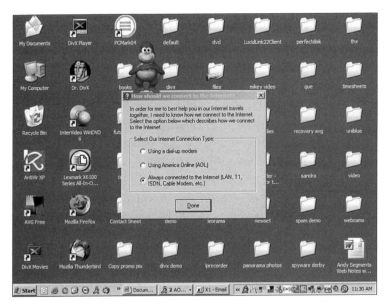

FIGURE 2.1

BonziBUDDY was an animated on-screen purple monkey that functioned as a talking virtual helper. The software, however, was also a well-known piece of spyware. Thankfully it was discontinued in 2004.

note Not all free downloads contain spyware. Many programmers release their programs free for the good of the Internet community and they are spyware-free.

Types of Spyware: Snoops, Adware, Cookies, and More

Like the term *virus*, which is often used as a generic term for all malicious attack software, the term *spyware* has a similar catch-all usage. It encompasses a family of malware that all has some snoop capability. Let's have a look at the various types.

Spyware: I Spy with My Little App

Spyware includes programs that can record what you do on your computer and share that information with a stranger via an Internet connection. Some can watch and record your web-surfing habits. Some, called *key loggers*, record everything you type. Spyware can also capture user IDs and passwords. It might have the ability to see where you have been on the Web. If there's information on your computer that is of interest to someone and can make them a little money, there's probably a spyware program to capture it.

The motivation to spy this way can be criminal (capturing information for identity theft, perhaps), but most often it's commercial in nature. A company wants to understand you better so that it can trigger customized ads or analyze your behavior and sell that marketing data.

Adware: Attack of the Pop-ups

Adware is equally annoying because it not only spies on you, but then it shows you ads. Some adware spies on you because its mission is to show you ads customized to your tastes, usually via pop-up ads on your computer's desktop.

Sometimes adware is a legitimate part of a free program. Software publishers often bundle adware in with free programs they offer, using it as a revenue source. Many warn you of the adware during installation in the End User License Agreement, also referred to as an EULA. (That term always make me think of a slightly portly aunt that you hate to kiss, but who makes good cupcakes.)

In a computer, the EULA is that scrollable box of soporific text (which probably earned some lawyer a Jacuzzi) that we all have to agree to before we can install a software package.

The EULA's legalese often says that in return for use of the program for free, you must allow the installation of the adware (see Figure 2.2).

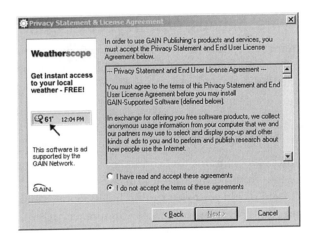

FIGURE 2.2

The End User License Agreement (EULA) for Weatherscope warns you that in return for giving you use of the software, information about you will be gathered.

Marketing companies that publish and distribute adware often take offense if their products are called spyware. Then again they take offense if you call it anything but install-this-now-because-it's-really-good-ware.

To thwart any potential legal action, computer security companies sometimes call these products *potentially unwanted programs* or PUPs. Security company McAfee—famous for its antivirus software—coined the term.

In any event, it pays to at least skim the EULA before just clicking the Next button. If you see anything suspicious, cancel the installation and do a Google search on the software you're installing. Chances are that if it contains spyware, adware, or any other undesirables, someone will be railing about it on the Internet somewhere.

Snoopware: I Wanna Know What You're Up To!

Snoopware watches your computer habits on behalf of someone else, usually someone you know. This can include parental monitoring software—programs designed to track children's computer habits. Windows Vista has built in snoopware called Parental Controls, so parents can keep tabs on the children's computer habits.

Employers might install snoopware to keep an eye on employee computer habits to ensure they're not spending too much time looking up old flames on facebook.com.

One of the most popular uses of snoopware is to track the behavior of a spouse. Usually it's purchased by wives who suspect their husbands are up to no good on the Internet, though it can equally track wives who might be sending the pool boy spicy emails.

The software can grab screen captures (snapshots of a screen) and record email, chat conversations, and other computer communications. In some cases it can deliver that information in real time across a computer network.

I'll skip any moral judgments on snoopware and leave that for the nice ladies over at the garden club. Needless to say, it creates lots of controversy.

One of the most famous snoopware software companies is called SpectorSoft from www.spectorsoft.com (see Figure 2.3).

FIGURE 2.3

SpectorSoft makes a line of snoopware that is designed to record a person's computer habits and report them to someone else.

Browser Hijackers: Turn This Browser Around, We're Going to Cuba.com

Browser hijackers are perhaps the most malicious spyware programs because they are so hard to remove. When you first open your web browser your home page pops open. Most people set this to Google.com, a news site, or their favorite web page.

Browser hijackers override this setting and reset a browser's home page to one of their choosing, usually a commercial web page. Why? Well, the link to the web page they set can be something called an *affiliate link*. The hijacker's author makes money when you are sent to the affiliate link.

Sometimes the web page you are directed to contains further affiliate links. Money is earned from affiliate links if you click and buy something or sometimes if you simply just click the link.

Affiliate programs are a legitimate way for many web content publishers to make income. Unfortunately, it's also a revenue source for spyware makers as well.

note Many affiliate links are 100% legitimate. For example, when surfing the Web, you'll often come across a link to a product that takes you to the manufacturer's or third-party reseller's site to purchase the item. The website placing the link on its site earns a kickback. These links generally aren't malicious, but they are capitalistic. The point here, however, is that all affiliate marketing isn't bad. It's just a shame that browser hijackers ruin the party for everyone.

Often browser hijackers direct you to a web page that looks like search sites such as Google or Yahoo!. The most famous browser hijackers are ones that redirect to a website called Cool Web Search (see Figure 2.4). The owners of the Russian-based site say they terminate affiliate arrangements with anyone who writes a browser hijack. Still, lingo has been born from the practice. The worst hijacker offenders are referred to generically as *CWS hijacks*.

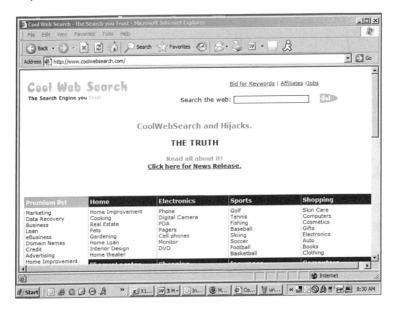

FIGURE 2.4

Many browser hijacker programs set Internet Explorer home pages to open to the website Cool Web Search.

Why the notoriety? Because this type of spyware can be extremely difficult to remove. At one time, Webroot, an antispyware software maker, listed CoolWebSearch (CWS) as its top spyware threat on the Net. These days it lists a series of Trojan horses as its top threats (see Table 2.1).The hijacker program works by initially setting

> **tip**
> I show you how to rid yourself of a browser hijack on in Chapter 8, "Damage Control: How to Manually Remove Viruses and Spyware," **p. 260**. Make sure you bring your happy face. It ain't pretty.

your browser to the home page it wants. If you reset it, the hijacker's code runs and resets the home page again the next time your computer restarts or your browser is opened. It's as frustrating as cleaning doorknobs at a finger-painting festival. And worse, removing a browser hijacker requires some serious tinkering behind the scenes in Windows.

Key Loggers: Snooping on Your Typing Skills

Key loggers can be either hardware or software. The software versions run secretly in a computer's memory and capture everything typed into the computer. They then save it for later analysis by a third party. A key logger can also be a piece of hardware that is attached between a computer's keyboard and its keyboard port.

Sometimes Trojan horses install software key loggers and then give access to the computer to someone on the Internet so that they can fetch the log file containing the captured data remotely or "phone home" across the Internet to send it.

Dialers: Dial In, Dial Out, Dial Often

Dialers are programs that initialize a computer's modem and call out silently to a toll line and connect to a web page.

It's the computer equivalent of one of those psychic help lines they advertise on TV. The longer you are connected, the more you pay. The one difference is the "psychics" on the destination site you're connected to by dialers are not so psychic and they seem to have forgotten their clothes.

Victims can find themselves on the hook to pay a huge phone bill for a lengthy long distance call. Typically it's the charges to a toll number that cause the most pain, however.

The good news is dialers are ineffective if your computer's modem is not connected to a phone line with a dial tone.

> **note**
> More computers use broadband Internet connections these days, so dialer threats aren't as prolific as they used to be.

Trojan Horses: Pretty Ponies with Deadly Insides

I list Trojan horses here because antispyware programs often detect and issue spyware signatures for them. A *Trojan horse*, named after the famous hollow wooden horse that got the Greeks secretly into Troy, is an innocent-looking, innocuous program that contains a virus or some other nasty malware in its belly (for more on Trojan Horses, see Chapter 1, "Viruses: Attack of the Malicious Programs").

Even though Trojan horses are classified as a form of virus, they are also spyware because they can allow malicious people to connect remotely to your computer over the Internet. These are sometimes called *backdoor Trojans* because after they are installed on your computer, they can open an electronic backdoor so that someone bad can sneak in from the Internet.

Table 2.1   Top 10 Nastiest Spyware in the Wild, September 2006 to September 2007

Source: Paul Piccard, Director of Threat Research, Webroot Software, Inc.

Spyware Name	Type	Payload
Trojan-Downloader-Zlob	Trojan downloader	Downloads and installs rogue security programs such as SpywareQuake, SpyFalcon, and WinAntivirusPro. Can install other malware. Some variants have backdoor functionality.
Virtumonde	Adware	Downloads and displays popup ads.
Trojan-Phisher-SABanks	Phishing Trojan	Installs a key logger to grab login details for online banks in Spanish- and Portuguese-speaking countries.
Trojan-Busky	Trojan downloader	Downloads other threats to the compromised PC.
PurityScan	Adware	Installs advertising on a computer, including pop-ups, pop-unders, banners, or links within web pages or parts of the Windows interface.
Trojan-Peacomm	Trojan downloader	Downloads and executes malware.
Lopdotcom	Adware/Browser hijacker	Sets home page on browser to Lop.com.
SDBot	Trojan horse	Opens a backdoor and allows a remote attacker to control a computer using Internet Relay Chat.
Trojan-Phisher-Bzub	Phishing Trojan	Harvests personal information such as usernames and passwords to access financial accounts.
Trojan-DNSChanger	Trojan horse	Changes the DNS server settings on a compromised PC and redirects its web browser to potentially malicious sites.

Cookies: Does My Oreo Have a Tape Recorder in It?

Cookies are tiny text files stored on your computer (see Figure 2.5) to help websites track your movements through their pages. They also record sign-in data and other site logon information that allows easy access to the site when you come back later. Web shopping baskets also use cookies to keep track of what you have selected to buy as you move from page to page on a shopping site.

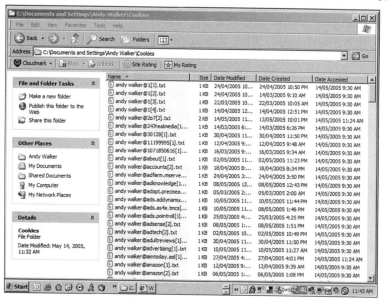

FIGURE 2.5

Cookies are stored as tiny text files on your computer for access by the websites that put them there.

Some antispyware programs classify these cookies as spyware. They can be classified as spyware because they do deliver information about your web surfing habits to someone else. But they are not all bad. In fact, some computer cookies are helpful.

Although it might seem objectionable to have your movements tracked on your own computer, it's not as insidious as you might think. Web programmers who code their sites to put cookies on your computer are the only entities that know the cookies are there. And they are the only ones who can access the information.

But cookies should be the least of your worries. Be more concerned about spilling guacamole on the cat.

If you visit, let's say, www.drunklazyhusbands.com, and it gives you a cookie to store on your computer, www.annoyedwiveslookingfortheirhusbands.com won't know about that cookie. There is one exception, however. Third-party cookies can potentially track your progress across the Internet. For example, if an Internet ad company is used across a variety of sites, then it could hand you a cookie on one site and read it when you visited another.

If you are worried, you can delete all or individual cookies that concern you from your computer. (Found out how in the "Clean Cookies" section on **p. 79** to learn how to do that.) If you delete a cookie for a specific site that you visit regularly, it won't know who you are anymore after the cookie is deleted. (A cookie can contain preference information you have set.)

Shopping sites use cookies frequently, so if you delete your cookies, you will have to re-enter information you have provided previously. Also note that deleting a site's cookies as you buy stuff on it would empty your shopping basket.

Cookies that are considered spyware are issued by web ad networks (see Figure 2.6). These keep track of the kind of ads you respond to so that they can provide more targeted material to you.

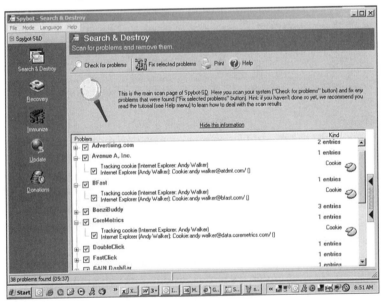

FIGURE 2.6

The antispyware program Spybot Search & Destroy earmarks the cookies on your computer that it considers to be spyware.

And in case you were wondering, if you visit keebler.com or oreo.com, you do get sent cookies, but sadly, not the delicious kind.

Who Is at Risk?

Spyware is the most widespread security threat to Windows-based computer users today. Depending on who you talk to, and how they define spyware, the vast majority of PC users have some form of spyware on their computer. If you include cookies, we all do.

Now you're probably thinking "almost everybody, but not me!" Let me reiterate. If you have never switched your computer on and you live alone, you don't have any spyware on your computer. Everyone else pretty much does.

And a word to those people (men: pay attention) who spend time on free websites that feature pictures of naked people—that's a great place to get spyware, especially the drive-by download kind.

> **tip** Some antispyware scanners might freak you out because they include cookies in their scans. It might look like you have hundreds of spyware infections, but if they are browser cookies they are mostly harmless, though purists will want to clean their cookies on a regular basis.

> **tip** You might have already surmised this, but cookies are an excellent way for others to easily see what kinds of sites you've visited lately. If you don't clean these out, your spouse, buddies, or co-workers can easily open the Cookies folder.
>
> To see your cookies, in Windows XP, navigate to Documents and Settings/Username/Cookies. On Vista they are hidden. First type **Folder Options** in the search bar of the Start menu. Then click Folder Options when it appears in the Start menu. Next click the View tab and scroll down to the item Hide Protected Operating System Files (Recommended) and uncheck the box. A warning dialog box will pop open. Be sure to click Yes on this. Next, check the radio button next to Show Hidden Files and Folders. Finally, browse to the cookies folder, which will now be revealed at c:\Users\[username]\AppData\Roaming\Microsoft\Windows\Cookies. Note that the [username] is your user folder and will be the name you use to log in to Vista.
>
> If you have any particular proclivities that you'd rather others not know about, delete the incriminating cookies. See the "Clean Cookies" section later in this chapter for more on how to deal with unwanted cookies.

2

2

How Do I Know If I Have Spyware?

Spyware is easy to spot, especially when there's a lot of spyware installed on a computer. Here are some symptoms:

- **Sluggish PC performance**—Spyware takes up computer memory and can bog down performance.

- **Weird pop-up ads**—If lots of annoying pop-up ads start to appear on your computer even when you are not surfing the Internet, chances are you have adware on your computer.

- **New toolbars you can't delete**—If a strange toolbar appears on your desktop or in your web browser and won't go away, it's probably spyware.

- **Unexpected changes to your home page settings**—If your web browser starts opening to a web page you've never seen before, your computer is likely infected with a browser hijacker.

- **Internet connections go awry**—If one day you can no longer connect to the Internet, it could be because spyware has been messing with your connection settings.

- **Unusual search results**—When you search for something on the Internet, a strange or unexpected search site produces results. Your web browser has probably been redirected by spyware to a search engine of its choosing.

- **Software malfunction**—If a program you use was working fine and then one day it won't start or it produces weird errors, it could be that spyware has corrupted files that your program requires to run or messed with the way it works.

- **Frequent computer crashes**—Spyware can cause a computer to crash either because a system is overwhelmed or because the spyware programming is badly written and causes the crashes.

tip Macintosh computers don't have the same problem with spyware as PCs. Each software install on newer Macs (which run the operating system called OS X) requires a user to type a password for the installation to continue, so self-installing spyware is stopped. That said, there has been spyware created for the Mac and it can find its way on to your Mac when you install legitimate software. It's safe to say that spyware is not a major problem on the Mac, while on PCs it's a plague. But do note that snoopware for the Mac does exist. Cookies are also a feature of web browsers on the Mac. Things may be about to change. A spate of Mac Trojans started appearing toward the end of 2007. They don't spread by themselves like a worm does, but it's the first concerted effort to infect Macs in a while. It may be the beginnings of a trend, especially as Mac computers are getting more

Defend Yourself Against Spyware

Spyware is more annoying than scary, though you do have to be on your guard against the worst of its ill effects, because it can be used to capture online banking information. Luckily, it is relatively easy to defend against. In this section I'll show you how to scan, cleanse, and defend your system against it. For the more advanced spyware infections, please see **p. 81**. Okay, let's get busy.

Spyware Countermeasures: 10-Minute Tactics

Here are a series of tasks that should take no more than 10 minutes each. When these tasks are complete, you'll be a lot less vulnerable to spyware.

Download a Free Antispyware Program

Spyware can be detected and cleansed with an antispyware program. It works similarly to an antivirus program except that its purpose is to keep your system free of spyware and adware.

The good news is there are many antispyware programs out there. The bad news is there are many antispyware programs out there. It's hard to choose the good from the bad. Some are great, some are not, and some are really awful and don't do much except find your cookies and flash overanxious alerts at you. So what to do?

The three products I recommend you use to protect your system are:

- Windows Defender
- Spybot Search & Destroy
- Ad-Aware 2007 Free

All three are free. In the case of Windows Defender (see Figure 2.7), it used to be called Giant AntiSpyware until Microsoft bought it. The happy news is it's one of the better products out there. (Say what you want about Microsoft, they never cheap out when it comes to key acquisitions.)

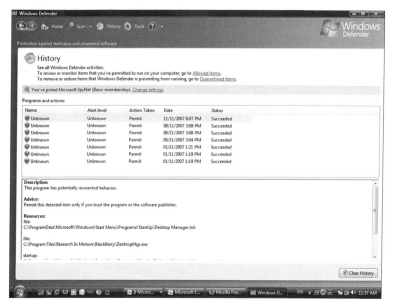

FIGURE 2.7

Windows Defender is an easy-to-use, highly effective antispyware tool for Windows XP, 2000 and Vista that's free.

Microsoft also built the program into Windows Vista. If you use Windows XP or Windows 2000, you can download Windows Defender for free from Microsoft's website. Note that it won't work on older versions of Windows.

Downloading and installing it takes about 10 minutes. So go do that now and then do a quick scan to cleanse your system of most of the pressing spyware threats. Then go back to your regularly scheduled life, until you have more time to think about the problem.

Windows Defender on Vista

Windows Defender comes built into Windows Vista. To run it, follow these easy steps:

1. Click the Windows button at the bottom left side of your screen and type **defender**.

2. To launch it, click Windows Defender when it appears in the Start menu.

> **tip**
> If you have an older copy of Windows such as Windows 95, 98, or Me, I suggest you get yourself a free copy of Spybot Search & Destroy from http://www.safer-networking.net or Ad-Aware 2007 Free from http://www.lavasoft.com.

3. When the program opens, click Scan at the top to run a quick spyware scan of your system. A Scan Now button will also be evident if the system hasn't done a recent scan. You can click that instead.

> **tip** Windows Defender also works on Windows 2000.

4. To do a more in-depth or custom scan, click the down arrow next to Scan and choose Full Scan or Custom Scan.

Windows Defender on XP

Windows XP doesn't come with Windows Defender, so you'll have to download and install it. Here's how:

1. Open Internet Explorer, and visit www.microsoft.com/defender/.

2. Find the Download It Here button and click it to get to the download page.

3. On the download page locate the Continue button. You'll see a "Validation Required" notation beside it.

> **caution** Make sure you have Windows XP Service Pack 2 in place before you get your hands on Windows Defender; otherwise, you won't be allowed to install it.

4. Click the Continue button (see Figure 2.8).

FIGURE 2.8

Before you can download Windows Defender, you have to go through the Windows validation process to ensure you have a legal copy of Windows XP.

5. The program takes you to a page where a plug-in called Windows Genuine Advantage will start to download. (But if you have done this recently for another piece of Microsoft software, it will skip this step and take you straight to the Windows Defender download page.)

6. Click Install on the dialog box. The plug-in will download. It used to do a full validation check here, but now it lets Windows Defender do that when it installs.

caution If you fail the validation test, you are not allowed to continue with the download. Microsoft gives you two options. If you send in your CD, show proof of ownership, and fill out a piracy report, the company replaces the CD with a free valid copy. If you don't have the CD, you can fill out a piracy report and get a discounted full version of Windows XP.

7. If your XP installation is legitimate, you'll be taken to another download page. This time you'll see a Download button that says "Genuine Microsoft Software" next to it.

8. Click it to download WindowsDefender.msi and choose either Run (or Save to download for a later installation) on the dialog box.

9. Windows Defender will then start to install (see Figure 2.9).

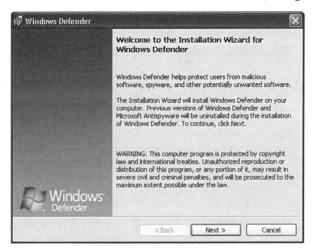

FIGURE 2.9

After you have jumped through Microsoft's download hoops, you can download Windows Defender and install it.

note If you do the validation with the Firefox web browser, the process has a few extra steps.

10. Click Next on the initial Windows Defender install screen.

11. Microsoft will get you to do another validation of XP at this point. Click Validate.

12. When you see a license agreement, read it and click the option I Accept the Terms in the License Agreement (if you agree).

caution To curtail software piracy, Microsoft requires you to run the Windows validation process each time you download an XP add-on. The exception is Windows security updates.

13. Click Next. On this screen (see Figure 2.10) you'll see an option to join the Microsoft SpyNet community, which gathers information from members' computers to build more effective spyware defenses. If you choose Recommended Settings, unwanted programs that Microsoft has assigned with a "high alert" designation will be removed automatically if detected on your system. Information from your system will also be sent via the Internet to Microsoft about Defender's actions on your system. Microsoft says this information will not be used to identify you personally.

14. Alternatively, you can opt out of this and choose Install Definition Updates Only. This opts you out of Microsoft's SpyNet program. Or you can choose later by selecting Ask Me Later.

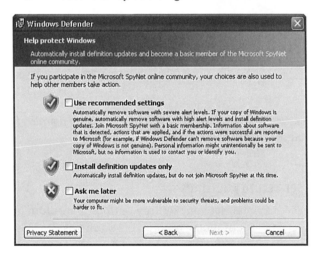

FIGURE 2.10

During the installation of Defender you'll be ask to join the Microsoft SpyNet community.

2

15. After you choose, click Next. Then choose whether you want a Complete installation or a Custom installation. Choose Complete as there aren't, ironically, any customizable options under Customize, at least not when I ran this installer. Of course, future versions may add custom options.

16. Finally, click Install. The program will take a few minutes to install.

17. On the installation completion screen, you'll see a check box to enable an update of Defender's spyware signatures (from the Internet) and to run a quick scan (see Figure 2.11). Check the box to say yes to this option. Uncheck to skip it. Click Finish.

18. If you opted in, Defender will fetch new signatures and do a scan.

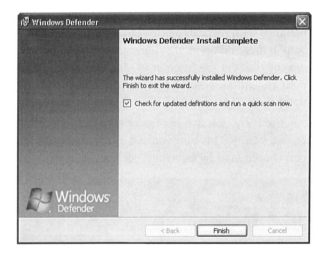

FIGURE 2.11
Before you are finished, you might want to select the option to download new spyware signatures and run a quick spyware scan.

Increase Browser Security Settings

In Internet Explorer, set your security settings to medium or high. This provides you with a reasonable amount of security as you surf the Web, and you'll see a warning if anything tries to download to your computer without your permission.

To set up Internet Explorer 7 so it's more secure, follow these steps for both Windows Vista and XP:

1. Click Tools on the top right and, in the drop-down menu, click Menu Bar so that the classic menu bar appears across the top.

2. Then click Tools on the menu bar and choose Internet Options.

3. Click the Security tab.

4. Click the Internet icon in the Web Content Zone box if it is not selected.

5. Click the Default Level button to reset the Security Levels For This Zone slider.

> **tip** You can see which version of Internet Explorer you have by clicking the Help menu and choosing About Internet Explorer. Version 7 shipped with Vista and is available for Windows XP at www.microsoft.com/ie/. In the future, when Internet Explorer 7 becomes yesterday's browser, you'll want to install the latest version.

6. The slider will be set by default to Medium-high (see Figure 2.12). If not, set it there unless you want to use the High setting. Note that the High setting may cause some websites to work poorly.

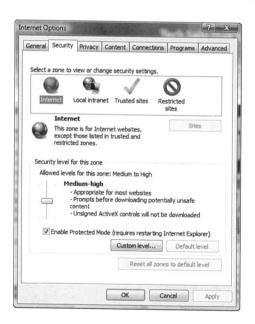

FIGURE 2.12

Set your Internet Explorer security settings to Medium-high or High.

ANTISPYWARE WEB-SURFING TIPS

If you remember these three tips, you'll be on your way to preventing spyware from getting onto your computer:

- Only download files or programs from websites you trust.

- Read a website's privacy statement and software license agreements. These provide you with clues to any misuse of your personal information when using these sites or about programs you download.

- Make sure you have the latest browser updates so that you are not vulnerable to drive-by downloads, where spyware is downloaded without your knowledge as you surf the Web.

- If you can't close a pop-up window, never click OK, Agree, or Close inside the body of the window. Only close the window by clicking the X in the top-right corner of the window.

Run Windows Update Frequently

You'll see this recommendation a lot in this book. Run Windows Update every week if it's not set to do this automatically. It's a good idea to run it manually anyway to see what noncritical updates may have become available.

Windows Update downloads all the latest security fixes for Windows XP and Vista.

In XP, click Start, then All Programs, and click Windows Update. In Vista, click the Windows button (the button formerly known as Start) on the bottom left side of your screen and type **update** in the Search box, and then click Windows Update when it appears in the menu above it.

Update Your Spyware Signatures

If you already have an antispyware program installed, be sure to update its spyware signatures regularly. These are like mugshots of bad guys. The antispyware program compares the spyware signatures to potential threats as they arrive on your

> **tip** If your computer uses Windows XP, the most critical fix available is a huge security update from Microsoft called Service Pack 2 (SP2). Note that sometime in 2008, SP3 will also become available. Learn more about installing SP2 on **p. 324.**

computer. If there's a match, the program stops the spyware. Some antispyware programs update these signatures automatically. On others you have to do it yourself. For example, Windows Defender automatically updates its signatures, while Spybot Search & Destroy does not (see Figure 2.13).

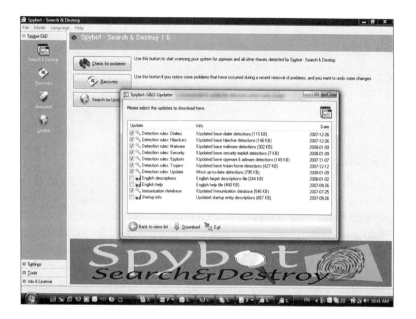

FIGURE 2.13

To keep Spybot Search & Destroy up to date, you need to check for new spyware signatures using the program's update feature.

Ban All Spies: Strong Spyware Defense in an Afternoon

Here are a few techniques you can employ to make your system more resistant to spyware and safeguard it further.

Run a Full System Scan

Most antispyware programs offer both a quick scan feature and a full system scan feature (sometimes called a *deep scan*). When you have more time, be sure to run a full system scan (see Figure 2.14). The program digs deeper into your system to look for less obvious spyware.

FIGURE 2.14

Windows Defender features a full system scan option that should be run every couple of weeks or when you have time to check every nook and cranny of your computer for spyware.

Install a Second Antispyware Program

The antispyware program you choose will not stop and clean all spyware infections. There are so many kinds of spyware that many antispyware programs only capture a portion of them. So to be vigilant, it's advisable to use two antispyware programs on your computer. I've had good luck with using both Windows Defender and Spybot Search & Destroy together. I also like Webroot Spy Sweeper which is bundled in as part of Webroot's security suite (see Figure 2.15), a commercial antispyware product available from www.webroot.com that is very effective at catching more spyware than the freebies. PC Tools Spyware Doctor from www.pctools.com is also a good commercial product.

A third free antispyware tool is Ad-Aware 2007, free available from http://www.lavasoft.com.

I recommend at a minimum that you run Windows Defender and Spybot Search & Destroy together. The most potent combination is to run those two and a third commercial antispyware product.

It may seem like overkill, but spyware infections can be nasty.

caution I strongly recommend you take this advice if you run the poorly defended and extremely vulnerable Windows XP.

FIGURE 2.15

I recommend using two antispyware programs. Besides Windows Defender and Spybot, I like using Webroot Spy Sweeper which is integrated into the company's security suite (shown).

Inoculate Your System

Windows Defender comes with a feature called Real-time Protection (see Figure 2.16). This feature watches 100 key areas of your computer looking for spyware behavior. If a setting is changed or an Internet connection is made, it alerts you to the behavior with an information pop-up box. If the alert is deemed severe, it asks you for a decision.

Spybot Search & Destroy also has a similar feature. It's called Immunize. It tweaks settings in Internet Explorer to block installation of known spyware.

caution In Vista, the Immunize feature on Spybot won't work unless you run Spybot with "Elevated privileges." To do that, instead of simply clicking in the icon on the program to start it, you first right-click the icon and choose Run as Administrator. When you do this, Windows will grey out the screen and trigger a User Account Control (UAC) alert. Click Continue and the program will start with elevated privileges. That will allow the Immunize feature to run properly when you activate it from inside the program.

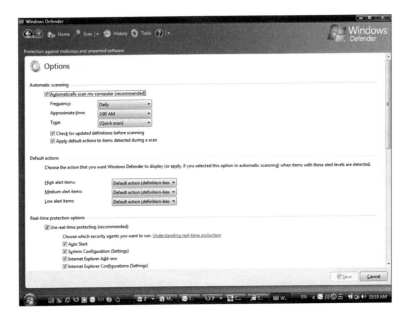

FIGURE 2.16

Windows Defender has a feature called Real-time Protection that watches over 100 key entry points used by spyware to get onto a computer.

Use Firefox As Your Primary Browser

If anyone is to blame for the spyware problem, it's Microsoft. That's because it produced Windows XP without proper attention to security at a time when really fast consumer Internet connections became available. At particular fault is Microsoft's web browser Internet Explorer (IE).

IE has all kinds of functions that are exploited by spyware writers. These include software called Browser Helper Objects (BHOs), which are add-ons for the browser that can auto-install from the Web. IE also uses something called ActiveX, which allows mini-programs to self-install on a computer. Many people stop using IE as their primary browser. Instead they install Firefox (see Figure 2.17), a really nice alternative from Mozilla.org that doesn't have the security holes that plague IE. I highly recommend it. Installing and using it should be a high priority for you. Not only will you have a more secure Internet experience, but the browser is also better designed.

caution If you install multiple anti-spyware products on your system, then it is important to turn on real-time protection (or its equivalent feature if it's called something else) for only one of them.

FIGURE 2.17

Using Firefox as your primary web browser closes one door on spyware on your system because its mechanisms won't allow spyware to come onto your system automatically.

That said, Microsoft has since made lots of repairs to IE. Internet Explorer 7, which is available for XP and comes with Vista, is a lot more secure than its predecessors. Note that IE8 will be released sometime in 2008.

You can't totally abandon IE because some sites, including Microsoft's own Windows Update, won't work without it.

However, installing and using Firefox most of the time is a good stopgap against getting a machine chock full o' spyware.

IE7's Protected Mode on Vista

One critical new antispyware feature in Internet Explorer 7 is called Protected Mode. It's designed to stop automatic downloading of spyware in the background on Vista. (The feature is engineered to work with Vista's security system. You won't find it in IE7 for XP.)

Spyware harnesses a technology called ActiveX to download in the background. Unfortunately ActiveX controls, which are little bits of Microsoft programming, can also add exciting features to websites.

Protected Mode stops ActiveX controls from doing unauthorized tasks.

However, it can also block legitimate website features. I recommend you leave Protected Mode on all the time and if it causes problem on a specific website, then deactivate it temporarily, as follows:

1. First, turn on Internet Explorer's classic menus by clicking the Tools button at the far right side of the browser near the top. Choose Menu Bar. It'll activate the traditional IE menu options (that is, File, Edit, View, and so on) across the top of the browser.

2. Next click the Tools item in the menu bar and choose Internet Options.

3. Click the Security tab.

4. Uncheck Enable Protected Mode. Click OK and close Internet Explorer (see Figure 2.18).

5. Open Internet Explorer again. Protected Mode will be turned off and you can see this because at the bottom you'll see the notation: Protected Mode: Off.

6. To turn it on again, go back to the Security tab as before and put a check mark in the Enable Protected Mode box, close IE, and restart the browser.

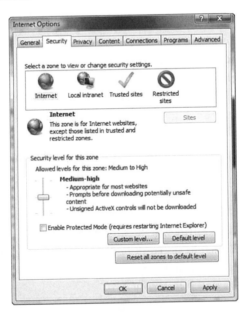

FIGURE 2.18

If you encounter a website that won't work properly in Internet Explorer on Vista, uncheck the Enable Protected Mode box temporarily in IE7's Security tab.

Clean Cookies

If you'd like to clean browser cookies in the Internet Explorer web browser (see Figure 2.19), take the following steps in both XP and Vista:

1. Open Internet Explorer 7.
2. Click Tools on the top right and, in the drop-down menu, click Menu Bar so that the classic menu bar appears across the top (if it's not showing already).
3. Then click Tools on the menu bar and choose Delete Browsing History at the top of the menu.
4. Click the Delete Cookies button in the Cookies section.
5. When the dialog box says Are you sure?, choose Yes.

To selectively delete cookies, follow these steps:

1. Click Tools on the menu across the top of the browser and choose Internet Options.
2. On the General tab, click the Settings button in the Browsing History section.
3. A dialog box will open. Click the View Files button and the Temporary Internet Files folder will open (see Figure 2.20). Locate the cookie files. They will be named like this: cookie:andy@deathtobeets.com
4. In the preceding example, my user name "andy" is used in the cookie's name. In your cookies your username will be used. After the @ sign the site that the cookie was created by will be listed.
5. These listings are actual files, some of which are cookies, so delete them selectively.

FIGURE 2.19

In Internet Explorer's Delete Browsing History dialog box, you can clean all your cookies with one click.

2

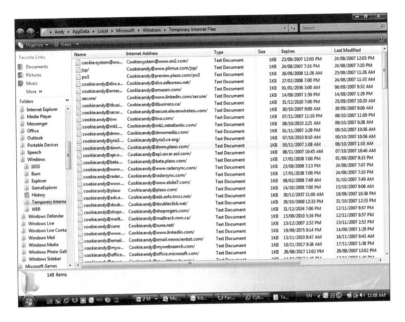

FIGURE 2.20

You use Internet Explorer to access the Temporary Internet Files folder and selectively delete cookie files.

If you'd like to clean your cookies in Firefox 2.0 (see Figure 2.21), do the following:

1. Start Firefox.

2. Click the Tools menu, and then click Options.

3. On the top menu, click the Privacy icon.

4. In the Cookies section, click Show Cookies then click the Remove All Cookies button. To selectively delete them, select the site (or click a plus sign and expand a site and choose single cookies), then press the Delete key or click the Remove Cookies button.

5. Click OK when you are done.

> **caution** It's inevitable that Mozilla will release Firefox version 3.0 and beyond. So some of the features described here may be moved around. However, the cookie management tools won't likely go away. So when you upgrade to version 3.0, be sure to read these instructions to get the gist of what to do and then poke around the Firefox 3.0 menus to find the new tools if these instructions don't quite fit what you see.

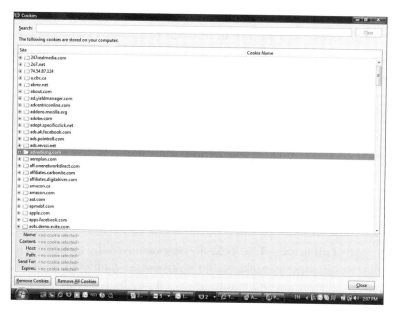

FIGURE 2.21

In the Firefox Cookies dialog you can wipe out cookies all at once or selectively.

Spyware Infection Found!
How to Scrub Your System

Despite your best efforts, you might still get infected by spyware or adware. In fact, because of the pernicious nature of this kind of malware, it's almost a certainty. So this section will come in handy. Here's how to clean spyware and adware from your system.

> **caution** If you clean your web browser's cookies, you could wipe away the good with the bad. Cookies can be used to remember user IDs, passwords, and other settings you use to log on to membership-based websites. So be aware that if you wipe your cookies clean, you'll have to re-enter this info the next time you visit a membership-based website such as your online bank.

Clean, Yes! Spyware, No!

I am going to show you how to use Windows Defender to remove threats. The process that most other antispyware programs use is not that different.

First, you'll want to run a system scan to detect infections. When you do this, the software does the following:

- It examines all the files on your computer looking for traces of spyware.
- It scours your computer memory looking for active spyware.

■ It checks the Windows registry, which is a massive storehouse of settings and data used to run your computer.

■ It also examines web browser and system settings as well as the startup areas of Windows.

Antispyware programs usually offer two kinds of scans:

■ **Quick scan** —This kind of scan checks the likely hiding places that spyware set up camp in, but it doesn't delve too deeply into the deep, dark areas of your hard drive. A quick scan catches most active spyware on your system, but misses the ones that are dormant or that have cleverly obscured themselves. This is handy to run a couple of times a week or when you think your system might have recently been compromised.

■ **Full scan** —This looks at the same areas the quick scan looks at but also deeply combs the hard drive seeking any sign of spyware. It checks every nook and cranny, every bit and byte. As a result, it takes a while to complete. This should be done weekly. This is sometimes called a deep scan.

Windows Defender has both modes. Let me take you through a full scan. Before you start, check to see if there are any spyware signature updates.

1. Make sure you are connected to the Internet. (If you can check email or surf the Web, you are connected.)

2. Start Windows Defender. On the Start menu it can be found under the All Programs menu in both XP and Vista.

3. Click the down arrow to the right of the blue circle with the white question mark on the top right side of the main Windows Defender window. Choose Check for updates. (In Vista, you will also have to click Continue on the UAC warning.)

4. Choose Check for Updates.

5. The program will check to see if there are any new updates on the Microsoft server and downloads and installs them and pops open a message when it's done (see Figure 2.22).

To do a full scan for spyware on your system, follow these steps:

1. Click the down arrow to the right of Scan on the menu at the top of the main Windows Defender window.

2. Choose Full Scan.

3. The program will start to scan your system. Let it go to completion.

FIGURE 2.22

Windows Defender will alert you if new updates are available and download them.

When the scan is complete, Windows Defender lists all the threats it found, rates their severity, and recommends an action (see Table 2.2).

Table 2.2   How to Interpret Windows Defender Alerts

Alert	Explanation	Recommended Action
Severe	A really wide-reaching malicious program that is similar to viruses or worms. Compromises your privacy and your system's security. May damage your PC.	Remove it as soon as possible.
High	Programs that might snatch personal data and compromise your privacy or damage your system. May change system settings without your knowledge or permission.	Remove it as soon as possible.
Medium	Programs that can invade privacy or edit settings on your PC that could impair your use of the system.	Read the information in the alert to understand why the software was detected. Consider blocking or removing the software if you don't like what it does.
Low	Potentially unwanted program. It may collect personal information or modify settings on your PC. However, it runs in line with the licensing terms you agreed to when you installed it.	If you're ok with the licensing agreement, leave this in place. If you didn't install it, remove it. If in doubt, remove it.
Not yet classified	Programs that won't hurt your system unless they were installed on your computer without your knowledge.	If you recognize the software, leave it be. If not, seek further information on the Internet.

What to Do When an Infection Is Found

When Windows Defender finishes its scan, it gives you the option to remove it. Click Continue. Hum merrily—spyware killing can be fun. Be sure to reboot your system after the removal process is done to stop spyware from regenerating. As long as it's in memory, some spyware and adware can re-install, self-repair, and download new infections from the Internet.

If the Removal Routine Fails

If an antispyware program has a problem removing a threat, you may want to do a scan with it in Windows Safe Mode.

Safe Mode is a Windows troubleshooting mode that allows you to run Windows without loading anything unnecessary in memory. You can get into it by restarting your computer and hitting F8 repeatedly as the computer starts. This takes you to a menu where you choose Safe Mode and boot into Windows in a raw state. This is useful to remove spyware and viruses because in Safe Mode nothing extraneous is loaded into memory, except key Windows components. Since program components spyware uses are not in memory in this state, they can be easily removed. Think of it like this: You can't put a ladder in the garage if you're standing on it. And you can't delete a program if it's running.

Running a scan in Safe Mode increases your chances of successfully removing the threat completely. Before going into Safe Mode, don't forget to update your spyware signatures first, by using the Update button in the program (see the previous section).

note Booting in Windows Safe Mode causes Windows to start up using only its most basic components (mouse, monitor, and keyboard drivers, for example). When in Safe Mode, Windows doesn't load a bevy of other drivers, startup applications, and the like, meaning any spyware lurking on your PC will be peacefully snoozing when you take the wood stake to it. Think of Safe Mode as Windows Unplugged, if you will. It's still Windows, just without all the frills. Here, you are better able to nix spyware (it's a good place to deal with viruses too). After you're done removing spyware, reboot your computer in Normal Mode and enjoy your spyware-free computer.

The Absolute Minimum

- Spyware is software that installs secretly and snoops on you on your computer.
- Low-risk spyware invades your privacy. High-risk spyware can steal banking information.
- Adware is like spyware; it snoops, but it also pushes unwanted advertising at you.

- You have to accept some adware if you want to run certain free programs.

- Other types of spyware include snoopware, Trojan horses, dialers, browser hijackers, key loggers, and cookies.

- Not all cookies are bad. Some are needed for online shopping and remembering user settings and passwords when you return to a website.

- All PC users are at risk of getting spyware. Spyware is almost nonexistent on a Mac.

- Spyware comes from web pages, free software, and email attachments. Trojan horses can also secretly download spyware onto your computer.

- Spyware compromises your privacy and can put you at risk for identity theft. It can also slow down your computer by using up system resources.

- Your first line of defense against spyware is an antispyware program. Three good free ones are Windows Defender, Spybot Search & Destroy, and Ad-Aware SE. I also recommend the payware products Webroot Spy Sweeper or its security suite (which includes Spy Sweeper) and PC Tools Spyware Doctor.

- Scan once a week and keep your spyware signatures up to date.

- You should scan with at least two spyware programs because no single program catches all infections.

- Service Pack 2 (SP2) should be installed on your Windows XP computer to help defend against spyware. Install SP3 for XP when it becomes available. Be sure to install SP1 for Vista if you run a computer that uses Windows Vista.

- Windows Vista has improved defenses against spyware because it uses a new feature called UAC or User Account Control.

Rootkits: Sneaky, Stealthy Toolboxes

Rootkits are not so much malware themselves, as they are deviously clever toolboxes that make malware vanish even though it is still there. In this chapter you'll find out how they work, how to scan and remove them, and how Sony made the term famous.

What Is a Rootkit?

Let's say you're toodling around the house one Saturday morning, perhaps tidying up, when you notice some odd things about your home. The back door is ajar. Strangely, your checkbooks and bank statements have been moved from your desk to a pile by the door. There's luggage in the living room that contains valuable things that are clearly not yours. The phone dials people on the speed dial by itself.

You may initially attribute these oddities to wayward children, a forgetful spouse, or the odd behavior of a visiting neighbor who recently stopped by to say hello on their way to Hawaii. But if you put things back to the way they should be and the oddities reoccur or even stranger activity happens, you might suspect ghosts—if you're inclined that way—or worse, intruders.

If I told you it was a criminal with an invisibility cloak, you'd think I was crazy.

Let's say this wasn't your home where all this happened, but instead your computer; then maybe the weird activity might be more plausible. A port out to the Internet is open. Your personal data has been copied or removed. Large ZIP files containing information you don't recognize have been stored in a folder. People in your address book start receiving e-mails from you that you didn't send.

A Trojan horse, a virus, or spyware might all be responsible for this behavior. But then again, a quick scan would reveal what is going on and which malware is responsible.

But what of that invisibility cloak? In the world of computer security, the invisibility cloak exists—and it's called a rootkit.

What Are Rootkits Used For?

Imagine if you had an invisibility cloak. You could have some real fun and, if you were inclined, do some real damage. You could spy on people undetected. You could use other people's property without them knowing. You could win contests, spy on people in their underwear, steal money, and commit all these crimes undetected.

This is what rootkits are used for in the computer world. A rootkit is simply a digital toolbox that can be added to malware—a Trojan, spyware, or a virus—to conceal it and provide it with unfettered access to your computer.

A decade ago, malware creation—especially virus-writing—was an ego-trip for its authors. The more the malware's impact was felt (and as a consequence the more visible it was to the victim), the more successful its creator considered it to be. Massive virus or worm infections conferred bragging rights on their authors.

Not so any more. Malware writing is a business; a dirty business perhaps, but a business all the same that can generate hundreds of millions of dollars for its creators.

The longer a computer is infected with malware, and the longer it remains concealed, the more time there is for it to generate its illicit revenue.

So rootkits are used to hide digital infections so that they can continue to produce money for their authors.

> **note** The term rootkit came from the Unix world. Unix is an operating system (a family of operating systems actually) used traditionally by businesses. These Unix-powered computers are used by companies, governments, and universities to share files, storage, and information resources in a large enterprise. "Root access" on a Unix system is the uber-account that gives the person who logs in superpowers on the system to do anything they want. So rootkits are toolboxes that give a program access to the most sensitive and highest-level folders and files. They not only provide deep access to the system and its files, but because they are all-powerful, they can also conceal that a program has been given privileged access.

Rock Star Rootkit: Sony's Famous Malware

Back in 2005, "rootkit" was not a well-known term in the popular culture of the Internet. All that changed when music company Sony BMG decided to use a rootkit in digital rights management software (a program that limits copying) on 102 of their music CD titles.

At the time, the music industry was sweating over the perceived losses that they were suffered over music piracy. Music consumers were ripping songs from CDs to MP3 files and sharing them on the Internet, especially on an infamous website called Napster (which has since gone legitimate).

In response, Sony BMG executives decided to put one of two copy protection technologies on their discs: XCP or MediaMax.

When CD buyers inserted the protected disc into their Windows computer, anti-copying software was quietly installed on the computer without the user's permission. Part of this package was a rootkit to conceal the anti-copying mechanism.

The problem was that the Sony-installed rootkit could also be harnessed by malware writers who knew it existed to conceal their nasty programs.

When technology writer Mark Russinovich discovered the DRM and associated rootkit programming on his system, he wrote a post on his blog that exposed what Sony BMG was doing. It resulted in a public backlash that forced Sony BMG to remove the offending software from its discs and issue an apology.

note Read Mark Russinovich's famous blog post (see Figure 3.1) that unveiled the Sony BMG DRM and rootkit strategy here: http://blogs.technet.com/markrussinovich/archive/2005/10/31/sony-rootkits-and-digital-rights-management-gone-too-far.aspx, or use this shorter address: http://tinyurl.com/y94s8m

FIGURE 3.1

Blogger Mark Russinovich chronicled how he found a rootkit on his system installed from a Sony BMG music CD.

How to Recognize a Sony Copy-protected CD

You may be wondering whether one of the CDs in your collection has the Sony copy-protection technology (called XCP or MediaMax) on board. Here's how to tell:

1. Look at the spine of the CD. You'll see a notation that says "Content Protected". (See a picture here: http://www.eff.org/cases/sony-bmg-litigation-info.)

2. On the back of the CD, you'll see a box that includes the words "Compatible with" that explains what system requirements are needed to play the CD.

3. If the CD uses XCP, you'll also see a web address as follows: cp.sonybmg.com/xcp/. The tip-off is the XCP in the address, the name of the offending copy-protection program.

4. If the CD uses MediaMax you'll also see a web address as follows: www.sunncomm.com/support/sonybmg. The tip-off is the SunnCom.com in the address. It's the name of the company that makes MediaMax.

5. You should also check this official list of CD titles that included the controversial copy protection: http://sonybmg.com/xcpcdlist.html.

How to Remove Sony BMG Copy-protection

If you discover that one of your CDs has the Sony BMG copy protection and you know that you've played it on your computer, you can remove it by using an uninstaller provided by the company.

There are two types of copy protection: XCP and MediaMax. Each one has its own removal method as follows.

> **tip** Most major up-to-date anti-virus programs will detect the flawed Sony rootkit technology and remove it.

How to Remove XCP

You'll need to use the Sony-provided program to remove or update the XCP copy protection.

If you remove it, you will not be able to play the CD on your computer. If you update it, the programming with the security flaw will be removed and you'll continue to be able to play the CD.

The program to remove or update the XCP software can be downloaded from this web site: http://cp.sonybmg.com/xcp/english/updates.html.

Sony's web site also provides this manual removal procedure:

1. Locate the c:\Windows\Downloaded Program Files folder.

2. Look for the file: "CodeSupport Control".

3. Right click on the file and select Remove.

4. If that file is not found in the directory, your computer is not affected.

How to Remove MediaMax

Sony provides a free uninstaller to remove the MediaMax software on this website: http://cp.sonybmg.com/mediamax/english/updates.html. To manually remove the program:

> **tip** Go to the Sony BMG XCP Frequently Asked Questions web page for more detailed information: http://cp.sonybmg.com/xcp/english/faq.html

1. Locate the folder called C:\Windows\Downloaded Program Files or C:\WINNT\Downloaded Program Files.

2. Look for a file called "AxWebRemoveCtrl Control."

3. Right-click the file and select Remove from the pop-up window.

4. If you can't find the file, it is not installed on your computer.

How a Rootkit Works

A virus or spyware scanner works by looking at digital signatures or snapshots of the virus or its component parts. They may be detected by looking for entries in the Windows registry (a filing cabinet for programs that contains settings) or references in system boot processes.

Rootkits conceal this trail of evidence (see Figure 3.2) by suppressing their existence by interrupting how the operating system accesses files and information and filtering out evidence of files or settings before an operating system displays it to the user.

This makes it invisible to the user and potentially to any malware detectors that may be installed on the computer.

> **tip** Learn more about how rootkits work here: http://www.informit.com/articles/article.aspx?p=408884&seqNum=5.

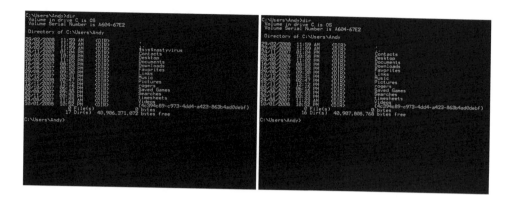

FIGURE 3.2

Here's a simulation of what a rootkit does. The folder sysnastyvirus exists on both systems, but in the one on the right it's being concealed by a rootkit.

Rootkit Detection and Removal

The problem with rootkits is that they make their changes invisible and conceal themselves. So if you keep an invisibility cloak in the attic, how do you find it if you can't see it? Good question.

The simplest way to detect a rootkit is to use an antivirus or antispyware scanner. Most well-branded and modern malware detection products have tools built into them to detect and remove rootkits.

Rootkit writers and security program writers engage in a bit of a cat-and-mouse game analyzing each other's approaches and writing new programming to hide or detect rootkits, depending on which side of the fence they're on.

So if you use a security utility from Norton, McAfee, F-Secure (see Figure 3.3) or any of the other big-brand security suites on Windows XP or Windows Vista and you pay for annual updates so that the programs are current, then you can assume that you are mostly protected from most rootkits that may find their way onto your system.

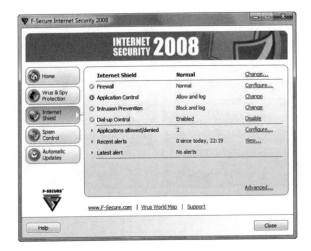

FIGURE 3.3
F-Secure Internet Security and other big-brand security suites have built-in rootkit detection and removal capabilities.

Mostly Protected? You Can Do Better Than That!

Of course, that phrase "mostly protected" means that a few rootkits may slip through and go undetected by your security software. That's like detecting most of the mad cows in the herd but letting one or two through. It's not particularly acceptable.

The safest strategy is to scan with more than one security program. So be sure to scan with a current antivirus program and perhaps two antispyware programs.

That said, the easiest way to remove a rootkit is to use Windows System Restore. This utility can be used to roll back the operating system to remove any programs that have been installed—including malware and the rootkits that hide it—since they were installed.

A step-by-step procedure showing how to use System Restore for this purpose in both Windows XP and Windows Vista is offered at the end of this chapter on **p. 98**.

You might also try one or more of the free rootkit scanners described in the next section.

> **tip** You can also try the free antivirus programs mentioned in Chapter 12, "Tools of the Trade," starting on **p. 379** to do rootkit detection.

Free Rootkit Scanners

There are several decent rootkit scanners available for free download from the Internet. Here are several you can try.

F-Secure Blacklight

This freebie scanner (see Figure 3.4) is a standalone version of the rootkit detection technology that has been built into F-Secure's Security Suite (one of my favorite payware security products). It works on both Windows XP and Windows Vista. It's easy to use and perhaps the best freebie anti-rootkit utility out there.

Download the scanner from http://www.f-secure.com/blacklight/.

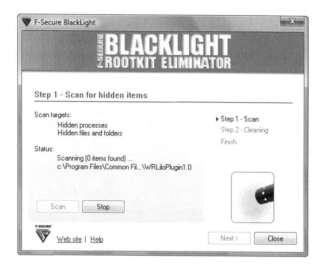

FIGURE 3.4

F-Secure's Blacklight is a free and easy-to-use rootkit scanner.

RootkitRevealer

RootkitRevealer is a free rootkit scanner (see Figure 3.5) written by Bryce Cogswell and Sony rootkit sleuth Mark Russinovich, whom I mentioned earlier. Note that it is only a detector. If it finds a rootkit, it'll let you know what it's called, and then you'll have to do some research on the web to figure out to remove it. This program doesn't like Vista much, so I only recommend it for use with Windows XP (its authors say it works on Windows 2000 or Windows NT4, but I didn't test it on these).

Download the scanner from http://technet.microsoft.com/en-us/sysinternals/ bb897445.aspx.

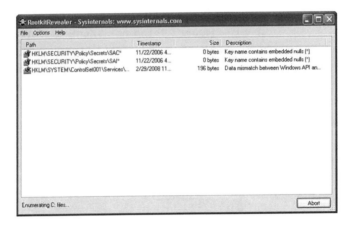

FIGURE 3.5

RootkitRevealer can detect rootkits, but you'll have to figure out how to remove them yourself.

Microsoft Windows Malicious Software Removal Tool

This free scanner and removal tool from Microsoft (see Figure 3.6) is designed to seek out well-known worms and viruses that plague Windows, including the Hacker Defender rootkit, and eliminate them. It's worth downloading to scan for that named rootkit, but note that other rootkit detection capabilities may be made available in future with this tool.

The program works on Windows XP and Windows Vista as well as business-specific operating systems Windows Server 2003 and Windows 2000.

Download the program from http://www.microsoft.com/security/ malwareremove/.

tip It's possible that you already received a copy of the Malicious Software Removal Tool and it may have already run on your system. Windows Update made it available to everyone. If you downloaded it that way, it'll run in the background and will only be evident if an infection is found. To run it more frequently, download it to your computer and put it in a place where you can find it later and then run it as you see fit.

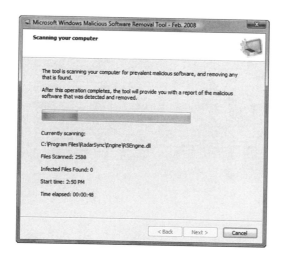

FIGURE 3.6

Microsoft provides the free Malicious Software Removal Tool, which can detect and remove the Hacker Defender rootkit.

Rootkit Hook Analyzer

This free tool can sniff out programs that are hooked into the heart of Windows (called the kernel) and may be able to intercept and modify information to and from the kernel. When you run this tool you'll see what programs (see Figure 3.7) are using this approach. The application is worth a run to see if anything weird turns up. It runs on Windows XP and Windows Vista, as well as Windows Server 2003 and Windows 2000.

Download the tool from http://www.resplendence.com/hookanalyzer.

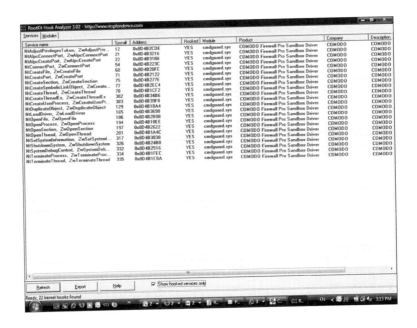

FIGURE 3.7

The Rootkit Hook Analyzer shows what programs have hooks into the Windows kernel. In this case, it's the Comodo firewall.

How to Use System Restore to Turf a Rootkit

The easiest way to get rid of a rootkit and its associated malware infection is to use the Windows utility System Restore to roll the system back to the way it was the day before the system was infected.

This is only possible if Windows creates a restore point (like a bookmark for your system setup) as far back as the day before the infection took hold. By default Windows sets a restore point every day. Some programs will also create restore points before they are installed.

So as soon as you know your system is infected, it's a good idea to try this technique.

caution Note that some malware will erase restore points to stop you from rolling the system back to get rid of them.

Here's how to activate a restore point:

For Windows XP:

1. Click the Start button, All Programs, and then Accessories.
2. Choose System Tools, then System Restore.
3. Select Restore My Computer to an Earlier Time and click Next.
4. Use the calendar to choose the date that most closely matches the day before the infection occurred (if you know) or choose the date an appropriate amount of time back so that it would be before the infection. If a restore point is available for a particular day, it will be bold-faced in the calendar. Click the date to see what's available for that day and select the one you want.
5. Click Next and shut down all unnecessary programs. Then click Next again to start the process. Your system will shut down and will be restored to the way it was on the selected date when it reboots, hopefully without the pesky infection and rootkit.

For Windows Vista:

1. Click the Windows button and type **System Restore** in the search bar.
2. Click System Restore when it appears. Click Continue on the User Account Control alert.
3. Then Select the Choose a Different Restore Point radio button and click the Next button.
4. A list of recent restore points with times and dates will appear (see Figure 3.8). Put a check mark in the box that says Show Restore Points Older Than 5 Days and scroll down to see what's available. Choose the date that most closely matches the day before the infection occurred if you know, or choose a date an appropriate amount of time back so that it would be before the infection. Select that date by clicking on it.
5. Click Next, then Finish. The system will reboot and when it starts up again it will look like the system on the date specified (hopefully without the rootkit and associated malware infection). Note that your personal data, including e-mail, will not be regressed to that date (that is, won't be deleted). Only programs and registry changes and system settings will be undone back to the day specified.

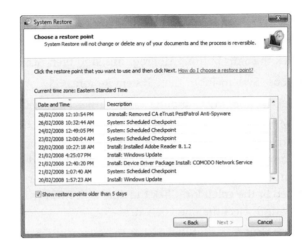

FIGURE 3.8

Use System Restore on both XP and Vista (shown) to regress your computer back to the way it was on a particular date, before an infection.

The Absolute Minimum

- Rootkits can conceal and give deep access to a computer system to any program, including malware such as a virus, spyware, or a Trojan horse.

- Sony BMG put a rootkit on their protected CDs that installed on users' systems and yet could be used by malware writers to conceal viruses or spyware. The company later backpedaled when the strategy was revealed by a blogger.

- Rootkits can be hard to detect. Do a scan with more than one security suite, including an antivirus program, an antispyware program, or one of the free rootkit utilities.

- You can use Windows System Restore to roll back a system to the date before it was infected, thus removing an installed rootkit and associated malware.

Hackers: There's a Man in My Machine

I f your computer is a fortress, hackers are the interlopers with pointy metal hats who charge the gate, scale the walls, or use stolen keys to get inside. Their mission? To steal your crown jewels or carve graffiti on the walls, such as "The king is a weenie.!" In this chapter, I'll tell you why they want access to your computer, how they gain access to it, and what you stand to lose if they do. There's also a really exciting section on how to stop them and what to do if one of them succeeds. It's like a medieval video game, but scarily, it's real.

What Is a Hacker?

Hacker is one of those terms that has a different meaning depending on who uses it. Among programmers, to be a hacker is to be a star. Hackers are programming code jockeys who can throw together bits of miraculous pieces of programming seemingly at will. They are gurus. People who modify computer and other types of electronic hardware are also sometimes called hackers.

note You might hear the terms *white hat* or *black hat* in reference to a hacker or cracker. A black hat is a bad person who gains unauthorized access to a computer or network for non-altruistic reasons. A white hat is a security expert who attempts to gain access to a computer or network to detect vulnerabilities so they can be patched. Pink hats are just fashionable.

Being a hacker can also be a bad thing. A hacker or *hack* can sometimes be someone who has no grace or elegance in his work and throws his projects together haphazardly. Among the general public (thanks to the media and perhaps Hollywood), a hacker is a person who gains illicit access to a computer and steals stuff or breaks into military networks and launches missiles for fun and with no conscience.

To complicate things even further, those who are hackers in the break-and-enter sense consider themselves *crackers* or *black-hat hackers*.

And among people who eat cheese, crackers are savory biscuits.

So you see the problem here. For simplicity's sake, I am going to use the popular mass-media definition of hackers interchangeably with crackers. Both terms refer to bad people who divine access to your computer across the Internet by compromising its defenses or using electronic loopholes.

Who Are the Hackers?

Hackers and crackers are usually highly intelligent social misfits who tend to have a strong curiosity and often have an anarchist or, at the very least, anti-authoritarian bent. They see the Internet as a playground and they tend to believe information should be free. Sometimes they are described as digital joy riders.

In an interview on SafeMode.org, one hacker—who used the nickname xentric—explained why he hacks:

"It's just that feeling when you finally get something done. You put lots of effort into some hacks and I feel a rush of excitement whenever I succeed in doing something. What is the incentive that keeps (me) doing it? Curiosity…"

It's safe to say that the vast majority of people who try to gain illegal access to computers are young men. Many high-profile hackers are in their 20s and

30s. However, many are simply teenagers who have access to publicly available hacking tools that can be downloaded easily from the Internet.

There's a hierarchy in the hacker community. High-status crackers write their own tools and develop their own break-in mechanisms to gain access to computers. Lower down on the hacker food chain are script kiddies. These electronic intruders use freely distributed tools designed by others to engage in computer vandalism, break-ins, or electronic theft.

What Damage Can Hackers Do?

Hackers like to subvert computer security without permission. They are cyber criminals. This can mean gaining access to a computer across the Internet for illicit purposes. They might engage in any of the following activities:

- **Vandalism**—Destruction or digital defacement of a computer or its data for destruction's sake. Sometimes this is ego-driven. They break in and leave their mark to show they've been there.

- **Hacktivism**—A form of vandalism or electronic civil disobedience with a political agenda. Usually hacktivists have altruistic motives.

- **Theft**—Gaining access to intellectual or proprietary technology or information, sometimes for resale.

- **Hijacking**—Many of the financially motivated hackers are interested in using viruses and Trojan horses to hijack your computer so they can control it remotely for their own purposes.

- **Identity theft**—Electronic theft of personal information that can be used to steal financial resources from an individual or corporation.

- **Terrorism**—Some experts believe that terrorists will eventually launch an attack using hacking techniques.

Targets of a Hack Attack

Hacker interests lie in many types of computers on the Internet. Following is a discussion of the types of targets and their appeal to the perpetrators.

Corporate Networks

Corporate computers are often heavily fortified, so hacking into one has high cachet. Behind corporate firewalls are repositories of customer information, product information, and sometimes, in the case of a software publisher, the product itself.

Web Servers

Web servers are computers that contain websites. While some contain customer financial information, web servers are usually targets for vandals because they can be defaced to display information the hacker chooses to the public.

Personal Computers

A personal computer by itself has little appeal for the high-profile hacker. However, it has its use in cyber crime. If it can be commandeered, it can be used to engage in hiding the perpetrator's identity. There are several key uses for these hijacked computers, as follows.

Denial of Service Attacks

A hacker can gain control of a computer by planting a program on it called a *bot*, usually by using a virus or Trojan horse. After infection, the hijacked computer, called a *zombie*, can be used as a weapon to attack another computer. It's commanded to blast chunks of data at a target computer in a coordinated effort with thousands of other zombies. This overwhelms the target machine and it stops functioning. This is called a *distributed denial of service attack (DDoS)*. Sometimes a DDoS attack is used against companies that have policies with which the hacker disagrees.

It's also used in extortion schemes. Gambling websites, typically located off-shore, regularly receive threats of DDoS attacks unless they pay protection money. These threats are known to intensify around Super Bowl weekend in the United States, when the volume of bets is at an all time high.

Spam, Spam, Spam, Spam, Spam, Spam, Spam

Hackers are also interested in getting malware onto personal computers so they can be turned into spam machines. Sending large volumes of unsolicited email from one computer gets your Internet connection shut down. If you can hijack thousands of other computers to do the spam-sending, however, you retain your anonymity and have a spam network that's hard to shut down because each sending machine has to be blocked one at a time.

Storage

A web server computer of mine was hacked before and used as a depository for illegal software or programs that are being shared. Someone used a loophole to get into it and left gigabytes of data on it, presumably for others to fetch as needed.

Hacker Motivation: I Think, Therefore I Hack

Hackers' motivations vary. For some, it's economic. They earn a living through cyber crime. Some have a political or social agenda—their aim is to vandalize high-profile computers to make a statement. Others do it for the sheer thrill.

When asked by the website SafeMode.org why he defaces web servers, a cracker replied, "A high-profile deface gives me an adrenalin shot and then after a while I need another shot; that's why I can't stop."

Tools of the Trade: Pass Me a Trojan Horse, Would You?

There are a series of tools that crackers use to gain access to computers:

- **Trojan horse**—This is a program that looks safe and useful but contains nasty programming inside that does bad stuff. If you are fooled into installing one of these on your computer, it can open what's called a backdoor. A *backdoor* is an access point created from inside a computer's defenses that allows outsiders to circumvent security and gain access to the machine from the Internet.

- **Virus**—A piece of self-replicating programming that infects a computer after being run by a human. It then installs tools that fulfill the attacker's agenda. This could provide access to an outsider, hijack the system to do nefarious tasks, or install tools that can be commanded from afar. People who release viruses aren't traditional hackers, but virus code is one tool in a hacker's toolbox.

- **Worm**—A self-replicating program that does not need human intervention to spread. It travels across networks looking for computer vulnerabilities and exploits them when encountered. People who release these programs aren't traditional hackers, either. They are virus writers.

- **Vulnerability scanner**—A program that checks a computer for known weaknesses, such as programming errors or security holes.

- **Sniffer**—A program that is looking for security information such as user IDs and passwords in data as it flows over a network such as the public Internet. This would be like a malcontented postal worker reading postcards as they moved through a sorting facility.

- **Social engineering**—This is simply the art of fast talking. The easiest way to break security is to have someone give you access. You might have all kinds of security on your computer, but if I call you and ask for access (and maybe convince you I am a technician who can help or a co-worker who should have access) and you give it to me, I have used social engineering to gain illicit access by fooling you.

- **Root kit**—This is the equivalent of digital camouflage. It is a programming toolkit that is used to conceal a virus, spyware, or other piece of malware to keep it from being seen by an operating system and discovered by a security program.

- **Exploit**—A program that takes advantage of a known security weakness in a computer.

Firewall: Shut Out the Hackers

This book discusses many of the security tools you can use to defend your computer against digital threats. An antivirus program and antispyware programs are critical; however, the third key tool in your defenses should be a firewall, which can be used to keep out intruders and worms (a type of virus that is self propelled). A *firewall* is an electronic wall used to keep out an intruder or unwanted communication. It sits between your computer and the Internet (see Figure 4.1).

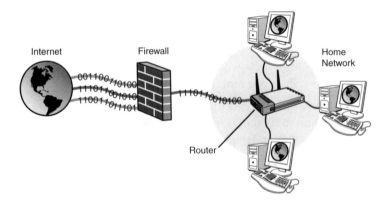

FIGURE 4.1

A firewall is an electronic barrier between your computer or your home network and the Internet.

In construction, a firewall is a physical wall that is designed to stop the spread of fire from one part of a building to another. Firewalls are also used in vehicles to separate the engine compartment from the passenger compartment. In the case of a network, a firewall stops unauthorized communication from the public Internet to a computer.

Think of a firewall as a big wall with lots of doors in it. These doors are called *ports*. When you use your web browser to access a website such as Google.com, you open a port (an electronic door) from inside the firewall and make contact with a server (a computer that sends information on request).

Let's say the server belongs to Google. Now that you have made contact with Google, it is allowed to communicate back to you. So data flows two ways through the port because you have initiated contact first and the firewall knows this.

There are potentially thousands of ports on a firewall. For example, email goes through port 25. Web browsers use port 80, and MSN Messenger uses ports 1863, 6891–6900, and 6901.

You don't have to know what ports are used. Programs on your computer figure that out for you. Some programs, such as file-sharing applications, however, need ports to be specially configured to work.

Crackers use port-scanning software to look for holes in a firewall. These scanners yell out to your firewall on various ports, "Yo dude, are you there?" Your computer would normally respond, "Yep, I am here. Ready to yak." The port scanner then knows that there's an opportunity to exploit a security hole and crawl through that door.

There are two basic types of firewalls at your disposal:

- **Software firewall**—Windows XP and Vista come with a built-in firewall, but you can install a third-party software firewall with better features. If you do that Windows disables the built-in firewalls.

- **Hardware firewall**—These firewalls are physical devices. For home users, their home network router has a firewall function, but advanced hardware firewalls are built for businesses.

Software Firewalls: Programs That Stop Hackers

A good software firewall for home users should have the following attributes:

- It's easy to configure.
- It's frugal with system resources, so it doesn't bog down the computer.
- It doesn't bug you much.

But not all firewalls are created equal. Let's look at a few.

Windows Firewall: Built-in Defense

The easiest software firewall you can use is the built-in Windows Firewall. It is a feature of both XP and Vista.

In the original release of XP, Internet Connection Firewall was a feature hidden deep inside the connection settings and wasn't turned on by default. However, Microsoft remedied that when it issued XP Service Pack 2 (SP2), a great big security fix that was released in the summer of 2004. If you installed SP2, the firewall was activated for you.

In Vista, the Windows Firewall is easier to find and configure (see Figure 4.2). It is turned on by default and accessible in the Windows Security Center (type `Security Center` in the search box on the Start menu to access it) .

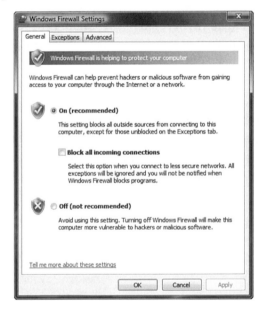

FIGURE 4.2

Windows Firewall is included with Windows Vista (pictured) and Service Pack 2 in XP and is easily accessible via the Windows Security Center.

The built-in firewall features in XP SP2 and Vista are good for several reasons:

- The firewall is invisible and always present. On Vista and XP SP2, it is turned on by default.

- On XP, you never hear from it. It silently does its job without needing much user intervention.

- On Vista, you only are notified by it if an unrecognized program on your computer attempts to gain access to the Internet.

- It doesn't slow the system by any perceivable measure.

> **tip** If you bought a new computer with XP installed since the Fall of 2004, you already have SP2 installed. If your machine is older and you haven't installed SP2 yet, what are you waiting for? Do it now. Learn how to install SP2 in Chapter 9, "Ground Up Security: Wipe Your Hard Drive and Build a Secure Windows PC from the Ground Up."

That said, the Windows Firewall does have some flaws:

- In XP (including XP SP2), inbound traffic is inspected by the software, but data traffic coming from the computer and flowing out to the Internet is not examined. That can be a problem because if there is a virus, spyware, or other malware on your computer trying to communicate with the outside world, the firewall does not catch it on the way out.

- Critics complain that even though Windows Vista checks both inbound and outbound traffic, that its outbound monitoring is lackluster and won't catch all malware that is trying to phone home across the Internet.

- The user interface for the XP SP2 firewall and the Vista version is minimally configurable. Microsoft did add a more advanced firewall configuration tool. You can find it by typing **Firewall** in the Start menu and then click on Windows Firewall with Advanced Security. Unfortunately, it is so advanced it's not usable by anyone but the alpha geeks.

> **tip** There's a nice little free application called Vista FireWall Control (see Figure 4.3), which lets you monitor what the Vista firewall is doing with outbound requests from programs on your system and customize its actions to your liking. Get it from www.sphinx-soft.com. There's also a Plus version that has extra features and an XP version available for a nominal cost.

4

FIGURE 4.3

The freeware program Vista FireWall Control gives you more control over the built-in firewall in Vista.

Third-Party Software Firewalls

For the best firewall protection possible on both Windows XP and Vista, install a third-party software firewall. These programs defend a computer in both directions. They inspect data coming into a computer from the outside world and they look at data leaving the computer to ensure that it's valid traffic and not being generated by spyware, a Trojan horse, or a worm.

These programs also use a question-and-answer process to learn your habits and your system's Internet use. They are particularly bothersome when they are first installed because every time a program attempts to move data across the firewall, an alert is generated by the firewall that requires the computer user to respond.

Here are some of the features that you can expect in third-party firewalls as well as the two-way firewall in Windows Vista.

- **Two-way communication filtering**—When a third-party, two-way firewall is installed, all outbound communications are new to the program and so you will see a lot of alerts. After a few days of clicking Allow or Block on a firewall's dialog boxes (see Figure 4.4), most of the key communication requests will be familiar to the firewall and so it won't interrupt nearly as much. (Windows Vista's built-in firewall is also very good from this perspective.)

- **Intuitive advice**—Good firewalls should offer you usable advice on how to respond to an alert. Esoteric Windows processes that are stopped by your software firewall can sometimes be difficult to deal with because their purpose isn't always clear. (They remind me of my first encounter with an artichoke.) However, Vista handles these (Windows processes, not artichokes) very well because Microsoft knows what they are and manages them accordingly.

FIGURE 4.4

The free PC Tools Firewall Plus detects that Firefox is trying to access the Internet and asks the user to allow or block the request.

- **Custom alert levels**—Communication from outside the firewall is less problematic because, unless the user initiates communication with the outside world, inbound communication from the Internet is ignored. Some firewalls can be configured to alert you to all or severe inbound requests, but you'd be surprised how often your computer is probed by someone or something on the outside. In this mode, the alerts can become tiresome. It's like a cat licking your forehead. It's fun at first until you get chafed. For curiosity's sake, you may want to turn this firewall feature on (if you software has the capability), for a little while at least, until you get fed up with it.

- **Stealth mode**—Stealth mode makes the firewall and the computer behind it invisible to the Internet. Most good firewalls have this feature available and often it's turned on by default. Stealth mode works like this: You walk by my house in the middle of the darkest night and you yell, "Is anyone there?" If I turn on the porch light, come out, and say, "Yes, I am here," you know that I'm home and you can engage me in a conversation. If you're a bad person, you can find a way into my house by either tricking me or finding an open window or door when I am not looking. If you yell, "Is anyone there?" as you walk by and I stay in my house and don't respond, you don't know I am there, so you keep going. This is the equivalent of a firewall in stealth mode. It's also a good way to avoid neighbors that want to borrow your lawnmower.

- **Threat management**—Besides playing traffic cop, some software firewalls offer threat management features. They can inspect inbound data and compare it to threat signatures to help block virus and spyware infections. It can also be configured to stop you from sharing personal information with fraudulent websites, helping to defend you against phishing.

> **tip**
> If you really like the idea of a firewall scanning for viruses, spyware, and other threats as they cross the digital threshold, consider purchasing an antivirus-filtering firewall, such as those manufactured by Check Point. See http://www.zonealarm.com/store/content/catalog/products/z100g/index.jsp.

Recommended Firewall Freebies

Hopefully I have convinced you to upgrade your firewall if you don't have one already installed. Note that if you have a security suite from a large security software maker, it likely includes a premium firewall. You can find out by checking the Security Center in both XP and Vista. Under the Firewall settings, it'll indicate if a third-party software firewall is installed and in use (see Figure 4.5).

> **caution**
> Windows Security Center will report if both a third-party firewall and Windows Firewall are turned on. Most third-party products will turn the built-in firewall off before installing. If not, you'll have to turn it off yourself as running two software firewalls will slow your system down. Controls to deactivate the Windows Firewall can be found on the left side of the Security Center windows.

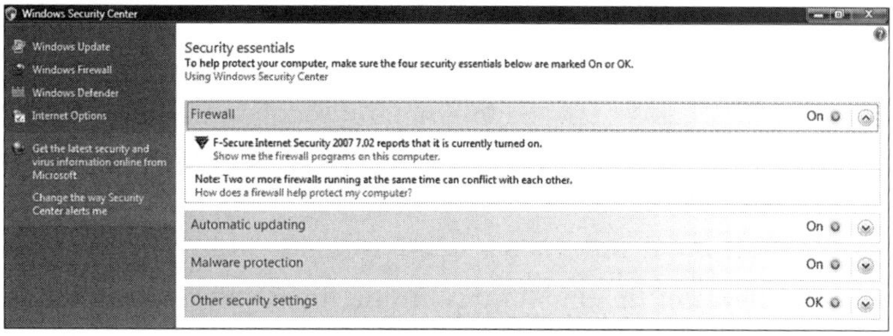

FIGURE 4.5

Security Center (shown on Vista here) will let you know if a third-party firewall is installed.

A couple of good free firewall programs you might consider installing include:

- PC Tools Firewall Plus
- ZoneAlarm from www.zonealarm.com
- Kerio Firewall from www.sunbelt-software.com

tip If you install a third-party firewall on Windows XP, the XP Security Center should detect it and turn off the Windows Firewall because running two is redundant, could cause conflicts, and can slow down the computer unnecessarily. If for some reason you find that both Windows Firewall and a third-party firewall are running at the same time, simply open the Control Panel, choose Security Center, click on the Windows Firewall button, and turn off the firewall.

note Note that the ZoneAlarm freebie only applies to the basic product. When you go to download it, ZoneAlarm will try hard to upsell you to the security suite. Not a bad thing as the paid product is decent, but just be aware of it. To get the freebie, go directly to the download page here and click carefully:

http://www.zonealarm.com/store/content/company/products/znalm/freeDownload.jsp. The Kerio Firewall, recently renamed as Sunbelt Personal Firewall, runs in full mode as trialware for 30 days and then shuts down to basic freebie mode after that. Get it here: http://www.sunbelt-software.com/Home-Home-Office/Sunbelt-Personal-Firewall/.

Hardware Firewalls

Hardware firewalls are devices that physically sit between your computer and the wire that goes out to the Internet. Although businesses usually use a device that is physically separated from their other network gear, at home you'll find a firewall built into home network routers.

Some of the many advantages to hardware firewalls are

- They are "fire and forget." Install them and you are protected. No tweaking needed, although enthusiasts can certainly tweak them if they desire.

- They are included in the price of a device that shares your Internet between computers (meaning you can share your Internet connection with other computers in your home). No fees or extra costs.

- They have no impact on the system performance of your computer.

Easy Defense with a NAT Firewall

Home network routers have a firewall feature built in that uses a technology called *network address translation (NAT)*. NAT is not a firewall technology per se, but it offers a firewall-like feature that provides natural protection from Internet nasties, such as hackers and worms.

NAT was invented because of a shortage of IP addresses available to the ever-growing Internet population. Sounds complicated but it's not really. An IP address is like a phone number for each device connected to the Internet. Every device on the Internet has an IP number. An IP address is a set of four 3-digit numbers that can't be any lower than 0.0.0.0 or higher than 255.255.255.255.

If you can surf the Internet on your computer right now, it has an IP address. Because there's a shortage of IP addresses, not everyone can have her own. So NAT devices were invented to help (see Figure 4.6).

FIGURE 4.6

This Netgear router uses network address translation (NAT), which hides the identity of computers connected to it.

NAT routers work like this: Every large company has a switchboard. Everyone dials one central public phone number to talk to the company operator. When they reach the operator, they ask for an extension and they are put through.

NAT works like that. The router has an IP address that everyone on the Internet can call (it's like the switchboard). Behind the router is a home network. Each computer on the network has a private IP address (like a phone extension).

When data from the Internet arrives for one of those computers, it is sent to the NAT router and the NAT router looks up the computer on its network (in a handy little directory it keeps) and checks to see which one made the request.

The router hands the data off to that computer. This is built-in security because no one on the Internet can send data to a computer behind a router directly. They always have to go through the router first.

> **note** Under the current IP address scheme, called IPv4, there are only 4,294,967,296 possible addresses in the world (although not all of those addresses are available for reasons that only bona fide, card-carrying geeks care about). Experts predict that those addresses could all be used sometime before 2020 unless our uber-geek friends come to the rescue. However, under a new plan called IPv6 there are 340 undecillion addresses, which is a really, really, really big number. According to wikipedia.org, that's 670 quadrillion IP addresses per square inch of Earth. If that is too big to fathom, trust me when I say that if I had that many mallomars, I'd be fat and probably dead.

> **note** The acronym NAT can stand for network address translation or natural address translation. Like a cookie and a biscuit, it's the same thing.

Stateful Inspection: The Meticulous Traffic Cop

There's one more level of security built into a NAT router that offers great and easy security. Let's say your child's computer, your computer, and your spouse's laptop are all behind a router. Suddenly, in comes communication from a server on the Internet that hosts bumfluff.com.

The router looks at a list it keeps of all computers attached to it to see who initiated a request with bumfluff.com. When it discovers that none of the computers did, it realizes that bumfluff.com is a bad website that is actually a front for hackersncrackers.com. So it discards the request, and all is right with the world again.

You see, in order to communicate with a computer behind a NAT router, that computer has to first communicate with you (see Figure 4.7).

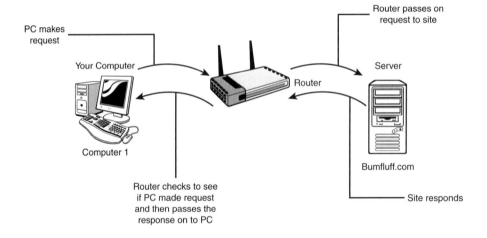

FIGURE 4.7

In stateful packet inspection, a router only allows information through to a computer if the computer requested it.

So if I use my computer to contact cyberwalker.com to see the latest tech help articles, the router notes that I am making contact. When cyberwalker.com comes back to the router with tech help information, the router says, "Oh yeah, Andy's computer has been communicating with cyberwalker.com, so I'll let it through."

This is called *stateful inspection* or sometimes *stateful packet inspection*. All NAT routers engage in stateful inspection.

How to Detect a Hacker Attack

If a hacker breaks into your computer, just noses around, and makes no changes to your computer, it's not easy to tell he's been there. There's no alert that says, "A hacker was here at 9:16 p.m. He works at the joint where you order your favorite pizza. His phone number is..." That said, it is possible that someone can come onto your system, romp around in your data like a dog on a dead fish, and leave without your knowledge.

Fishy signs that a hacker might have visited include the following:

- The appearance of strange data, perhaps files or programs stored on your computer. A hacker might be using your computer as a temporary storage area or repository for pirated software.

- Your computer might start sending spam. A hacker could have added software to send spam from your address.

- Your computer might start sending large volumes of garbage data to another computer. The hacker might have turned the computer into a zombie that can be commanded from afar to attack another computer in a distributed denial of service (DDoS) attack. In these attacks, bad guys harness thousands of computers to attack a single computer to overwhelm it with data and make it crash.

- The first sign of a hacker could also simply be theft of money from your bank account. If you keep your banking information, including user IDs and passwords, in a file on your unprotected computer, it's entirely possible that someone could sneak on, find this information, and disappear again. However, phishers, key loggers, and other data capture schemes could also be responsible for this.

All that said, hackers tend not to actively snoop around in single computers personally (as a rule) unless there is a really good reason to be there. That's not to say they won't with yours, but typically they use automated malware such as viruses, Trojans, and spyware to do their dirty work.

What's more likely is that script kiddies (a.k.a. bored teenagers using downloadable hacker tools available from the Internet) may try to hack your system for fun.

LOG THE HACKERS

Windows XP and Vista include a log file function that can record firewall and connection activity. However, the contents of these files are not particularly easy to interpret. Still you should have the option to explore. Here's how to turn the feature on:

In XP:

1. Click Start, then Run, and type `firewall.cpl` and then click OK.
2. Click the Advanced tab.
3. Under Security Logging, click the Settings button.
4. In the Log Settings dialog box, check the Log Dropped Packets and Log Successful Connections boxes.
5. You can also specify here where the system should store the log file.
6. Click OK and then click OK again to exit.

In Vista:

1. Click the Windows button and type `Advanced Security` and then click Windows Firewall with Advanced Security when it appears in the Start menu.
2. Click Continue on the UAC warning.
3. Click Properties on the right side of the Windows Firewall with Advanced Security window.
4. Select the appropriate profile tab: Domain Profile, Private Profile, or Public Profile. On your home network, you'll likely want to choose Private Profile.
5. Click the Customize button under the Logging section.
6. Use the drop-down arrows beside Log Dropped Packets and Log Successful Connections to select Yes. This will enable logging for the option you select. Then click OK.
7. Note the location of the firewall log file or change it to a location more convenient to you. I like to create a folder called Firewall in my Documents folder at c:\Users\Andy\Documents\Firewall and direct the system to put the log file there.
8. Click OK to save the changes.

Once you enable security logging on either Vista or XP, firewall activity information is written to the pfirewall.log file.

In Vista, you won't be able to open the log file while it's in use by the system. Instead, right click on it, and choose Copy. Then in an empty part of the desktop right-click and choose Paste. A copy that you can open with Notepad (or your word processor) will be put onto your desktop.

Most people will find that wading through all the data can be befuddling. Curious geeks (like you) might get a kick out of it, and of course it may be useful to system administrators who have a degree in Microsoftology.

How to Fix a Hacker Attack

After a computer has been hacked it can never be trusted again. So say the pros, and security expert Steve Gibson, of GRC.com, in particular.

"There is no way to know what might have been altered or changed. Any component could be Trojaned, or TimeBombed, or anything. The only thing to do if you want to *ever* be able to really trust your machine again is to wipe it and start over," says Gibson.

There, you heard it from the man himself. Gibson is one of America's pre-eminent computer security experts.

A Trojan, of course, is a nasty piece of malware that looks harmless but has a program inside that can give someone outside your system remote access or it can contain a virus or spyware. And *TimeBombed*? That's just malware on a timer, set to go off at some future time.

caution If you've been visited by a hacker, you might wonder if you absolutely have to wipe your computer clean and start fresh. If the computer is just used for games or general recreation and no lifestyle-critical tasks, maybe you don't need to. Be sure to continue to scan for viruses and spyware, however, and to install a firewall. That said, if you do your banking on your computer and keep personal files and valuable data on it, the idea of having someone return and rifle through it again is rather distressing. If it were me, I'd wipe and start clean just for peace of mind.

Steps You Can Take Immediately After Being Hacked

If you think a hacker or his automated tools have been on your system and you want to take some instant security measures, here are steps you can take to reduce the risk of further visits.

Disconnect While You Assess

The first measure you can take that's instantly effective against a hacker is to disconnect the computer from the Internet. If you have a high-speed Internet connection, locate your modem, usually a box connected to your phone line or cable wire, and turn it off.

Install a Firewall

You have three options when it comes to firewalls:

- Turn on the Windows Firewall.
- Install a third-party firewall.
- Install a home network router that has built-in firewall capabilities (though running a software firewall in addition to your router's hardware firewall isn't a bad idea).

I detail how to do this at the end of this chapter. On **p. 123**, you'll see how to turn on the Windows Firewall or how to install a third-party software firewall. On **p. 129**, I detail how to install a hardware firewall, which is built into a home network router.

Assess the Damage

Scan your system with your antispyware and antivirus programs to see if anything strange has been installed on your computer. Be sure to update your virus and spyware signatures first. You'll have to turn your Internet connection back on (briefly) to update these.

Also look for any new data that has been added or changed. To search for changes, use the Windows search function, following these steps:

In Windows XP:

- Click Start, Search, and choose All Files and Folders on the left. Leave the All or Part of the File Name and A Word or Phrase in the File fields blank. In the Look In field, choose My Computer.
- Then click When Was It Modified? and select Specify Dates. From the drop-down box you can choose Modified Date to see files that have been changed. To see files that have been opened and examined, choose Accessed Dates and use Created Date to see new files. Set the From and To dates to the period you are interested in; typically just look at the previous 24 hours.

- Then click Search. A list of the files you've requested begins to show up in the right pane.

In Windows Vista:

- Click the Windows button, then Search on the right side, and click the down arrow next to Advanced Search on the top right of the Search window. In the Location field, choose Computer.

- Then click Date to reveal a pull-down menu and choose Date Modified. (Use Date Created to list newly created files.) Then in the box that says Any, choose the option "Is After" and in the box to the right of that, choose the previous day (or the date of the day before you think your system might have been compromised).

- Also, check the box that says Include Non-indexed, Hidden, and System Files. Note that this will slow the search down, but it will be more thorough.

- Next click the Search button. The system will list all files that have been changed since the date you specified.

This search process might freak you out, because you'll see many files listed that have been accessed in a 24-hour period.

Remember that Windows accesses many files by itself, even when your computer is idle. So this is not indicative of hacker activity. However, this process is useful in determining what files have to be created or changed.

Wipe the System and Start Fresh

Remember that wiping your system and restoring it is the best way to start fresh and give yourself peace of mind. It's not a simple task, so steel yourself for a bit of hard work.

You'll need either the original Windows installation CD/DVD if you purchased it retail, or the installation CD/DVD provided by your computer maker. The company might have provided a full copy of Windows or a restore disc that wipes your computer and sets it back to the way it was the day you bought it, including all the preloaded software.

I detail the step-by-step procedure for wiping and restoring your system in Chapter 9, starting on **p. 271**.

4

If you own a Mac, which uses the Mac OS X operating system, be sure to make a backup of all your personal data to CD or DVD first and then follow these steps:

1. Insert the Mac OS X Install Disc 1 CD and double-click the Install Mac OS X icon.

2. Follow the onscreen instructions. In the panel where you select the destination disk, select your current Mac OS X disk (in most cases, it is the only one available).

3. Click Options. If you want to save your existing files, users, and network settings, select Archive and Install, and then select Preserve Users and Network Settings. If you want to erase everything on your computer—and this is recommended to ensure you are completely starting fresh—select Erase and Install. Note that you can't recover erased data.

4. Click Continue. Then click Install to perform a basic installation.

5. After installation, be sure to reinstall any programs you might have wiped out from their original installation CDs.

6. Update the operating system with any updates provided by Apple.

After scrubbing your Mac, check the Mac OS for any updates since you originally installed it. Here's how:

1. Open System Preferences and click Software Update.

2. Select Check for Updates.

3. From the pop-up menu, choose Daily, Weekly, or Monthly.

4. If you want your Mac to download important updates automatically, select Download Important Updates in the Background. When the update finishes downloading, you are notified that it is ready to be installed.

5. When the installation is finished, Software Update looks for updates one more time. This is because some updates require the presence of previous updates before they can install.

> **note** If you bought a standalone version of Mac OS X, installation instructions are included in a booklet that comes with the Mac OS X disc. Of course, if you need additional help with Mac OS X, I highly recommend picking up a copy of Que's *Easy Mac OS X, v10.4 Tiger*. If you are running Leopard, I recommend picking up a copy of Que's *Mac OS X Leopard On Demand*.

Batten Down the Hatches—Ten-Minute Tactics

The simplest way to defend your computer quickly *against hackers* is to use a firewall. So let's look at your two fastest options. Either can be done in 10 minutes.

Turn on Windows Firewall

If you have Windows Vista, your Windows Firewall is already turned on (unless you, your cat, or someone else turned it off). Here's how to check:

1. Click the Windows button and type `Firewall` in the search box.

2. Click Windows Firewall when it appears in the Start menu.

3. Your Windows Firewall dialog will show the firewall status. If it's off, click Change Settings in the main window. (It may also show it's set to off but that a third-party firewall is in use instead.)

4. When you do, the UAC will throw an alert. Click Continue.

5. In the Windows Firewall Settings dialog, click On (see Figure 4.8). Then click OK to enable the firewall.

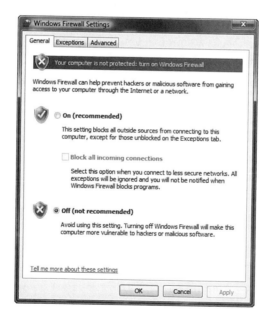

FIGURE 4.8

Did someone turn the Windows Firewall off by mistake?

If you have Windows XP Service Pack 2 installed, the Windows Firewall should also already be turned on. Here's how to check:

1. Click Start and then click Control Panel.
2. In the Control Panel, click Windows Security Center.
3. Click Windows Firewall.
4. Click the button next to On (Recommended) and click OK. The firewall is turned on.

WHEN THE WINDOWS FIREWALL IS OPTIONAL

If your computer connects through a wire to your high-speed modem, which in turn connects to the Internet, I highly recommend that you use a firewall to protect your computer. However, there are other circumstances where the Windows Firewall is optional:

- **Wireless connection**—If you use a wireless connection to connect to the Internet, you are going through a box called a home Internet router. This has a built-in firewall, so turning on the Windows Firewall is unnecessary because you are already protected. Turning on the Windows Firewall as an additional measure won't hurt, however. In fact, it will protect your system in case other machines on your home network get infected.

- **Dial-up connection**—If you use a dial-up connection to get on the Internet (meaning your computer's modem uses a phone line to dial your Internet service), when it is not connected a hacker cannot get on the computer.

   The other quirk about this is that your computer changes its Internet Protocol (IP) address each time it dials up the Net. That's the numerical address that other computers on the Internet use to send you data. It would be difficult for a hacker to find you repeatedly because your IP address changes when you use a dial-up service. Conventional wisdom says that a Windows Firewall is unnecessary on a dial-up connection.

   However, turning on the Windows Firewall as an additional measure won't hurt and it protects against Internet worms.

- **Third-party firewall**—If you already have a software firewall installed, such as ZoneAlarm, PC Tools Firewall Plus, or Norton Firewall, it's not necessary to use Windows Firewall as well.

If you haven't already installed SP2, you need to do that soon. In the meantime, the original version of XP does include Windows Firewall (it's called the Internet Connection Firewall). Though less friendly than the one on SP2, it's better than nothing until you can get SP2 installed. Here's how to activate it:

tip If you run Windows 95, 98, or Me, there is no built-in firewall, but you can install a free third-party firewall such as ZoneAlarm or Firewall Plus from PC Tools.

1. Click Start, Control Panel, Network and Internet Connections, and then click Network Connections.

2. If you don't see Network and Internet Connections, click Switch to Category View (on the left side of the Control Panel window).

3. Highlight the connection you want to protect by clicking on it once. Then click Change Settings of This Connection from the list on the left. If you use a high-speed Internet connection, such as a cable modem or digital subscriber line (DSL) service (high-speed Internet from your phone company), look for Local Area Connection.

4. Click the Advanced tab and then click the Protect My Computer and Network by Limiting or Preventing Access to This Computer from the Internet check box.

Installing a Firewall on a Mac OS X System

The latest operating system from Apple, called Mac OS X, comes with a software firewall that's turned off. You can switch it on by going to System Preferences, Sharing, Firewall, and clicking on the Start button.

Wall Off the World—Install a Better Firewall in an Afternoon

More advanced firewalls can be time-consuming to install, but they are not difficult to use. Take the time to fortify your defenses. It is really worthwhile.

Install a Two-way Software Firewall

Installing a third-party firewall gives you two-way protection in XP and arguably better two-way protection in Vista.

It stops hackers and worms from coming into your computer from the Internet. And if your computer becomes infected, it stops worms, spyware, and viruses from communicating out to the Internet.

Earlier I recommended three free third-party firewalls. (See the section "Recommended Firewall Freebies" on **p. 112**.)

My favorite of the three is PC Tools Firewall Plus (see Figure 4.9) from www.pctools.com.

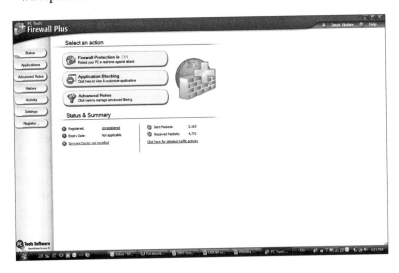

FIGURE 4.9

PC Tools makes the free and nicely customizable Firewall Plus.

I like it because

- It's easy to install.
- It's easy to use.
- It works well on XP and Vista.
- It's customizable.
- It's free.

Sold? Okay, here's how to install the free version of PC Tools Plus, my favorite:

1. Use Internet Explorer or Firefox to visit www.pctools.com.

2. Click Download and then scroll to PC Tools Firewall Plus from the list of products.

3. Click the Download button next to the Firewall Plus product listing.

tip If you already have Norton Firewall or McAfee Firewall, these programs are as good as the pro versions of the free firewalls recommended in this chapter, though both are resource hogs and could cause your computer to perform like a college student with a Sunday morning hangover.

4. Click the Start FREE Download Now button. In Firefox click Save the File in the dialog box when it opens. In the Firefox Downloads window, click Open next to the file after it is downloaded.

5. In Internet Explorer, click Start FREE Download and when you get a dialog box, choose Run.

6. On Vista you will get a UAC warning. Click Continue.

tip Because websites change from time to time, it's possible that my instructions on navigating the PC Tools website may become out of date over time. If so, do your best to locate the installation file on the site and download it to your computer and then resume the instructions at step 4 or 5, as appropriate.

7. The program will start to install. Click Next, and if you're okay with it, accept the legal agreement by clicking I Accept The Agreement, then click Next.

8. Choose a folder to install Firewall Plus in and click Next.

9. Choose whether to install a trial copy of PC Tools Spyware Doctor (this is their upsell). You don't have to for the firewall to work. Click Next.

10. Choose either Normal user or Expert user. I recommend Normal as you will get simplified information. Expert mode will give you more advanced options when network traffic is detected.

11. Let the software install and if challenged by UAC (in Vista), click Continue.

12. When the installation is done, click Yes Restart the Computer Now to reboot.

13. When a program tries to access the Internet from your computer, you see a pop-up alarm (see Figure 4.4, earlier in this chapter). If this program is known to you, choose Yes and choose Remember This Setting so you're not bugged again next time you run that program. It is normal for some programs to use the Internet to check for updates (especially antivirus programs and antispyware software), but you'll be surprised how many programs will try to communicate with the Internet.

14. Of course, if something weird tries to communicate with the Internet from your PC and Firewall Plus alerts you, choose No and block it. Firewall Plus will give you a sense of what it is. Be sure to record that information and do either a virus and/or spyware scan. Also research the program on the Internet to try to figure out what it is. It might be a background Windows process and could be legitimate, but it's worth finding out.

4

15. You'll have to suffer the alerts for a few days until all the programs that access the Internet are caught by Firewall Plus and approved by you. Then you shouldn't be bugged much after that until you install new programs or there's a legitimate infection that is caught by the firewall.

note Steve Gibson, of GRC.com, coined the term *spyware* when a program on his computer started to communicate out to the Internet as he was testing an early version of ZoneAlarm.

tip If you would like to check your firewall's defenses, check out Steve Gibson's free firewall test called ShieldsUP! (see Figure 4.10) It's an excellent and well-documented online test available at www.grc.com that runs tests against your computer or home network and explains in careful detail where you are vulnerable.

FIGURE 4.10

Steve Gibson's ShieldsUp! offers a free security test for your personal computer from his website at grc.com.

DOUBLE YOUR DEFENSE WITH A DOUBLE FIREWALL

If you have a home network router, your computer and other computers on the network (such as your spouse's laptop and your children's computer) are protected from the outside world.

However, you are not protected from the computers inside the router. So you might want to leave on the Windows Firewall or a two-way firewall such as ZoneAlarm or Firewall Plus on your computer. Here's why:

- Maybe your children or roommates have their own computers and they haplessly infect them with spyware or viruses.

- A friend or family member sometimes comes over with an infected laptop and connects it to your home network.

- You leave your wireless network unsecured and a wireless network snoop connects and exposes your computers on the network to viruses, spyware, or their own curiosity. (Learn more about wireless network snoops in Chapter 7, "Wireless Network Snoops: Lock Down Your Wi-Fi Network," on **p. 183**.)

Install a Hardware Firewall

For sheer firewall simplicity, I recommend installing a home network router with built-in network address translation (NAT) firewall capabilities (discussed earlier in this chapter on **p. 114**).

Here are some things to keep in mind when it comes to a NAT firewall:

- It does not use any memory on your computer, so the firewall is invisible.

- It works silently to defend your network. You'll never see pop-ups, alerts, or other annoyances.

- It stops inbound threats but won't stop outbound nasties that might be on your computer.

To take advantage of a NAT firewall, you need to buy an Internet-sharing device called a home network router (see Figure 4.11) from any one of several well-known vendors, including:

- **D-Link**—www.dlink.com
- **Netgear**—www.netgear.com

- **Linksys**—www.linksys.com
- **Belkin**—www.belkin.com
- **SMC**—www.smc.com
- **Apple**—www.apple.com

FIGURE 4.11

Like all home network routers, the Belkin N1 Router has a built in hardware firewall.

These routers will cost you about $60 to $100 (and sometimes less) unless you choose Apple's Airport Extreme and then you're in for $200. A router connects to your high-speed Internet modem from either your cable TV or telephone company and shares that connection with several computers in your home. Your computer(s) in turn connect to the router via network cables or using a wireless connection (also known as Wi-Fi).

> **tip** If you choose a wireless connection, most new laptops have built-in capabilities for this. You can, however, buy wireless adapter cards for both a PC and laptop without built-in wireless.

The router configuration is fairly straight-forward. When you set the device up, there is a walk-through wizard that configures your computers and the router so they work together. Both Macs and PCs can coexist on a router together and even share files with each other.

> **tip** If the idea of setting up a router scares the ham out of your sandwich, you should check out Mark Edward Soper's excellent book called *Absolute Beginner's Guide to Home Networking*.

When you install the network, you need settings from your Internet provider to input into the router during setup. Be sure to check Chapter 7, starting on **p. 183**, to learn about wireless network snoops and how to configure your router to be secure. After the router is set up and running and you can connect to the Internet with your computer(s), there's nothing further to do. That NAT firewall runs automatically.

The Absolute Minimum

- Among geeks, the word *hacker* has many definitions, including a good programmer, a bad programmer, or a person who modifies technology hardware. In the mass media, it's a person who accesses a computer they don't own without permission.

- A cracker is what computer break-in artists called themselves, but we call them hackers.

- Crackers' motivations are varied. They hack to steal, to protest, to make money, to terrorize to prove a point, or—as George Mallory said about Mount Everest and a very nice donut earlier that day—"because it's there."

- Personal computers are usually hacked so they can be turned into zombies and be controlled remotely to attack other computers, used as a storage for illicit information, or used to send spam. Sometimes they are hacked by identity thieves who steal personal financial information.

- Windows XP has a built-in firewall. When Service Pack 2 is installed, it turns the firewall on for you. Windows Vista has a built-in two-way firewall.

- A third-party firewall is a program that acts as an electronic wall on a computer to stop inbound traffic and, usually, outbound communication that contain viruses, spyware, and other malicious programs.

- A hardware firewall is a device that blocks inbound traffic from the Internet. Network address translation technology in a home router provides a firewall function.

- It's hard to tell if you have been hacked. The only way to have complete peace of mind after you have been hacked is to wipe your computer clean and start fresh.

- You should ensure you have at least one firewall—either hardware or software—turned on, protecting your computer from viruses and worms.

4

5

Identity Thieves and Phishers: Protect Your Good Name and Bank Account

This chapter explains how the Internet is playing a part in one of the largest growing crime trends in the world: identity theft. It also demystifies phishing, an Internet-powered phenomenon used to steal your identity by tricking you into giving up personal information. And there's a warning about pharming, which is phishing with a bigger net. But never phear, the chapter gives you phoolproof tricks to phight back!

What Is Identity Theft?

If you wanted to pretend you were me, what would it take to fool my devastatingly gorgeous girlfriend? Well, you'd need to learn to walk, talk, and look like me. Plus you'd need plastic surgery to web together your toes like mine (my grandmother said I'd never drown!). And you'd have to be a good kisser. It would take some effort.

But if you wanted to convince my bank that you were me, it wouldn't be quite as difficult. You'd need my wallet, my address, a good forged driver's license, and certainly the ability to sign like me. It would be an easier impersonation, but still would take some effort.

But what if you had my online banking user ID and password and an Internet connection? You could log on to the Web as if you were me and then it would be bye-bye savings account and the $637.34 in it.

That's what's called *simple identity theft*. You obtain the electronic keys to my digital piggybank, smash it open, and disappear into the bits and bytes flowing across the Internet. But identity theft can be more complex. It's not always just a smash-and-grab proposition.

It starts with thieves obtaining your personal information, such as your name, Social Security number, credit card numbers, or other identifying information. They then get financial and identity tools issued to them in your name, including bank accounts, checks, and even government-issued documents. Think of it as creating a clone of a person's paper trail.

Crooks can then apply for credit and nurture and protect the accounts, perhaps even making small payments to generate more credit. They might do this over the course of two to three years to generate a decent credit portfolio.

The big payoff comes when they cash out, making a purchase worth $20,000 to $100,000, and then disappear, leaving you on the hook to pay off the debt and deal with a devastated credit history.

Some identity theft basics are discussed next. Later in the chapter, specific technology threats that impact identity theft are covered.

Techniques Thieves Use to Steal Your Identity

Identity thieves use myriad techniques to steal your identity. To start, all they need is some initial seed information to build on.

Think about the kind of information organizations ask you for when you apply for anything: perhaps a membership, say with your health club; a financial tool such as a credit card or bank account; or even an entry for a contest.

The basics would be your name, address, and phone number. While this information can be publicly available to anyone who cares to look, you become vulnerable when a potential identity thief can pair it with more detailed information about you. Your birth date might be common knowledge among your friends and family but no one else needs to know. Be careful about providing any piece of identification or information that wouldn't be listed publicly.

After thieves have gathered the basics on you and have one critical identity tool, such as a driver's license number or Social Security number, they can then use that to research more information about you and create an identity document. What they do is build a portfolio on you until they have enough information to apply for a credit or financial tool in your name.

After they have that, all they need to do is use the tool and nurture it. They'll make deposits and withdrawals in an account. Or use a credit card to make modest payments and pay off the balance. This can go on for months. Slowly they build up creditworthiness that allows them to apply for more credit.

The endgame is to create such a large credit facility that they can cash out. They'll extract the most money they can out of the credit tools they have nurtured and leave you on the hook. When the credit-offering organization attempts to collect, they will come to you and not the thief because by their records it looks as if you are the one who has been using its credit services.

How They Become You: Identity Theft Techniques

According to the U.S. Federal Trade Commission, here's how thieves get their hands on your identity:

- They steal or buy information from insiders at businesses that keep records on you.
- They engage in dumpster diving, where they retrieve information and documents from the garbage.
- They illicitly gain access to credit reports, using tools available at their workplace.
- They scoop your credit or debit card information using a special electronic tool when a credit card transaction is processed. This is called *skimming*.
- They snatch purses or steal wallets.
- They steal mail that contains financial or tax information. Sometimes this is achieved by redirecting your mail to a new address.
- During a burglary, information and documents are stolen from your home.

- A scam artist fools you into filling out what seems like a legitimate form or survey that reveals personal information.
- They steal a person's identity after their death by applying for a replacement birth certificate, especially if a person died in a different jurisdiction from where they were born.

Preventative Measures: How to Not Become a Victim

Avoiding identity theft takes just a few slight adjustments in the way you run your life. Here are some tips:

- Avoid providing personal information to anyone you don't know or who doesn't have a pressing need for it.
- Safeguard your identification numbers such as driver's license, Social Security number, and passport number. Provide them only when absolutely necessary and to verified employees of organizations that request them.
- Your Social Security number is the key that unlocks all of your personal information. Guard it like it is the last chocolate in the box because it's precious. It's the virtual key to your personal vault of information. Some people like to print their SSN on their checks, which is a secure as printing it on a billboard by the freeway.
- Be sure to keep your passport, original social security card and other highly important documents in a safe at home or preferably a safety deposit box at the bank. That way, if you are ever burglarized, you don't need to worry about these essential items being whisked away.
- Destroy with a shredder all unneeded documents that contain personal information, especially old bank account statements, financial records, and discarded or incomplete application forms. Make sure you destroy your junk mail, too, if it has personal address information on it. It's a good idea to buy a personal shredder from your local office supply store for $50 to $100.
- Keep an eye on your credit report. Later in this chapter I list all the credit bureaus in key countries around the world where identity theft is rife. Check with your credit bureau annually at a minimum and better, every quarter, to see what credit activity is being tracked against your name.

> **tip** Most standard shredders cut your paperwork into strips. This technique is called a strip-cut and is considered not as secure as the more advanced (and expensive) cross cut technique where the shredder turns paper into confetti.

- Simplify your financial life. Keep only one or two credit cards on hand so it's easier to track those accounts. Cancel credit and bank accounts you don't need.

- Photocopy the contents of your wallet or purse and keep those documents in a safe place. If your wallet is stolen, you'll have a record of everything that is in there. Also photocopy your passport and any other documents you carry when you travel that are vulnerable to loss or theft.

- Pay your bills electronically. Minimizing a paper trail reduces the risk that paper documents will fall into the hands of the wrong people.

- Never give out your credit card number on the phone or in an email. Only deal with people and organizations you trust.

Signs You're a Victim

Victims often don't know they have become victims of identity theft until it's too late. Here are some signs you might already be a victim or might be at risk:

- Strange items on your credit card statements or activity in your financial or other accounts you don't recognize.

- A call from a collection agency demanding payment for a debt you didn't incur.

- New accounts created on your credit record for which you haven't applied.

- A declined credit application, even though you believe your credit is good.

- Strangely missing or stolen identity documents or records.

- A call from law enforcement about a crime that has been committed that they believe you have been involved in or traffic citations for offenses you didn't commit. Someone may be using your ID to represent themselves to authorities.

What to Do If You're an Identity Theft Victim

You're going to be very busy if you discover you have been victimized by an identity thief. Clearing your name is not easy and can take a lot of time. Here are some key steps you should take to make the process easier:

1. Immediately make contact with the fraud departments of the credit bureaus in your country. There's a list on **p. 156**. The bureaus can

place a fraud alert on your accounts and ask creditors to call you before they open new accounts in your name. Ask for credit reports so you can track the abuse.

> **tip** There are some really good identity theft resources available at http://www.ftc.gov/bcp/edu/microsites/idtheft/consumers/resources.html and http://www.ftc.gov/bcp/edu/microsites/idtheft/tools.html. They are United States–centric, but even those outside the U.S. will find much of the information useful. Also have a look at www.idtheftcenter.org.

2. Close or suspend your tainted accounts. Contact your credit card company and bank to report your ATM or credit card stolen. Have your bank stop payment on stolen checks and contact its check verification companies.

3. Call your local police department and file a report with details about the fraud. Provide the police with as much documentation as you can. Credit bureaus might only take action if you can provide them with a copy of your police report.

4. Have all identity documents reissued by government and other issuing organizations.

5. In the United States, file a complaint with the Federal Trade Commission. This can be done online at http://www.ftc.gov/bcp/edu/microsites/idtheft/consumers/filing-a-report.html. It maintains a database of ID theft cases for federal investigators. In other countries, find out if there is a government body that tracks identity theft and file a complaint with it, if possible.

What Is Phishing?

Phishing is a technique used by identity thieves to steal your personal information, usually so they can gain access to financial accounts.

To understand phishing, let's consider what fishing is. A fisherman casts a line out in the water repeatedly with a lure attached. The lure is a deceiving piece of gear that looks like a tasty smaller fish, but it's actually a nasty hook. Eventually, the lure catches the attention of a fish, which then bites it. The fooled fish is then reeled in on a hook and meets its demise in a frying pan with a sprig of dill.

Phishing is kind of the same, but without the dill. The phisher uses email (or sometimes a pop-up message on the web) as his lure. He casts out zillions of emails that are designed to trick the recipients into giving up personal information such as user IDs and passwords used to access their bank accounts.

Phishers use a variety of emails to fool their unsuspecting victims. One of the most common is the email that claims to be from a business or organization you deal with: perhaps your Internet service provider, an online payment service, or a government agency. Very often phishers pretend to be your bank.

The email includes realistic company branding and logos and reads like typical communication from the real institution (see Figure 5.1). This sometimes includes, ironically, warnings about protecting yourself from fraud.

> **note** According to the website www.antiphishing.org, the term *phishing* was coined circa 1996 by hackers who were stealing America Online accounts from AOL members. The buzzword was first used on the alt.2600 hacker newsgroup in January 1996, says the site, adding that it might have been used earlier in the printed edition of the hacker newsletter *2600*. It is in no way related to the jam band, Phish.

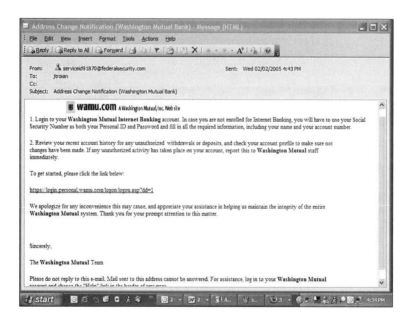

FIGURE 5.1

This email appears to be from Washington Mutual. Clicking on the link, however, would lead to a website run by a phisher, who is trying to gather personal banking information.

Notice that this email, purportedly from a legitimate banking institution, asks the recipient to enter sensitive, personal information—something reputable banks do not request via email. The email asks for validation of personal information including account numbers, user IDs, and passwords. It asks you to click on an included link that takes you to the institution's website so you can enter your information. Of course, it also looks exactly like the institution's website, but it, too, is bogus.

Although many phishers pretend to be major global banks, they have been known to use regional credit unions and community banks. Among other favorites are online companies such as Amazon, eBay, and PayPal (see Figure 5.2).

Notice that this email redirects to a suspicious website address in Russia and not eBay. The consequences of not providing the requested information are fairly dire and are proof that this email isn't what it seems.

caution Phishers are starting to use spyware to collect personal and financial information by employing a key logger. That's a program slipped onto your computer via a surreptitious web download or installed by a freebie program that can capture what you type on your computer. These can also be installed by viruses or Trojan horses. This information is then grabbed by the bad guy across the Internet. The best defense against this is the use of one or more good anti-spyware programs. Learn more in Chapter 2, "Spyware: Overrun by Advertisers, Hijackers, and Opportunists."

FIGURE 5.2

This email looks as if it came from eBay, an online auction website. However, it secretly directs the recipient to a website with a Russian web address.

PHISH FINDER: IDENTIFYING PHISHING EMAILS

Here are some tips you can use to help identify emails from phishers, as suggested by the Anti-Phishing Working Group at www.antiphishing.org:

- Phishers use false statements in the email they send to you, hoping they will upset or excite you, and that you'll react immediately to their request. They might threaten dire consequences if you don't respond, such as terminating an account or instituting a steep fee for reactivation of the account. If the consequences to not replying or acquiescing to their demands seem unnecessarily steep, contact the real organization in question, via phone or email, and ask if this email is theirs.

- They will ask for things such as usernames, passwords, credit card numbers, Social Security numbers, name, address, and other personal data. You will never be asked by a reputable company or institution to provide this kind of information via email.

- Phishing emails are rarely personalized. They rarely address you by name in the text of the email. Valid emails from your bank or e-commerce company generally do. This isn't to say that an email addressing you by name isn't a phishing email or that emails that don't address you by name are phishing emails. I'm talking in generalities here. If it seems phishy, er, fishy, then it probably is. When in doubt, contact the institution in question before doing anything.

How Does Phishing Work?

A phisher's email looks as if it has been sent from an organization you trust, such as your bank, but of course, it hasn't been. The trickery is achieved using a technique called *spoofing*, which is a techie term that basically means to fool electronically. Phishers use a series of tricks to deceive you and make you think you are corresponding with a legitimate organization. Here's how they do it.

Email Address Spoofing

First off, phishers change the sender's address in an email to make it appear as if your bank and not a tongue-pierced kid in a dumpy apartment in

Warsaw sent the correspondence. This is done by simply changing the coding in the header of the email (see Figure 5.3). The header is a set of information roughly equivalent to the address information written on an envelope.

Spoofed return address

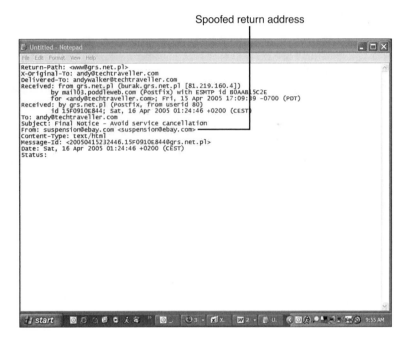

FIGURE 5.3

This email header was taken from a phishing email that purported to be from eBay. The phisher has changed the information in the From: field to make it look like it came from the email address suspension@ebay.com.

Imagine if you sent your best friend a letter by mail but instead of putting your own return address on it, you put the return address of his angry ex-wife's lawyer. On receiving it he might freak out because he'd think that she might be trying to make a claim on his new golf clubs. All you've done is spoofed the return address.

Link Spoofing

The links you are urged to click on in some phishing emails are also spoofed. In the case of web address spoofing, the link looks like a legitimate address, but through some very simple technology it redirects to another link.

The phishing email is created with a programming language used to create web pages. In fact, when you receive an email with pictures, fancy fonts, and a nice layout, it is what's called an HTML email. It looks exactly like a web page because it is made with HTML—the same programming language used to create web pages. HTML is short for HyperText Markup Language.

To create a clickable link in HTML, you use programming code like this:

```
<a href="http://www.realsafebank.com">www.reallysafebank.com</a>
```

This results in a web link that looks like this:

www.reallysafebank.com

Note that the web address inside the angle brackets between the quotes and after the `<a href=` is the web address where you are taken if you click on the link (see Figure 5.4).

Phishers use this programming trick to make it appear as if you are going to one site, but really they put the address of a bogus page in the `href` tag, like this:

```
<a href="http://www.bogusbank.com">www.reallysafebank.com</a>
```

So you think you're about to go to www.reallysafebank.com but you're actually taken to www.bogusbank.com, which looks like your legitimate bank's web page and might actually contain a series of web pages to make it look like an actual banking site.

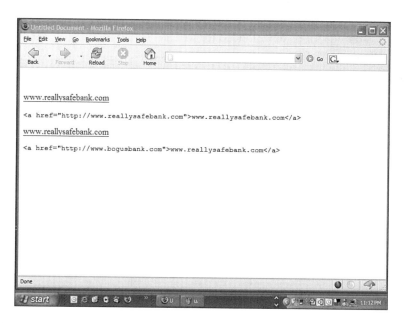

FIGURE 5.4

These two actual web links look exactly the same but the programming used to create them, which appears below each one, shows different destinations on the web.

Web Address Spoofing

Phishers have been exploiting a bug (an error) in the programming of Microsoft web browser Internet Explorer so they can display a fake web address in the browser. When you visit a website that exploits this bug, its web address is not displayed in the browser. Instead, another more trustworthy web address is displayed. So you could be fooled into visiting www.bogusbank.com by a phishing email but your web browser shows you are on www.reallysafebank.com.

The bug affects versions 5.01, 5.5, and 6 of Internet Explorer. However, patches for the vulnerable browser have been issued by Microsoft to fix it. If you run Windows Update and download the latest patches, you will have the patch already installed.

This bug has been fixed in Internet Explorer 7, which comes with Windows Vista and can be downloaded for free for Windows XP from www.microsoft.com/ie.

To test if you are vulnerable, open Internet Explorer and visit security firm Secunia.com at http://secunia.com/internet_explorer_address_bar_spoofing_test/. If your web browser is not up-to-date with the latest Microsoft fix, you'll see how the spoofing trick works and a fake address appears in your address bar. If the bug is fixed in your browser, you'll see a warning or a "This page cannot be displayed" In IE7, nothing happens when you click on the link.

tip Some email programs give you the ability to see the destination website of a link in an email before you click it. For example, in Outlook 2003 and 2007, if you hover your mouse over a link inside an email, the destination address appears in a floating box. In Outlook Express (or Windows Mail in Vista), this address appears in the status bar across the bottom of the window.

tip You can see the source code (and linking information) of an HTML email in Outlook 2003 by opening the email and right-clicking in the body of the message. A View Source option appears. If you click on this option, the HTML source code opens in Notepad. To do this in Outlook 2007, open an email and click Other Actions in the Actions area across the top. Then choose View Source. Windows will open up the source code of the email in Notepad.

tip You can tell which version of Microsoft's Internet Explorer you have on your computer by starting the program, clicking the Help menu, and then clicking About Internet Explorer.

What Is Pharming?

Even if you think phishing scams are as obvious as angry cats, there's one scary new form of scam that even an expert can be fooled by. It's a technique called *pharming*, which, when perpetrated, is invisible to web surfers until it's too late.

> **caution** Sometimes there is a form to fill out directly inside a phishing email. If filled out, this sends your information directly to a phisher's server. No intermediary fake website is necessary.

In a nutshell, here's what happens: You tell your web browser to open a website. It is secretly directed to a fake website that looks just like the original. And this all happens without any clue that you're being duped.

To understand how pharming works, pretend that surfing the Internet is like visiting the zoo with your niece.

You say to her, "What shall we see first?"

She says, "Let's go see the monkeys!"

So you take her up to the information booth and the nice information officer tells you to follow the banana signs. So you both follow the banana signs until you get to the monkey house.

That's kind of how the Internet works now. When you type a web address into your web browser, your browser makes contact with a domain name service (DNS) server, which is a kind of Internet information booth. The browser gives the DNS machine the destination requested. And in turn the DNS server (like the information booth officer) looks it up in the DNS cache. What comes back is a numerical address called an Internet Protocol (IP) address. The web browser uses the IP address to contact the correct server (a computer that contains a website) you want to visit.

In the case of pharming, the information booth officer has been fooled. He's been given the wrong map by the evil marketing guy at the zoo who wants everyone to go to the gift shop. So when you ask for directions to the monkey house, the information officer looks at his map and sees that the monkey house can be found by following the cabbage signs. That doesn't seem right, but that's what the map says, so those are the directions he gives you. (Actually the DNS server isn't smart enough to question the information. It just hands it out.) So you end up at the gift shop. To further the scam, the gift shop might even be decorated like the monkey house with banana wallpaper and stuffed monkeys.

Pharmers poison a DNS server by changing its cache so it stores the wrong IP addresses (see Figure 5.5). So when you browse to your bank's web page, the

DNS server that translates your bank's dotcom address will hand back the wrong IP address. Your web browser takes you to a fake bank site that looks like your bank but is run by a pharmer.

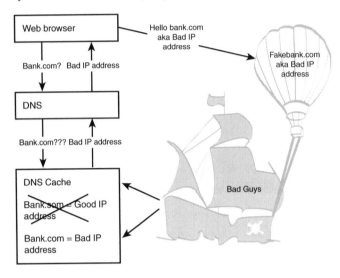

FIGURE 5.5

Pharmers can poison a DNS server with a bad IP number so when your web browser asks for the correct numerical Internet address of your bank (for example), it gets sent the IP address of a fake bank site.

What's alarming about pharming (besides that awful rhyme) is that it can cause a large group of innocent people to be herded off to bogus websites and scammed. Even scarier, during this process your browser looks as if you are visiting a correct site even though it's bogus.

caution Defending yourself against pharming is largely out of your hands. It's a problem being dealt with by Internet service providers, banks, and the telecommunications companies and organizations that own the DNS equipment on the Internet. That said, if you ever click on a website link and you see a message that indicates a mismatched security certificate like the one found at http://www.pharming.org/cert_no_match.jsp, then don't click Yes. The site may have been pharmed.

LOOK OUT FOR 419 SCAMS!

One of the most common email scams is what's called a Nigerian 419 scam or advance fee fraud. It's named after a part of the Nigerian penal code (section 419) that relates to fraudulent schemes.

Here how it works: An email (although in the past mailed letters or faxes have been sent) arrives from someone outside your country, often claiming to be from Nigeria (see Figure 5.6) or some other African nation, and sometimes from other countries. The person sometimes portrays himself or herself as a family member of a deposed Nigerian powerbroker, a Nigerian oil executive, or some other person who has access to oodles of trapped cash.

The author admits that they don't know you, but explains there is a substantial amount of money squirreled away that needs to be moved. If you help, you can keep a big chunk of it, usually millions.

If you bite and open a correspondence with the scam artist, you're led by your email address down a path that results in a request for money. It could be for bribes, taxes, or other fees that the scammer needs to help lubricate the system so the money can be freed. After the first payment the correspondence abruptly stops or you're told complications have set in and a further request for funds is made. This continues until you're tapped out or you get wise. There are also stories (although I couldn't verify them) of victims traveling to Nigeria to help further the transaction and the trip ends with kidnapping, theft, and even murder.

These email scams continue unabated today. My inbox receives at least one or two per day. However, to my amusement, I've discovered a group of people calling themselves "scambaiters," who make it a hobby of turning the tables on the scammers, often with humorous results.

See the correspondence here: http://www.419eater.com/html/letters.htm

5

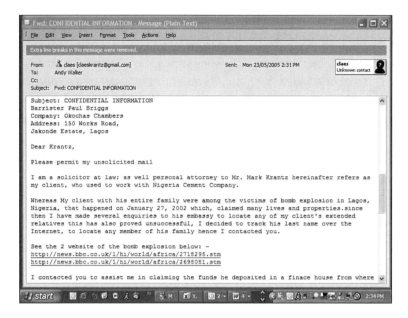

FIGURE 5.6

This example of a Nigerian 419 scam uses the guise of an English barrister representing a Nigerian national.

What Damage Can Be Done By Phishing?

Phishing and identity theft are scary threats because they can result in some severe consequences:

■ **Financial loss**—The most likely result of phishing is being ripped off and losing the cash in your bank or financial account.

■ **Bad credit**—If a wily phisher gets his hands on a credit vehicle such as a credit card or line of credit, he can put you into debt and leave you on the hook to pay the bill.

■ **More severe identity theft**—Although phishing victims typically suffer a one-time hit, in which their bank account is drained, the acquisition of personal information could lead to more severe identity theft. People whose identities have been stolen can spend years trying to clean up the mess made of their good name and credit profile. It can lead to a huge disruption in lifestyle, financial loss, and even being wrongly accused of crimes they haven't committed.

Who Is at Risk? Everyone!

Anyone who uses the Internet is a potential victim of phishing scams. Victims of identity theft cross age and gender boundaries almost equally. Even children and teenagers have been targeted. Mac and PC users alike are at risk.

You don't even have to be alive to be a victim of identity theft. One particular insipid technique is what police call *tombstone shopping*. A crook searches for the death of a child, perhaps by researching deaths at a public library or even visiting a graveyard. The criminal looks for someone who was born in one jurisdiction and died in another. Then she applies for a birth certificate at the dead child's place of birth. After they have that document, a whole new individual can be resurrected on paper and applications for government identity documents can be made.

Don't Get Phished: 10-Minute Tactics to Stay Off the Hook

Phishing is an Internet threat that can be easily avoided with a little common sense and some simple technical know-how. Here are several anti-phishing techniques you can implement in about 10 minutes each.

They Won't Ask, You Don't Tell

Banks and other financial institutions are tuned into phishing scams, so they never ask you to verify your user ID, password, or other personal information via email. If you are in any doubt, call the bank or institution and ask. The best course of action is to communicate with the company directly by phone or in person and delete the email. Never reply to it.

Use Caution and Cut and Paste

If you ever receive an email that asks you to click an included link, the safest thing to do is to cut and paste that link directly into your web browser's address field. This is the best way to avoid being fooled by phishing emails.

Follow these steps to cut and paste a link:

1. Place your mouse to the left of the link, hold the left mouse button down, and drag to the right and release when the whole link is highlighted.

2. Go up to the Edit menu in your email program and choose Copy (using the shortcut key Ctrl+C also works).

3. Open your web browser. Click in the address field (where the web address goes), click the Edit menu, and choose Paste (Ctrl+V also pastes the address).

4. Press the Enter key or click the button to the right of the address field to load the link.

caution Phishers are getting more sophisticated, so it won't be long before they implement secure web pages themselves to extend the illusion, but a web page that asks for personal information with an unlocked symbol at the bottom of the browser is a very good indicator that a site is a phake.

Communicate Securely

You will often have occasion to fill out a form on the web. When you do, be sure that the form is on a secure web page. These web pages use encrypted (scrambled) data. Anybody watching this data as it flows across the Internet sees a stream of nonsense information.

Here's how to check to see if you're on a secure web page:

- The web address of a secure page includes the prefix https://. Note the *s* in https://. Non-secure sites begin with http://.

- When on a secure web page, your web browser displays a closed gold lock in the browser window (see Figure 5.7). In Internet Explorer 7 that closed lock is to the right of the web address at the top of the browser. In the Mozilla Firefox browser, the closed lock shows to the right of the web address at the top of the browser as well at the bottom right corner of the browser window when a secure web page is loaded.

- I hate to scare you but there is a minor problem with the lock icon. Phishers have been known to create clever emails that disguise the parts of the web browser with an overlay (a digital version of a sticker). They have done this before with the overlay of the address bar that shows a bank's real address masking the fake address underneath. This technique is easy to do over the lock icon, too. The way around it: Move the browser window. The overlay stays in place but the browser window moves. This a rare trick, but worth a mention.

tip To improve your browser security, I recommend that you install and use the Firefox web browser as much as possible. Although it has had some security problems (that were promptly fixed) in the past, it's much more secure than Microsoft's Internet Explorer web browser. Firefox can be downloaded free from www.getfirefox.com and is available for the Mac, PC, and other computer platforms.

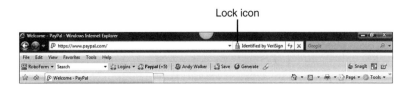

Lock icon

FIGURE 5.7

A closed gold lock to the right of the Internet Explorer address field shows that the web page is secure and data sent from it is encrypted.

Install an Anti-Spam Filter

Spam is unsolicited commercial email. It's the Internet equivalent of those letters addressed to Occupant that show up at your door offering furnace cleaning and raccoon removal, though spam often is much cruder ,offering low-cost prescriptions adult entertainment and products that enhance certain body parts.

I deal with anti-spam techniques in depth in Chapter 6, "Spam: Unwanted Email from Hell," but it is worth a mention here because spam filters can identify and filter phishing emails.

Of particular note is Cloudmark Desktop, a plug-in program that works with Microsoft Outlook, Microsoft Outlook Express, and Mozilla Thunderbird. More than one million Cloudmark Desktop users flag email they consider spam with the program. That information is shared on a common server at Cloudmark. The program works by comparing each email that arrives in your inbox with the Cloudmark database (see Figure 5.8). If an email looks like spam, it's moved to a separate Spam folder in your email program or it's deleted (your choice).

The software (available at www.cloudmark.com) is not free, but is definitely worth the $39.95 annual fee.

Block Phishing Sites with NetCraft

A really good freebie program called NetCraft rates the website you are browsing and tells you how trustworthy it is (see Figure 5.9). It also blocks websites that it has identified as phishing sites. I highly recommend you install this program. It can be turned off when you don't need it, and turned on when you encounter a site of which you are unsure. The program comes in versions for both Firefox and Internet Explorer and is available from http://toolbar.netcraft.com/.

5

FIGURE 5.8

Cloudmark Desktop filters email in Outlook by cross-referencing inbound messages against a database of known spam and phishing emails.

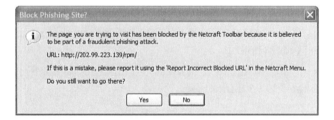

FIGURE 5.9

The NetCraft toolbar blocks a faked SouthTrust banking website, identifying it as a phishing site.

Carry a Big Spoofstick

You can install a free program called Spoofstick as an add-in (often called a plug-in) for your web browser that helps you identify if you're on a bogus website. The program displays the web address you're accessing in big text at the top of the web browser.

Some Internet crooks use slightly modified web addresses on their bogus sites. So if they faked my website Cyberwalker.com, they might set up a website called Cybewalker.com or Cyerwalker.com, two slightly misspelled addresses you might not notice. Spoofstick makes it easier to spot a spoofed website by jacking up the size of the text of the web address (see Figure 5.10).

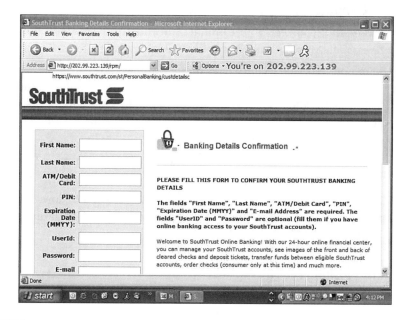

FIGURE 5.10

On this faked SouthTrust website, the IP address (displayed in large font by the Spoofstick program) is a good indication that the site is a fake.

A common phishing practice is to send a user to a website using its IP address. A clue to a spoofed site would be the presence of the IP address in the address field of your browser instead of the dotcom name. Spoofstick makes this more obvious, too.

Spoofstick is free and available for both Internet Explorer and Firefox from www.corestreet.com/spoofstick/.

Keep Your Antivirus and Antispyware Programs Up-to-Date

Many antivirus programs can detect malicious attachments that arrive via email. This includes Trojan horses and key loggers, two types of malicious software that install programs on your computer that can record your personal data and make it available to crooks via the Internet. So be sure to update your virus signatures by using the program's updater.

Antispyware programs, explained in Chapter 2, "Spyware: Overrun By Advertisers, Hijackers, and Opportunists" can also spot and block Trojan horses and key loggers.

Keep Your Computer Software Up-to-Date

Ensure that you keep your computer software up-to-date with the latest bug fixes. Both Microsoft and Apple issue regular security fixes via the Internet.

Microsoft issues its security fixes through the website http://windowsupdate.microsoft.com. This is also accessible by clicking the Windows Update icon on your Start menu or in Vista, typing **Update** in the Search bar on the Start menu, and then clicking Windows Update when it is listed.

Also check with the maker of your email program to ensure it is up-to-date with the latest security patches.

If you have Windows XP with Service Pack 2 (SP2) or Windows Vista, updates for your computer are downloaded automatically by default and you are alerted when they are ready to be installed.

Vista's Anti-Phishing Features

Windows Vista introduces new anti-phishing protections as an extra line of defense to your common sense. The features will also be helpful for those who are new to computers and phishing threats.

The anti-phishing technologies are integrated in both Windows Mail and Internet Explorer 7.

Windows Mail detects phishing, spam, and other suspicious email, puts it into the Junk E-Mail folder, and alerts you with a warning (see Figure 5.11). You can turn this feature on or off as follows:

1. In Windows Mail, click Tools, then Junk E-mail Options.

2. Click the Phishing tab.

caution You should see Windows Update alerts (at least once a month) that indicate the system has installed new fixes. If not, it could be that someone has turned them off. To check the Automatic Updates status, open the Security Center control panel as follows:

In XP, click Start then Control Panel then Security Center

In Vista, click the Windows button and type **Security Center** in the search bar and click it when it appears in the Start menu.

3. Use the settings on that tab to turn the anti-phishing detection on or off and to set Windows Mail to move suspected phishing emails to the Junk E-mail folder.

Suspected spam email

Content of suspected spam email   Windows Mail alert
regarding suspected spam email

FIGURE 5.11

Windows Mail detects phishing emails and moves them to the Junk E-Mail folder so they are out of harm's way.

If you ignore the Windows Mail warnings and end up on a phishing website anyway, IE7 will warn you (see Figure 5.12), at least most of the time. It relies on its own database of suspected websites. So if the phishing website you arrive on isn't in the Microsoft database, it might give the site a clean bill of health. So once again, a healthy dose of common sense is always your first line of defense. Still, kudos to Microsoft for attempting to protect us from ourselves and for developing good anti-phishing features in Vista.

tip Firefox 2.0, a web browser I recommend in this book over IE7, also has built in anti-phishing technology. It's available for free at www.getfirefox.com.

FIGURE 5.12

IE7 protects you from loading a phishing website.

Ensure You Are You: Take an Afternoon to Protect Your Identity

Defending yourself against phishing is not hard to learn. What really is at stake, however, is your identity. Here's how to protect yourself against identity theft.

Check Your Credit Reports

The easiest way to keep an eye on your identity and prevent thieves from using it is to check your credit report frequently with the credit bureaus in your country. Credit bureaus are for-profit organizations that keep track of the credit ratings of individuals and corporations.

Each time a financial institution does a sizeable financial transaction with someone, they post the experience with the credit bureaus. This allows the bureau to build a credit profile of every borrower, so that in future when a lender wants to determine a credit worthiness of a borrower, he has a credit history he can check against.

It's worth checking your credit record quarterly because you can see which lenders have posted activity on your profile. If there's been an application for credit that you don't remember making, it is likely that you might be a victim in the making.

Some credit bureaus send you a free credit report once a year if you write to them, as mandated by law. If you check your credit online or more frequently, there's usually a nominal fee.

United States

Here's a list of the three credit bureaus in the USA.

- **Equifax**—1-800-685-1111; www.equifax.com
- **Experian**—1-888-EXPERIA (397-3742); www.experian.com

In the United States, you can order your free annual credit report at www.annualcreditreport.com or by calling 1-877-322-8228. You can also request it by mail. More info is at www.ftc.gov/bcp/conline/edcams/credit/ycr_free_reports.htm.

Canada

In Canada, the two credit bureaus are

- **Equifax**—1-800-465-7166 or 514-493-2314; www.equifax.ca
- **TransUnion**—1-866-525-0262 or 905-525-0262; in Quebec, 1-877-713-3393 or 514-335-0374; www.tuc.ca

One free annual credit report is available for each person from each credit bureau by sending a request by mail.

United Kingdom

In the U.K., credit reports are available from three credit reference agencies:

- **Experian**—0870 241 6212; www.experian.co.uk
- **Callcredit**—0113 244 1555; www.callcredit.co.uk
- **Equifax**—www.equifax.co.uk

More information on identity theft in the United Kingdom is available from the Home Office Identity Fraud Steering Committee at www.identity-theft.org.uk.

Australia

In Australia, the three credit reporting agencies are

- **Veda Advantage (formerly Baycorp Advantage)**—+61 2 9464 6000; www.vedaadvantage.com
- **Dun and Bradstreet (Australia) Pty Ltd**—13 23 33; www.dnb.com.au
- Tasmanian Collection Service **for Tasmanian residents**—(03) 6213 5555; www.tascol.com.au

Also see: http://www.mycreditfile.com.au.

More information on identity theft in Australia is available from the Australian Government Attorney General's Department at www.ag.gov.au.

If Your Country Is Not Listed

If you live in a country other than the ones previously listed, you can very easily find information about identity theft and the credit bureaus that service your area by contacting your bank, financial advisor, or government information line.

Shred It Before You Chuck It

Be careful what you throw out. Even though the Internet can be a happy hunting ground for identity thieves, they also prowl the real world as well. If you chuck out mail, documents, and other paper records, be sure to shred them before they go in the bin. Your garbage is ripe for the picking in more ways than one.

Read Your Statements

It's not great literature, but it's worth reading every credit and bank statement you receive as it comes in. A vast majority of identity theft victims don't discover the problem until months have gone by. Early warning signs show up as weird or unexpected line items on bills or statements.

> **tip** Ideally, you want to destroy your documents into tiny pieces, so they can't be reassembled easily. Straight-cut shredders slice paper into strips and are less secure than cross-cut shredders that cut across two axes so that the document becomes confetti. Cross-cut shredders are slower and require more maintenance.

The Absolute Minimum

- Identity theft is the use of your personal and financial information to apply for credit in your name without your permission or knowledge. It is also the illegal use of your existing credit.

- Guard your personal information, especially identifying documents. Do not fill out unnecessary applications or provide information to unfamiliar people or organizations you don't trust. Simplify your accounts and credit cards, and destroy paper documents with a shredder. Keep an eye on your credit reports annually. Look at them quarterly if possible.

- Thieves steal your identity by acquiring personal information about you and building up enough data to apply for an identity document. Then they use this to apply for credit in your name.

- You know you're a victim when credit reports show accounts you did not authorize. Strange transactions appear on financial or credit card statements. Credit you apply for is declined. You are pursued by a collections agency to pay a debt you haven't incurred. You are accused of a crime or traffic offense you did not commit.

- If you have been victimized, file a police report, close tainted accounts, and place a fraud watch with the credit bureaus. Document the process. File an identity theft report with the FTC in the United States or the appropriate government body in other countries.

- Phishing is an electronic method of fooling you into providing personal and financial information to a crook on the web. It's most commonly perpetrated by email, but information can also be solicited using a pop-up window on the web.

- Pharming is an attack on special network computers called DNS servers that direct traffic on the Internet. These data traffic cops are poisoned with incorrect information so that when a web surfer asks to be directed to a specific website, they are unknowingly sent to a crook's site.

- Avoid any too-good-to-be-true offers of quick money and skip any communication with strange Nigerians that need dubious help. It's a scam to get money out of you. These schemes are called advance fee fraud. Nigeria is commonly used as a cover story, but they are perpetrated from all over the world.

5

- Your bank or other financial institutions will never request verification of user IDs, passwords, or other personal information through email. If in doubt, contact the institution.

- If you do send personal information via a financial website, be sure to first type the company's web address into your browser manually. And check to see if the site is secure—indicated by a closed lock symbol in your web browser and https:// in the web address bar.

- Be alert to misuse of your identity by regularly checking your credit reports with the national credit bureau in your country.

- Keep your antivirus and antispyware programs up-to-date and scan your system regularly. This protects you from key loggers and Trojan horses that can capture your personal information and send it to crooks on the Internet.

- Keep your computer's operating system up-to-date. And ensure that any fixes issued for your email program and web browser are installed.

- If you have a Windows Vista computer, note that it has built-in anti-phishing mechanisms in Windows Mail and Internet Explorer 7 that help defend against phishing.

- Guard your offline information as well. Read your financial and banking statements and shred mail and documents before putting them in the trash.

5

Spam: Unwanted Email from Hell

This chapter explains why you get all those emails about cheap Viagra, amazing fat-fighting plant extracts, and attractive pillow-fighting college students. Yes, it's a chapter about spam—the email kind, not the canned meat kind. In these pages I'll tell you what it is, where it comes from, and what to do about it. It's the amazing, natural, and safe chapter about fighting spam! No dangerous stimulants or damaging side effects!

What Is Spam?

Despite its namesake, spam is not a favorite Hawaiian breakfast ingredient, a pig byproduct, or my dad's favorite lunch meat. That's SPAM, the compressed ham in a can made by the Hormel Foods Corporation.

No, spam is something completely different. And it's so important that it merits its own chapter in a computer security book. Lowercase *spam* is unsolicited commercial email or electronic junk mail.

It's those emails you receive in your inbox from people you don't know that advertise everything from religious T-shirts (see Figure 6.1) to adult websites (see Figure 6.2). Sometimes these ads are offensive. Other times they're stupid. Usually they are just plain annoying, especially because they arrive in huge volume and rarely do they advertise anything you need. Don't you think spam would be less annoying if it offered to sell you a freshly baked pecan pie or a tasty piece of haddock? Spam never advertises anything good.

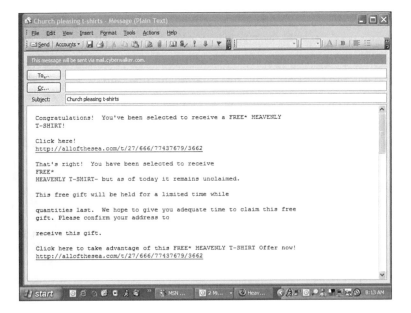

FIGURE 6.1

The site this spam links to offers a free "Wherever I go God is with me" T-shirt. It's odd, however, that the spammer has put 666 in the URL. Not a great marketing tactic when it comes to Christians.

FIGURE 6.2

This spam email features Alyssa, who has dark brown hair (isn't that blonde hair in the picture?) and black eyes (a little odd, too). Don't think she's interested in meeting you. The email clicks through to an adult website.

Why Does Spam Keep Coming?

Spam makes spammers money. It's hard to believe, but there are people out there who receive spam email, click the offer, and buy the advertised product. Now, you might think, why would anyone do that? Who knows, but they do because the spam keeps coming.

Personally, I think spam is perpetrated by people like that slightly evil kid in chess club. You know, the one who smelled vaguely sour and hiked his shorts too high in gym class. In reality, spammers are just business people—okay, slimy business people—bottom-feeding on yet another Internet opportunity.

caution Many reputable companies use email for legitimate marketing purposes. If you agree to receive email from an organization (that is to say, you opt-in), the email it sends you is not spam. If you find yourself in this situation, go back to the company's website and find out how to opt-out (unsubscribe). Most reputable companies have a mechanism that allows you to unsubscribe from their emails. Often, you'll find directions for unsubscribing at the bottom of the email in question.

6

Nevertheless, you don't need much more than Grade 9 math to figure out that if you send a lot of emails, a small percentage of the recipients read the email and an even smaller percentage buy the advertised product. Small as it is, it's income with a scaleable formula. If you can send millions of messages for the price of an Internet connection and a computer, you've got an almost free distribution system. And if it costs almost nothing to send and produces an income of any kind, it's profitable. So the spam keeps coming.

LOVELY SPAM, WONDERFUL SPAAAAAAM!

The origin of the term *spam* comes from a sketch by the British comedy troupe Monty Python. They did a bit on a restaurant that only featured dishes made with SPAM (note the uppercase), which is a canned ham product from Hormel. When the waitress describes items on the menu, a group of Vikings sing a song that goes something like "SPAM, SPAM, SPAM, SPAM. Lovely SPAM, lovely SPAM…" So spam was thus named because, like the song, it is an endless repetition of worthless text.

Specialty Spam

Spam distribution is a popular and effective way for Internet criminals to deliver their schemes or scams, however not all spam is made the same. Some custom spam techniques are used to for specific purposes or use distribution technologies outside of email. What follows are some curiosities in the specialty spam world.

Malware and Scam Distribution

Some bad guys use spam engines to send messages with attachments, which are actually viruses. When opened by unsuspecting recipients, the virus's payload turns the system into a zombie. A *zombie* is an infected computer that can be remotely controlled by a bad guy from the Internet to do bad things like send more spam or attack other computers by blasting nonsense data at them (often called a denial-of-service attack).

Spammers also use spam engines to distribute 419 scams and phishing emails.

> **tip** If you want to learn what a 419 scam is and how to protect yourself against them, check out Chapter 5 "Identity Thieves and Phishers: Protect Your Good Name and Bank Account."

Hobbit Spam

In the spring and summer of 2006, some odd spam started to appear in inboxes. The messages contained lines from the JRR Tolkien's novel *The Hobbit*.

Here's an example:

```
"the hobbit that was lost. That only makes eleven (plus one mislaid) and
not fourteen, unless wizards count differently to other people. But now
please get on with the tale. Beorn did not show it more than he could."
```

Besides the bit of hobbit prose, the messages weren't pitching anything. So where did they come from? The theory is that a teenager (or similar inexperienced mischief maker) got his hands on a spam distribution tool and was taking it for a spin. Another theory is that a spammer was testing well-crafted prose against spam filters to see if he could fool them into letting the message through.

SPIM and Non-email Spam

Spam can also be unwanted, voluminous, and usually commercially motivated messages posted to web discussion forums, newsgroups, and blog comments.

There is also a spam variant that arrives in instant messenger (IM) programs. That kind of spam is sometimes referred to as SPIM.

SPIM looks like a chat message that usually has an embedded link of some sort or a file attachment. When you click on it, your system can be infected with some sort of malware. Sometimes the link takes you to a site that tries to sell you something.

The chatter that sends the SPIM can be someone unknown to you or you might recognize them. If they are a friend, colleague or family member, it could be that their system has been infected by a virus, which is using their identity to send SPIM.

If you receive a suspicious chat message, then message the person back and challenge them. Automated SPIMbots (programs that distribute spim) won't answer back. Friends, of course, will, unless their chat identity has been hijacked and is being used by a SPIMbot.

Good antivirus programs will detect spim, especially spim laden with malware, and alert you to the hazard.

6

Why Doesn't Someone Stop the Spammers?

note A botnet is a loose network of infected personal computers connected to the Internet that can be remote controlled by a bad guy (who wrote the malware that infected them). Internet criminals use botnets to distribute spam and attack target computers in denial of service attacks.

Spammers are difficult to stop, partly because email as a technology is easy to use and hard to block. Each computer connected to the Internet has a unique numerical address called an Internet Protocol (IP) address. It's sort of like a telephone number. To send or receive information to or from a computer on the Internet, you have to know its IP address.

If a computer sends too much information—maybe too many spam emails— its IP address can be blocked by the recipient. This is what Internet service providers (ISPs) often do to curtail spam from a particular source. But if the owner of the sending computer changes the IP address, the ISP has to reblock the new address.

Because of this, spammers can evade being blocked by changing their IP address on a regular basis (or by sending from computers that they have hijacked and control through a botnet). They also move their operations overseas to countries that don't care or are more interested in making money than stopping spam.

Anti-spam laws have been enacted around the world in recent years by various countries, including the United States, to regulate commercial bulk email. Some high-profile spammers have been convicted but the laws have had little effect on reducing the total volume of spam. It keeps growing. However, spammers are being driven offshore to countries, such as China and Russia, where they are out of the grasp of anti-spam legislation.

According to a report by Message Labs, an email security company, the Australian Spam Act is one piece of legislation that has resulted in a "significant decrease in spam activity," driving known spammers to shut down activities or go offshore. Still, the volume of spam continues to climb (see Figure 6.3).

tip Get an intriguing handle on how much spam is out there and what malware or scams it is laden with on the Message Labs Intelligence web page at: http://www.messagelabs.com/intelligence.aspx

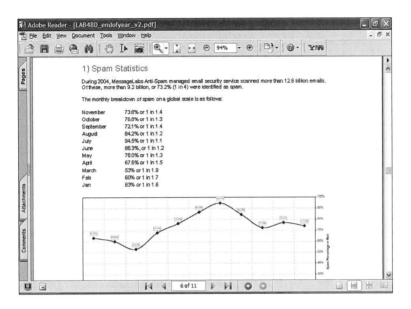

FIGURE 6.3
Email security company MessageLabs reported that spam constituted between 53% and 94.5% of email sent worldwide in 2004. Not much has changed; that volume is consistent today.

How Do Spammers Get My Email Address?

Spammers are a crafty bunch. They source email addresses wherever they can get their hands on them.

Website Harvesting

Programs are available that scan public address books on web-based email sites.

Spammers also have software that looks for email addresses embedded in websites. If you have a personal web page, an email address you post is almost guaranteed to be found by spammers. In fact, the people who receive the most spam tend to be webmasters. After emails are harvested they are compiled into lists and sold on the Internet.

Dictionary Spamming

There are also programs that combine random words and common names and pop them together in an effort to come up with valid email addresses.

6

With so many people using email, all the common names for email addresses such as Bob Smith are long gone at the big ISPs. So people make up their email addresses from common words. So let's say your ISP is called really-bigisp.com and your email address is topdog@reallybigisp.com.

Spammers might find you by running their dictionary program and combining the words *top* and *dog* together. They'll try sending an email to topdog@reallybigisp.com. They try this address combination against all the other major ISPs as well, so all the top dogs at aol.com, msn.com, and beyond get spam.

And don't think that becoming topdog1967@reallybigisp.com will help because after the spammers run through the most obvious words, they start combining them with numbers.

They'll even send email to aaaaaaa@reallybigisp.com, then aaaaaab@reallybigisp.com, then aaaaaac@reallybigisp.com, and so on.

Because computers do all this work the spammers can try billions of combinations in hours. Then they spam to all these potential addresses. If they don't receive a bounced email from the address, they log it as valid and put it on their active list.

Commercial Email Lists

Millions of email addresses are available for sale via Internet download or on CD-ROM. Out of curiosity, I bought a list of 10 million Canadian email addresses for $49. The company claimed they were all opt-in email addresses, meaning that the owners of the addresses had agreed to be put on the list. I found one of my addresses that is used for inbound mail only, however. It was never used to opt in to anything.

Newsgroups, Discussion Forums, and Interactive Websites

When you post your email address to the web to receive a newsletter or to sign up for a discussion forum, for example, you expose yourself to spammers. Email addresses can also be easily harvested from Internet-based discussion groups called newsgroups (see Figure 6.4) or discussion forums and the web at large. Some companies sell these lists of verified email addresses. Before making this information available, you might want to look for a privacy statement on the website to see what they are going to do with any personal information you give them. Credible websites stick to their privacy policies closely.

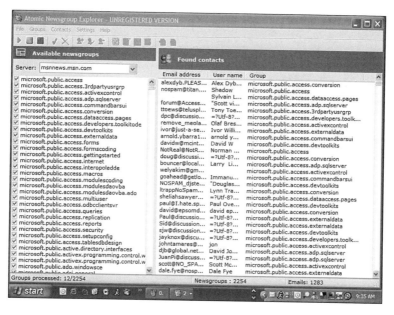

FIGURE 6.4

Atomic Newsgroup Explorer is a program that can extract thousands of email addresses and user names from Internet newsgroups in mere seconds. Here it has scanned the newsgroups at msnnews.msn.com.

Contests and Other Free Offerings

You can sign up to receive spam legitimately by entering contests or engaging in offers that appear to give you something for nothing. Oftentimes, these deals are email-harvesting schemes. Sometimes they even explicitly tell you in the fine print that you will receive bulk commercial email and you actually agree to this.

Email Forwarding

If you forward an email to dozens of people, make sure you send it to yourself in the To: field and put everyone else in the Bcc: field. *Bcc* means blind carbon copy. It's used to send a copy of the email to someone without revealing her email address (see Figure 6.5). If Bcc is not used, you expose everyone's email address to dozens of other people. It's been suggested that your email can be exposed to spammers that way. I know a few public relations people who have scooped my email for press release lists when another person has failed to hide my address in the Bcc field.

6

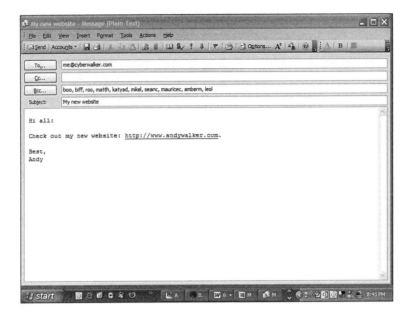

FIGURE 6.5
The Bcc: field is used when you want to send a copy of an email to someone, but hide her email address from others copied on the email.

Data Theft

Data is stolen from companies with alarming frequency. According to Privacyrights.org, as of December 4, 2007, 216,402,336 records containing sensitive personal information had been involved in security breaches since 2005 in the United States.

If you have ever registered your email with a company you do business with, and it is breached by a hacker, your email address could have been accessed and potentially sold by the perpetrators to spammers. Of course if that has happened, it is probably the least of your worries. This kind of data theft typically leads to identity theft or credit card fraud.

The Damage Spam Can Do

Spam might be free to send, but it is very costly to its recipients and the Internet community in the following ways:

■ **It costs you money**—Spam costs millions of dollars a year in Internet

tip For a list of data breach incidents since 2005 and an updated number of records exposed by a security breach to date, see http://www.privacyrights.org/ar/ChronDataBreaches.htm#Total

resources. It clogs Internet plumbing, forcing ISPs to buy bigger electronic pipes to carry all the information on the Internet. This drives up the cost of operations, which is passed on to you, the ISP's customer.

- **Wasted productivity**—If you're a business owner, spam wastes workers' time and productivity and increases expenses because it consumes helpdesk and IT resources to deal with it.

- **It wastes your time**—Spam wastes your time. Wading through spam to find the legitimate email takes time, especially if you get a lot of spam. If it takes you one second to delete a spam email and you get 900 spam emails each day (for a time I was getting more than 1,000), that wastes 15 minutes of your time.

- **It disconnects you**—If the flow of spam becomes too great, you have to abandon your email address in favor of a new one. This disconnects you from people who lose track of you because they don't update their email address lists.

- **It's annoying and offensive**—Spam is advertising you're not interested in, and that's just plain annoying. And often it comes with content that's offensive or at the very least distasteful.

- **It endangers children**—It exposes children to topics and images that they shouldn't have to worry about, including adult content.

- **It's a malware carrier** —Some spam carries email attachments that if opened can infect your computer with viruses or spyware. (Learn more about spyware in Chapter 2, "Spyware: Overrun by Advertisers, Hijackers, and Opportunists.")

- **It distributes scams**—Spam can also be used to mass-mail 419 scams or phishing emails. (Learn more about these scams in Chapter 5, "Identity Thieves and Phishers: Protect Your Good Name and Bank Account.")

- **It can get you kicked off the Net**—Some viruses can infect your computer so it turns into a spam-sending machine. And if your computer is identified as a source of spam, your Internet service provider may terminate your Internet account. Spammers use viruses to hijack other people's computers into sending spam because they create a

caution Be sure to run an up-to-date antivirus program on your computer to ensure your computer is not infected with a computer virus that has turned it into a spam distribution machine. Some viruses are engineered to install spam-sending software on a victim's computer.

6

massive network of spam-sending machines without worrying about having their own computers being identified as a spam sender. The spam also comes from thousands of computers and not just one, making it harder to stop.

Reduce the Flow—10-minute Tactics to Reduce Spam

You can do a few simple things to immediately reduce the flow of spam to your email address.

Don't Respond

First of all, never respond to spam. That means don't open spam, don't send angry responses to the spam sender, and definitely don't buy anything in a spam offer. If spam failed to work as an advertising medium, there would be little value in sending it. When you buy or respond to spam, you reinforce the notion that spam works as a marketing tool. And when you respond in any manner, you confirm that your email address is an active address. As a consequence, you'll receive more spam.

Don't Post Your Email Address on the Web

Don't give your main email address to anyone on the web. That's hard to do because many websites insist on your email address when signing up for their services. It's a good idea to maintain an alternate email address with Hotmail.com, Yahoo.com, Gmail.com, or any of the other free email services on the web. Check the secondary address occasionally to check for valid email, such as subscription confirmations, and if the volume of spam to that address gets to be too much, simply abandon it and get a new secondary address.

Webmasters Shouldn't Use mailto

If you run a website, don't post your primary email address to it using the HTML code called mailto.

A mailto link allows you to insert a link in a webpage that, when clicked, triggers the web surfer's email program and inserts the email address in the To field. A link that uses this technique looks like this:

```
Send me an email at <a href="mailto: me@mymailaddress.com">me@
➥mymailaddress.com</a>
```

Email harvester programs hunt for this code. Using a mailto is like wearing salmon-flavored socks at a cattery. You'll get bombarded with a lot of unwanted attention.

Instead, use the following JavaScript code, which achieves the same result but masks the email address. Be sure to customize the parts that say *me*, *example.com*, and *Link text* to your own needs.

```
<a href="email.html" onmouseover="this.href='mai' + 'lto:' + 'me' +
➥ '@' + 'example.com'">Link text</a>
```

Learn more about this at www.december14.net/ways/js/nospam.shtml.

Turn Off Image Display in Email Programs

Both Outlook and Outlook Express have a feature that turns off images in HTML email. (HTML is a web programming language that is used to create web pages.) HTML email can include pictures, fancy fonts, and layout like a magazine. If you see a picture displayed in the body of an email, it was mostly likely created with HTML.

The ability to put images in email can cause an increase in spam. That's because spammers put an invisible pixel (an image of a transparent dot) in HTML emails. When an email is opened or previewed, the invisible pixel is fetched from the spammer's server. That tells the server that the email address affiliated with that image is a good one and is ripe to receive further spam.

Outlook 2003, Outlook 2007, Outlook Express 6, and Windows Mail (on Vista) have the ability to block these images from displaying (see Figure 6.6). Here's how to turn the features on in all these programs.

Outlook 2003

1. Click the Tools menu and choose Options.
2. Click the Security tab.
3. Under the Download Pictures heading, click Change Automatic Download Settings button.
4. Put a tick mark in the box marked Don't Download Pictures or Other Content Automatically in HTML Email.

6

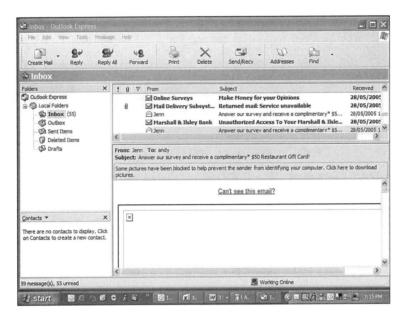

FIGURE 6.6

Outlook Express 6 can block images from displaying in HTML emails when they are opened or in preview mode.

Outlook 2007

1. Click the Tools menu and choose Trust Center.

2. On the left side, click Automatic Download

3. Put a check mark in the box next to Don't Download Pictures Automatically in HTML Messages or RSS Items.

4. Look at the suboptions and consider if you want to allow those. If you use the Junk Email feature in Outlook, you might consider checking off the box next to Permit Downloads in Email Messages From Senders and to Recipients Defined in the Safe Senders and Safe Recipient Lists...

note This feature is built into Windows Mail in Vista, but in Windows XP it only works in Outlook Express 6 if you have installed Service Pack 2 (SP2), a major security add-on released by Microsoft in August 2004. You can install it by running Windows Update. Learn more about SP2 on **p. 274**.

Outlook Express 6/Windows Mail

1. Click the Tools menu and choose Options.

2. Click the Security tab.

3. Under the Download Images heading, put a check mark in the box marked Block Images and Other External Content in HTML Email (see Figure 6.8).

tip The image-blocking function in Outlook 2003/2007 and Outlook Express/Windows Mail has a nice side benefit. When porn-related spam arrives with graphic images of naked people doing surprisingly agile things, the images won't automatically display, saving you some shock and perhaps a little embarrassment if your grandma is nearby.

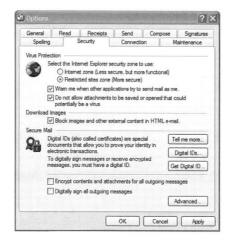

FIGURE 6.7

Outlook Express and Windows Mail has an image-blocking function to stop the display of embarrassing images and invisible tracking images.

Tweak Junk Mail Filtering on Your Mail Server

If your email provider allows you access to filter mechanisms on the mail server you should certainly tweak those filters to your liking. This is particularly useful if you have a vanity or company web domain and email addresses. This is like filtering junk mail at the post office before it gets put in the postman's delivery bag.

For example, I run the web site Cyberwalker.com and my company uses that domain (web address) for email. So on the server side of things I have access to spam filtering. I log on to my provider, Everyone.net, and can tweak spam filter settings (see Figure 6.8).

You might want to call your Internet service provider (if they provide your email address) or the third-party company that hosts your email to see if you can access these settings.

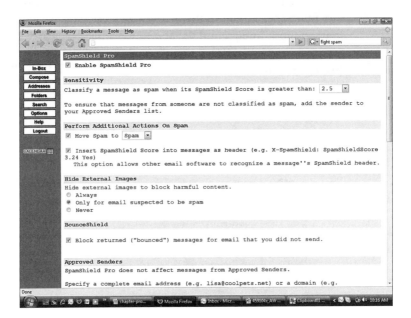

FIGURE 6.8
Some email providers, like Everyone.net, offer the ability to tweak spam filtering on the email server before it gets to your PC's email program.

Turn on Junk Mail Filtering

If you use Outlook 98, 2000, 2003, or 2007, turn on the Junk filter. It is not a foolproof method, but it stops much of the spam headed for your inbox.

Outlook 98, 2000, and 2002

To turn on the Junk filter, follow these steps:

1. In Outlook 98, click the Tools menu, and then click Organize.
2. Next, click Junk Email.
3. In the Automatically <action> Junk Messages list, select Move as the action, and then click to select the destination folder from the list. Click Turn On.

4. In the Automatically <action> Adult messages list, select Move as the action and then click to select the destination folder from the list. Click Turn On.

Outlook 2003 and 2007

Outlook 2003 and 2007 offer improved junk email tools over previous versions of Outlook. Here's how to turn the those features on:

1. Click the Tools menu and choose Options.

2. On the Preferences tab under Email, click Junk Email.

3. Select the level of protection you want (see Figure 6.9). If you receive a small volume of spam, choose Low. Note that High protection does a better job, but you will have to check your Junk email folder periodically to ensure that no legitimate emails have been mistakenly marked as spam.

FIGURE 6.9

Outlook 2003 (shown here) and Outlook 2007 offer vastly improved anti-spam tools over previous versions of the program, including conservative and aggressive sensitivity settings.

Kill More Spam—In an Afternoon

When you have a few hours to spare, here are a few more tactics to stop even more spam.

Install an Anti-Spam Program

Lots of anti-spam programs are available. All the big-name software security companies, including Symantec and McAfee, have their own. Choose one and install it; it will drastically reduce the flow of spam to your inbox.

I have had great success with Cloudmark Desktop (see Chapter 5, "Identity Thieves and Phishers: Protect Your Good Name and Bank Account," for more on Cloudmark Desktop). It's a plug-in for Outlook (see Figure 6.10), Outlook Express, and Mozilla Thunderbird that looks at each email as it comes in and electronically compares it to a database of spam email at Cloudmark. If a match is found, the email is marked as spam and is dumped into a spam folder or it can be automatically deleted; it's your choice.

Cloudmark toolbar

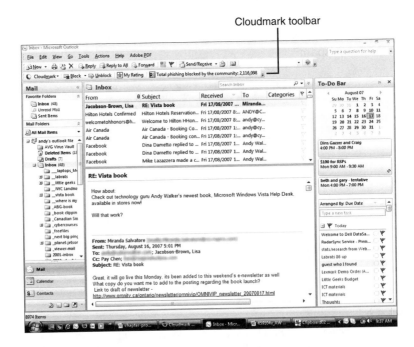

FIGURE 6.10
Cloudmark Desktop is a spam filter for Outlook, Outlook Express and Mozilla Thunderbird. It is shown here near the top of Outlook 2007.

The flaw in most anti-spam programs is that no matter how clever the detection engine, it will almost always misidentify some legitimate email as spam or let some spam through.

Cloudmark Desktop catches about 80%–90% of spam because humans look at each message. But fear not, there's no team of spam spotters on the

Cloudmark staff looking at all your email. The program relies on its users. When email comes in, you can mark it as spam using the program. This reports the message as spam to the company's servers. If enough of us report the spam, a spam signature is generated and everyone that gets that spam in future has it filtered automatically by the software.

The community approach results in no false positives, which is lingo for a misidentification of a legitimate email as spam.

So if I get an email from my aunt who talks about the cocks crowing on her farm and the pretty tits singing in the trees outside her window, the Cloudmark software is not going to treat her email as spam, while others might because of misread keywords in her message.

Cloudmark Desktop costs $39.95 per year, but it does have a free 30-day trial. It's available from www.cloudmark.com.

> **tip** If you use a web-based email service such as Gmail.com, Hotmail.com, or Yahoo! Mail, it's worth investigating their built-in anti-spam features to set spam filtering sensitivity.

> **tip** My pal Leo Laporte talks about his strategy for the Mac here: http://techguylabs.com/radio/Main/StopSpam

> **tip** I've found that turning on Microsoft Outlook's built-in Junk Filter and installing Cloudmark Desktop helps blocks 99% of the spam that arrives in my inbox.

If you don't want to use Cloudmark Desktop, you might consider using Norton AntiSpam or McAfee SpamKiller, though I am no fan of either.

For the Mac, check out SpamSieve from http://c-command.com/spamsieve/.

A series of free anti-spam programs for Windows PCs are available for download at www.snapfiles.com/Freeware/comm/fwspam.html.

Fight Back!

If youare angry enough to fight back against spammers, here's how. Forward a message with your spam complaint to the ISP that hosts the spammer's email account. For example, if you received spam from bobby1234@llamasarenice.com, go to the website www.llamasarenice.com and look for a Contact Us page. Often ISPs have an email account called Abuse for such purposes. In this example, you'd send a copy of the spam to abuse@llamasarenice.com. You could also try postmaster@llamasarenice.com or hostmaster@llamasarenice.com. Try to verify what the correct address is first so you don't waste anyone's time.

6

The big problem with this solution is that ISPs are deluged by spam and to investigate every source of spam is not possible. Still, the option is available to you and it may make you feel better.

You can also use SpamCop.net (see Figure 6.11), a spam reporting service. It analyzes an email's content and header information (where it came from and how it got there). Then if it is deemed to be spam, it sends a warning to the ISP that provides the spammer with Internet service. ISPs tend to not like spammers on their network, so they often revoke service from them if they receive valid complaints. SpamCop.net has free and paid versions of its service.

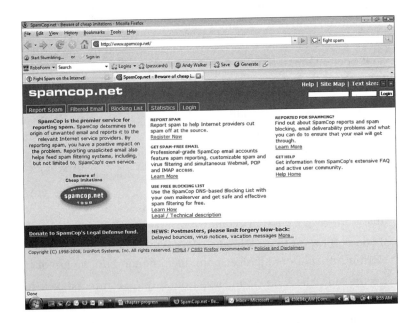

FIGURE 6.11
SpamCop.net analyzes your spam and reports it to the ISP that connects the spammer to the Internet.

More spam fight strategies are available here: http://spam.abuse.net

The Absolute Minimum

■ Spam is unsolicited commercial email or electronic junk mail.

■ SPAM is canned meat from Hormel.

■ Spammers send massive volumes of email because they make money at it. Someone, somewhere, buys the products they advertise.

- Spam is an effective distribution method for scams and malware.

- A spammer's computer can be blocked but it's easy for him to evade this by changing his computer's IP address, the numerical address used to identify his computer on the Internet.

- Spam is free to send but costs recipients time, productivity, money, and aggravation.

- Never respond to spam.

- Never post your main email address to the web. Instead, use an alternate email for web forums, subscriptions, and the like.

- Use the junk mail filters in Outlook, Outlook Express, or Windows Mail.

- Install an anti-spam program. I recommend Cloudmark Desktop.

- Fight back by reporting spam to the spammer's ISP.

6

Wireless Network Snoops: Lock Down Your Wi-Fi Network

Wireless networks are everywhere. You might even have one in your home. If you do, did you know you've just left an electronic door into your home wide open to anyone who walks by? In this chapter you learn the risks posed by a wireless network and how to lock it down so that no one pulls up to the curb outside your house and tiptoes through your personal data. Plus, you get to learn about exciting encryption technologies such as WEP and WPA and how to scramble data so that people can't read your bank statements or your grandma's top secret cookie recipe as it flies through the ether.

What Is a Wireless Home Network?

Better go look out your window. There could be someone lurking in her car outside your home connecting to your wireless network right now. I am not kidding. It happens every day. In fact, it could have been me. I've been at curbside in my car numerous times waiting for someone and checked my email on my laptop by connecting to someone's open wireless network. I didn't do anything bad. But I could figure out what brand of wireless router they had, what settings it had, and what computers were on the network. It would have even been possible to print a note on their printer—"Andy was here. Thanks for the toner."

I didn't, but I could have.

To understand how strangers can access your computer just by parking outside your house, it's important to understand what a wireless home network is. Let's first look at the basics. A *home network* is a way to connect computers and other devices together so they can share stuff such as files, access to the Internet, and printers.

Businesses have been networking for a long time, but the technology has recently become available to do this at home very cheaply. This is achieved by attaching wires from each computer—called CAT-5 cables—to a little box called a *home network router* (see Figure 7.1) or connecting them wirelessly across radio waves. The router, in turn, is connected to a high-speed Internet modem, which connects to the Internet. A printer can also be attached to this setup so that any computer on the network can print to it. And computers on this network can send or get files from each other.

To make wireless work, you need a router that has Wi-Fi or Wireless Fidelity capability and a computer with a wireless network adapter. Most home network routers these days come with Wi-Fi built in. Since Wi-Fi

> **tip** Wi-Fi is usually used with a laptop, but if you have a desktop computer, you can add Wi-Fi to it by buying a wireless adapter card. The adapter card, which contains an antenna and Wi-Fi circuitry, fits into an open slot (called a PCI slot) in the rear of the PC. This is useful if the computer is located in a different room from the Wi-Fi router because it saves running a cable.

> **tip** If you have a Wi-Fi router in your home, you probably already know it. But if you're not sure, here's how to check. Locate the modem that connects to your high-speed service. If it connects directly to your computer with a cable, you don't have a Wi-Fi network. If the modem connects to a small box with one to three pencil-sized antennas, that small box is likely a Wi-Fi router. That said, some Internet companies offer broadband modems with Wi-Fi modems built in. The giveaway is the antenna.

7

is turned on by default in these routers, any computer that has a Wi-Fi adapter can connect wirelessly to the router within a range of about 300 feet.

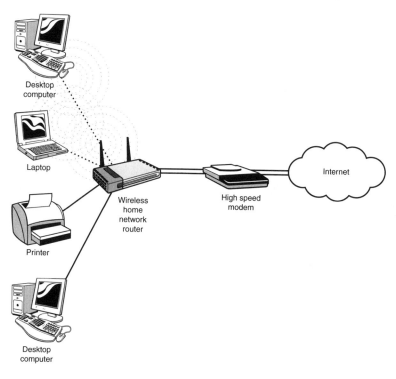

Desktop computer

Laptop

Wireless home network router

Printer

High speed modem

Internet

Desktop computer

FIGURE 7.1

At the heart of a home network is a router. It's a junction box that connects computers so they can share files. It also gives them access to the Internet and resources such as a printer.

This is useful at home because it means you can sit by the pool with your laptop and order urgent groceries, such as margarita mix, using the Web.

The bad part is you can also get email wirelessly from your egomaniacal boss who can chastise you about your expense report that includes a receipt for margarita mix.

note There is one thing a wired connection is better at: speed. Although the fastest flavor of Wi-Fi moves data at potentially 248Mbps, wired networks can be much faster. A wired connection, called Ethernet, comes in three speeds. It started at a pokey 10Mbps, but these days the 100Mbps version is most common. And now 1000Mbps, or Gigabit Ethernet, is available.

7

WHAT'S WITH THE WI-FI ALPHABET?

If you listen to Wi-Fi geeks chat, you'll sometimes hear some weird terms when they refer to different types of Wi-Fi technology: "Oh yeah, my Wi-Fi network uses eight-oh-two-dot-eleven-gee!"

If you want to play along with him, here's the magic decoder ring for that conversation.

There are four types of Wi-Fi: 802.11b, 802.11a, and 802.11g, plus one new one on the way called 802.11n:

- **802.11b** —This is the slowest version of Wi-Fi with a maximum speed of 11Mbps (and a real-world speed of 2–4Mbps). It's the oldest Wi-Fi technology around. It works in the 2.4GHz radio spectrum—the same part of the radio dial that your cordless phone, baby monitor, garage door opener, and microwave work in. It has a range of up to 35 meters (115 feet).

- **802.11a** —This version of Wi-Fi has a maximum speed of 54Mbps (with an actual speed of 20–30Mbps or so). It's the second oldest. It works in the 5GHz part of the radio spectrum where some cordless phones work. You won't see it used very often any more.

- **802.11g** —This is the most common version of Wi-Fi today that ships on most laptop computers. It's 802.11b on growth hormones. It works at a theoretical 54Mbps (or real-world 20–30Mbps), but it also works in the 2.4GHz radio spectrum. And it works with old 802.11b gear. It also has a range of up to 35 meters (115 feet).

- **802.11n** —This is a new, super-fast Wi-Fi that works at up to 248Mbps (but typically at 74Mbps). It has a range of 70 meters (230 feet). Most of the details of this new specification have been ironed out after a lot of geek-fighting. So manufacturers are issuing first-generation gear using what they call "draft-N," "pre-N," or "MIMO" technology. Expect the final specification to

note "Theoretical" speeds are maximum possible speeds that a bunch of technology scientists have demonstrated in a lab with all the walls, pets and coffee cups out of the way. It's unlikely that you'll ever get the maximum theoretical speed in your home.

be complete in the fall of 2008 with compliant gadgets to ship in time for the 2008 holiday season. Note that manufacturers say that the pre-specification products released in 2007 and early 2008 should be upgradeable to the final specification when it is released. All you'll need to do is download a free firmware upgrade (software that updates the router's programming) from the manufacturer's web site. Very early pre-N versions available in 2005 and 2006 will likely not be covered by that promise because there will be physical differences in the chips compared to final release products.

What Damage Can a Wireless Network Snoop Do?

Wireless network snoops tend to be curious, not malicious. In fact, most people who access your Wi-Fi network are just looking to borrow an Internet connection, perhaps to check their email (see Figure 7.2).

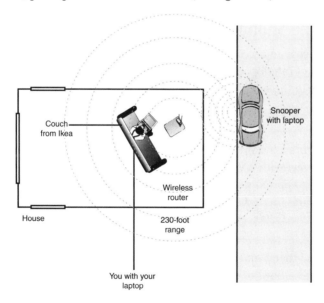

FIGURE 7.2

You can be sitting at home surfing HotorNot.com and a stranger in a car outside can be accessing your network with her wireless laptop.

That said, there are still real dangers to leaving your Wi-Fi network unprotected because a network snoop can also do the following:

- Use your Internet connection to anonymously download illicit material from adult content sites, including child pornography.
- Use the connection to hack someone else's computer and perhaps steal data.
- Use your network to send spam. This is handy for snoops because you'll get the blame for the spam, not the sender.
- Install viruses, spyware, or other malware onto your computer or network. This can also happen unintentionally. If the snoop's computer is infected, some malware looks for opportunities on nearby networked computers to infect them.
- Steal credit card data, other banking access information, or personal information from you to use for criminal purposes.
- Gain access to your company network via your home computer.

Who Are the Snoopers?

If it's easy to access a wireless network, who's snooping? Well, there are a few types of interlopers. Generically, I call them wireless network snoops, but they come in three basic varieties.

Wardrivers

Wi-Fi is such a huge phenomenon that all you have to do is drive down a city street with a Wi-Fi–enabled laptop to pick up dozens of open Wi-Fi networks. Approximately 61% of all wireless routers are unprotected by security measures, according to an study done at Indiana University (http://weis2006.econinfosec.org/docs/51.pdf).

These wireless networks make geeks curious. They can't resist probing them, poking them, and sampling them a bit. These geeks are kind of like kids around a bowl of cake icing. Most just sneakily sample a little bit of the wireless offering and move on. The problem is that more nefarious geeks take it too far. These are the people that (as kids) would steal the icing bowl, lick it clean, and wear it as a hat. They are the ones you should be concerned about.

The practice of probing wireless networks is called *wardriving*. All wardrivers need is a car, a Wi-Fi laptop, a snooping program downloaded from the Internet (see Figure 7.3), and optionally an upgrade antenna. Sometimes these are made out of cylindrical potato chip cans.

7

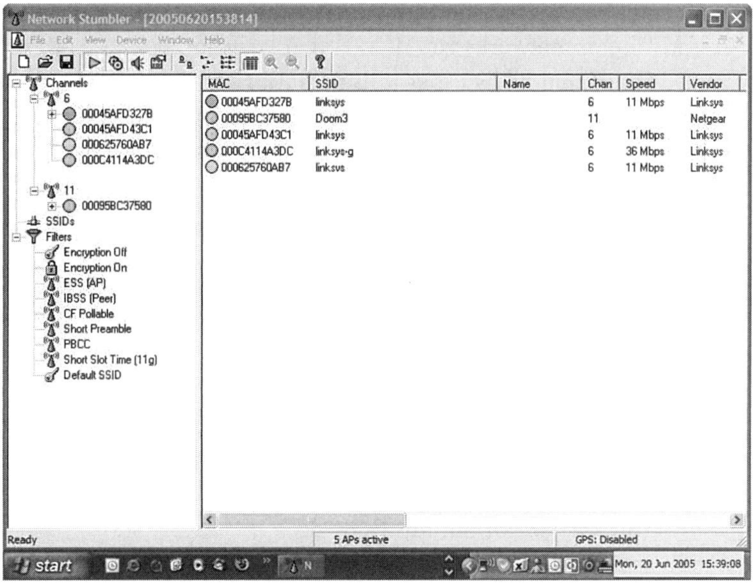

FIGURE 7.3

Network Stumbler is a free program that can be used to electronically sniff out Wi-Fi networks.

Wardrivers also sometimes use Global Positioning System (GPS) receivers to register the exact geographical location of an open Wi-Fi network. These coordinates are cataloged and sometimes published to the Web so others can locate the open networks when they need to connect to the Internet.

How Wardrivers Operate

Want to see what wardrivers see? If you live in a well-populated urban area, there are probably at least half a dozen Wi-Fi networks detectable right where you sit. If you live in an apartment building, there might be dozens. I once opened my laptop in an apartment in one of those clusters of high-rise apartments and detected 23 Wi-Fi networks.

note Wardriving is a modification of the term *wardialing*, a technique used by hackers to repeatedly dial phone numbers looking for computers they can potentially break into. The term was introduced in the 1983 movie *War Games*. In it, Matthew Broderick's teenage character programmed his computer to dial phone numbers sequentially, seeking other computers.

tip *Warchalking* is the practice of tagging pavement near an open Wi-Fi network to alert others that wireless access is available at that location.

7

Now, I am not advocating that you engage in wardriving practices. Trespassing on networks you do not own is illegal in Canada, the UK, and the United States and likely other jurisdictions. However, I want you to know how easy it is to do it so that you will take measures to safeguard your own wireless network. Here's the fail-safe: If you don't actually connect to the wireless network, you're not doing anything wrong.

That said, here's how to peek at the networks near you using your XP computer:

1. First you need a Wi-Fi–enabled computer. Almost all laptops are Wi-Fi–enabled today, so if yours is fairly new, you probably already have the capability.

2. You might need to turn Wi-Fi on with a switch. Some laptops have a slider that needs to be switched on to turn on the wireless capability.

3. Look for a little icon (a tiny picture) that looks like a screen with radio waves emitting from the right side of it. You'll find this in the System Tray on the bottom right side of your screen.

4. Double-click on the icon and the Wireless Network Connection Status box appears. Click on the View Wireless Networks button (see Figure 7.4).

> **tip** Windows 95, 98, and Me require an add-on Wi-Fi program to add Wi-Fi connectivity to the computer. It too will appear in the System Tray.

FIGURE 7.4

In the Wireless Network Connection Status box in XP, click View Wireless Networks to see what Wi-Fi networks are available to connect to.

5. The Wireless Network Connection box appears, listing all the wireless networks that can be detected by your wireless computer (see Figure 7.5). Next to the name of each network is the signal strength.

6. If the network has security measures, a little lock icon appears next to it and its security status appears below its name.

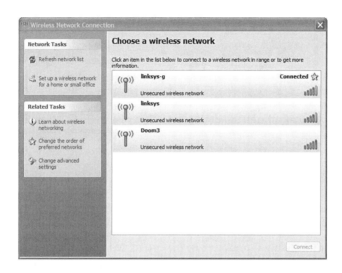

FIGURE 7.5

The Wireless Network Connection box in XP contains a list of the Wi-Fi networks detected by your computer that you might be able to access.

In Windows Vista, here's how to see the Wi-Fi networks near you:

1. As in the preceding list, you'll need a Wi-Fi–enabled computer.

2. You might need to turn Wi-Fi on with a switch. Some laptops have a slider that needs to be switched on to turn on the wireless capability.

3. In the System Tray on the bottom-right side of your screen, look for an icon that looks like one computer screen behind another.

4. Right-click on it and choose Connect to a Network.

5. The Connect to a Network dialog box will open. From the Show drop-down box choose Wireless. A list of wireless access points in range of your computer will appear. Next to the name of each network is the signal strength.

6. If the network has security measures, the words "Security-enabled network" appear next to it. If it is open, it'll say "Unsecured network" (see Figure 7.6).

7

FIGURE 7.6

In Windows Vista, the Connect to a Network dialog box lists nearby Wi-Fi networks.

Bandwidth Bandits

The most likely damage you can expect to your wireless home network is not really damage, but more of an inconvenience: People will steal your bandwidth.

Bandwidth is your Internet connection's capacity to carry data. In plumbing terms, bandwidth would be the diameter of the pipe that carries water through your house. This is not to be confused with bumwidth, which is the mathematical capacity for a plumber's pants to ride down based on the girth of his belly.

If you notice a slowdown on your Internet connection, it could be because a bandwidth bandit is accessing your network and sharing your bandwidth.

Because wireless connections are possible hundreds of feet from the Wi-Fi router, it's easy for someone outside your home to log on to your Wi-Fi connection, access the Internet, and get her email or surf the Web without your permission. By doing this, she is stealing your bandwidth.

> **caution** In many jurisdictions around the world—including the United States, the UK, and Canada—accessing a network without its owner's permission is illegal. In August of 2007, London police arrested a man who used his laptop to access someone else's wireless Internet connection. Police said it was not the first arrest of its kind, but no convictions have ever resulted from such arrests. More on this at http://tinyurl.com/3x6oba.

If you live above or very close to a coffee joint, bus station, or any place where people with laptops might gather, I can guarantee that the local bandwidth bandits love you and are happily using your open Wi-Fi Internet connection.

Long ago, before I wrote fun books like this, I commuted to work on a train into Toronto. (I also dressed before noon and shaved daily.) When the train stopped at a station on the way, I'd pick up a local Wi-Fi signal for a minute or so. This was long enough to download my email. Many of the people around me did the same with their laptops. If the person who owned the connection was trying to surf the Internet when the train pulled in, he'd see his Internet service slow drastically until all us bandwidth bandits disappeared out of range as the train pulled out of the station again.

> **caution** In the contract you have with your Internet provider, there is likely a clause that sets a ceiling on the amount of bandwidth you can use before being billed extra. This is probably more than you would ever use yourself. But if hordes of bandwidth bandits use your wireless connection, you could find yourself going over the limit and being surcharged or having your service cancelled.

DON'T GET WI-PHISHED

Here's a fun new tech term for you: Wi-Phishing (pronounced "why fishing"). This is a technique whereby bad guys set up wide-open Wi-Fi routers to lure bandwidth bandits to connect. When they do, all the data the victim sends and receives over the rogue wireless connection is captured.

If it's credit card, banking, or personal information, the Wi-Phisher steals it and rips the bandwidth bandit off.

When the term emerged in 2005, good geeks pondered if it could be a worrisome threat. It hasn't really manifested as that since. I like how the website of *The Register* (www.theregister.co.uk) put it: "The scenario is plausible. But… this is probably a well-understood risk given a catchy moniker, backed by an energetic marketing campaign."

A common-sense tip here anyway: If you borrow someone's connection, do not send sensitive data with it. Someone could be watching.

To learn more about phishing in general, see Chapter 5, "Identity Thieves and Phishers: Protect Your Good Name and Bank Account."

7

Wireless Hackers

Perhaps the most insidious wireless network snoops—besides pajama-clad book writers—are criminally minded people who are out to hack onto your network and steal your banking access information, identity, or other valuable data on your home network. Although these people are rare, they are also the most dangerous type of wireless network snoop.

If you work for a big corporation, these people might also be able to get onto your wireless network and access a computer that has security access to your company's network. If you have access to a virtual private network (VPN)—a secure connection that you use to access your company's servers from home—you are at risk.

A VPN uses the public Internet to tunnel like an electronic gopher across the public Internet into the company's network. The data that runs through this digital tunnel is protected from snoops because the data is scrambled. However, a wireless snoop can make his way onto your computer, access the open end of this electronic tunnel, and march down it into your company's network.

Dead-End Wi-Fi Access Points

Have you been in an airport with your laptop and noticed a Wi-Fi network called "Free Internet Access" or "Free Public Wi-Fi," yet when you try to connect, it doesn't work?

What's happening here is that your Wi-Fi–enabled computer has the capability to go into "ad-hoc" mode, meaning that it has a feature that can directly connect to another Wi-Fi–enabled computer nearby.

The bad news is if you connect to this ad-hoc Wi-Fi network, your system too will begin to send out beacons for that network. So if you connect to a "Free Public Wi-Fi" ad-hoc network in an airport lounge, and later switch on your notebook on the aircraft, your system will advertise as a "Free Public Wi-Fi" access point to others.

When other passengers connect to your ad-hoc network with their laptops, they will begin to advertise "Free Public Wi-Fi" too. These ad-hoc SSIDs spread as travelers open their laptops in new places.

To ensure that your computer doesn't suffer this problem, simply use a third party Wi-Fi utility to manage your wireless connections. A Wi-Fi client may have come with your wireless router. Or download the Boingo freebie from http://boingo.com/download.html.

7

If you want to let Windows manage Wi-Fi then here's a fix.

For XP system, follow these steps:

1. Right-click the wireless icon in the System Tray on the bottom-right side of your screen.

2. Choose View Available Wireless Networks.

3. On the left sidebar, click Change Advanced Settings.

4. Click the Wireless Networks tab.

5. Click the Advanced button.

6. Then select "Access point (infrastructure) networks only."

7. Click Close and then OK to close the dialog box.

Ad-hoc networks will no longer be detected when you browse for access points.

To do this on Vista, the fix is a little more geeky:

1. Click the Windows button and then in the Search bar type **cmd.**

2. When the **cmd** item appears in the Start menu, right-click and choose Run As Administrator.

3. Click Continue in the UAC dialog box.

4. When the Command box appears, type at the flashing cursor:

```
netsh wlan add filter permission=denyall networktype=adhoc
```

5. Press Enter and Windows should respond with: *The filter is added on the system successfully.*

6. To reverse this process, type:

```
netsh wlan del filter permission=denyall networktype=adhoc
```

7. Press Enter and if successful, Windows should respond: "The filter is removed from the system successfully."

Your Wi-Fi Network Is Full of Holes!

Is your Wi-Fi network secure? The answer to that question is the same as the answer to this question: Is your cold beer safe on a hot day with sweaty men around? Nope.

If you bought your Wi-Fi router and set it up without changing any of the factory settings on the device, you are a prime target for a wireless network snoop. That's because many Wi-Fi routers ship with security protections turned off.

7

Why? Because if they were all turned on, they would be difficult to configure. It would be like buying a minivan with the child locks on, the hazard lights flashing, and the parking brake engaged. It would take you a while to get the vehicle unencumbered so you could fishtail off the lot and speed home into the arms of your fashion-model spouse.

That said, some router makers are including activation of security settings in a wizard that is run during the initial setup.

In the next few pages, I am going to show you some critical steps you need to take to make your home network more secure. Many tips require that you electronically crawl inside the router using your web browser. This in itself can be a challenge, so before we get any further into these deliciously fun procedures, let me show you how to access a router's settings.

> **tip** A little lingo alert here. When I say *default*, I mean the way the settings were configured when they came from the factory. You might hear this word a lot in the context of computers and technology. It just means the way things are originally set by the manufacturer or programmer.

> **caution** Accessing your router's settings is a critical step in securing your home network, so make sure you don't skip this section. I'll refer to it often and without warning. Uh-oh. I sound like your ninth-grade history teacher, don't I?

How to Access Your Router Setup

To get into your router, you'll need to determine what its internal IP address is. Each device attached to your home network has one of these numerical addresses.

You can get this information by using a hidden Windows function. First open a DOS emulation box. Follow these steps for XP or older:

1. Click the Start menu, and select Run.
2. Type **cmd** (see Figure 7.7). If you have Windows 95, 98, or Me, type **command** instead.
3. Click OK and a DOS emulation window opens.

If you use Windows Vista, follow these steps:

1. Click the Windows button and type **cmd** in the Search box.
2. Click "cmd" when it appears in the Start menu.
3. A DOS emulation box will open.

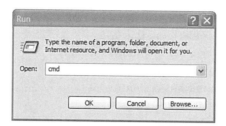

FIGURE 7.7

Type cmd into the Run box in XP.

Once the DOS emulation box is open, follow these steps:

4. In the DOS emulation box, you'll see a command prompt (flashing cursor) where you can type instructions (see Figure 7.8).

5. At the flashing cursor, type **ipconfig**.

6. Press Enter.

FIGURE 7.8

*Type **ipconfig** at the DOS prompt to display your network's settings.*

7. Information about your network appears below the line where you typed ipconfig. Look for the line that says Default Gateway. This displays the IP address of your network router. Make a note of it. It will probably look like one of the following IP addresses:

- 192.168.0.1
- 192.168.1.1
- 192.168.2.1

note In the early days of personal computers before Windows, computers used a command-line operating system called MS-DOS or Microsoft Disk Operating System. The DOS emulation window is "faked" DOS. It's not real; however, it still has functions that look and work like DOS.

This DOS window is useful because you can ask for very specific information about your network connection here.

7

■ 192.168.x.1—Where x is any number from 0 to 255. Normally this shows that the person who installed the router has customized it from its default settings set by the factory.

■ 10.0.0.1—Common in the Apple world.

To get inside the router and look at its settings, follow these steps:

1. Open your web browser and type the router's IP address you just retrieved (see Figure 7.9), like this, for example:

   http://192.168.0.1.

2. Press Enter or click Go on the web browser.

tip
If you use Windows 95, 98, or Me, type `winipcfg` instead of `ipconfig`. A Windows box appears with the network information you need.

tip
If you use an AirPort from Apple, you will have to use the AirPort Utility that came on the CD in the box or download it from the Internet. Mac users may be able to find it already on their systems. An older Windows version is available from http://tinyurl.com/lt6y8. Or use the following link if you have lost your AirPort CD: http://tinyurl.com/3c7uu8

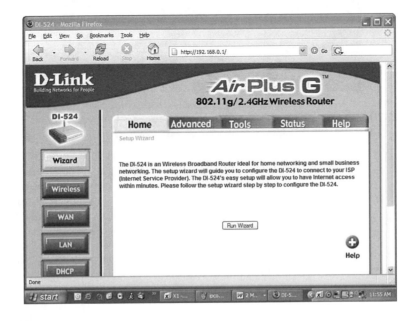

FIGURE 7.9

Type your router's IP address into your web browser to access the device's settings information.

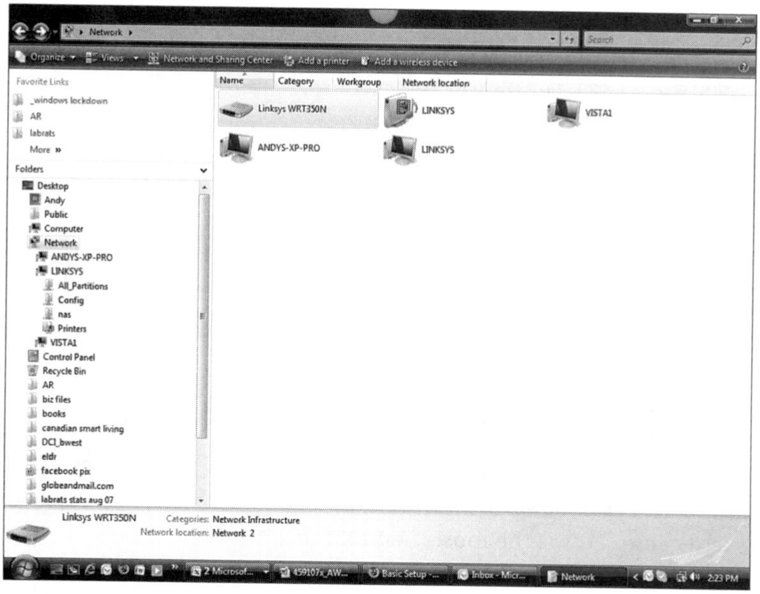

FIGURE 7.10
Access your router easily through the Windows Vista Network browser. A Linksys WRT350N is shown here.

3. Next, the router asks for a user ID and password. If the router has never been customized, you can obtain this information by checking the manual for the router or accessing the support area of the website of the router's manufacturer. If the site has a search engine, use these search terms: *router user ID password*.

4. Type the user ID and password into the router and you'll be given access to the router's settings page.

Table 7.1 shows some common user ID and passwords for various brands of popular routers. If it says (blank) next to your brand of router, don't type **(blank)**—that means enter nothing in that field when you access your router.

> **tip** An easy way to access your router, using Windows Vista, is as follows: Click the Windows button, then click Network (on the right side of the Start menu). Vista will display all devices connected to your network (see Figure 7.10). You should see your router in the list (though it doesn't recognize some routers). Access it by double-clicking the router's icon and entering the admin ID and password. The internal IP address is also available by right-clicking it and choosing Properties. You'll find it in the Troubleshooting section of the dialog box.

Table 7.1   Common Default Router User IDs and Passwords

Router Brand	User ID	Password
D-Link	admin	(blank)
Netgear	admin	password (Note: on older routers it's 1234)
Linksys	(blank)	admin
Belkin	admin	(blank)
SMC	admin	smcadmin

First Line of Defense: Secure Your Wi-Fi Network

Three key technologies are available to lock out wireless network snoops: WEP, WPA (and the newer WPA2), and MAC address filtering. This is your first line of defense. This is the most useful bit of information in the chapter. If you read nothing else, read this! Here's an explanation of each technology and how to activate them.

tip There's also a router password information here: http://www.routerpasswords.com and here: http://www.phenoelit-us.org/dpl/dpl.html

Turn On WEP

One of the most common security features on wireless routers (especially older routers) is a feature called Wired Equivalent Privacy (WEP). WEP is a way of scrambling information as it flies through the air between a computer and a router.

It's about as fun to set up as shaving with a piece of cheddar, but with a little patience you can get it going.

First you'll need to set up a *key*. That's a special code that's input to both the router and the computer that connects wirelessly to the router. The key is used to scramble all the data moving between the computer and the router. At either end the key is also used to descramble the information. You can think of it just like a key that locks and unlocks a door.

caution Most manufacturers ship consumer Wi-Fi routers with all their security settings turned off; however, they prompt you to turn them on in the setup wizards. This low-security environment minimizes the complexity of setting them up and reduces the likelihood of a support call (which costs them money).

caution The shaving with cheese analogy is an attempt at humor. Do not attempt, especially if lactose intolerant.

Wireless network snoops are shut out if WEP is engaged because they don't have the key to communicate with the router. Well, that's the theory. The problem with WEP is that it's not very tough as security measures go. WEP is like a paper door. It looks like a big thick door that blocks bad

> **tip** You might be thinking: If WEP is so weak, why bother? Good point. If you have a router security feature called WPA (or the newer WPA2), you'll want to use that instead.

people from entering. But you can put your fist through it and walk through the hole.

WEP is a good bandwidth-bandit repellent, but a wireless hacker can break the code using a piece of software called a sniffer if he has a little patience. All he has to do is use the sniffer to watch the data flow back and forth between a router and a computer and look for patterns, and eventually this can be used to figure out the key.

Here's how to turn it on. First, you blow in its ear. Wait, that's *Meeting, Mating, and Cheating: Sex, Love, and the New World of Online Dating*. Let me rephrase. Here's how to activate WEP.

I am going to use a D-Link router in all the examples in this chapter (see Figure 7.11).

FIGURE 7.11

The D-Link DI-524 router is an easy-to-use wireless home network router with a well-designed interface that can be used to configure the device with a web browser.

If you use another brand, your steps are different, but the settings are similar:

1. Access your router's settings by typing in its IP address in your web browser (as explained earlier in this chapter).

2. Locate the wireless settings. In a D-Link router, click the Wireless button to the left of the Home tab.

3. On the Security setting, click on the WEP radio button.

4. In Authentication, choose Open System.

5. In WEP Encryption, choose 64 bit, 128 bit, or 256 bit (if available). A bigger number of bits means more characters in your key (see Figure 7.12). The bigger the bit count, the longer it takes to crack.

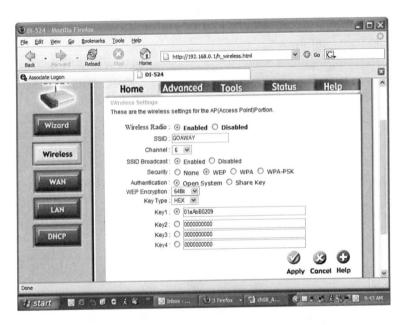

FIGURE 7.12

The WEP settings on a D-Link router can be found in the Wireless control panel.

6. Under Key Type, choose either HEX or ASCII. HEX means your key has to be written in hexadecimal format, which means it contains characters that include letters A through F and numbers 0 to 9. ASCII means plain text. The ASCII character set consists of the letters A through Z, numbers 0 to 9, and common punctuation marks, including a whitespace character. There's no way to make HEX and ASCII pretty. Read it again and when you understand it, reward yourself with a tasty cold beverage.

7. Now select Key1 and type in a sequence of letters called a key. Note there are four slots for keys, but only one is active. If you chose 64-bit HEX, this has to be a hexadecimal number, which consists of characters like this: A4B1C0DDE2. If you chose 128 bit, this has to be a 26-character hexadecimal number.

8. If you chose 64-bit ASCII, this is five ASCII characters, such as snack. If you chose 128-bit ASCII, it is 13 ASCII characters such as mmmmmmmsnacks. If you choose a 256-bit key, you have to a write a short sentence about snacks (29 characters).

9. When you click Apply, your router restarts and you are disconnected from it.

10. To reconnect, double-click on the wireless icon on the bottom right of your Windows XP screen and choose View Wireless Networks.

11. In Vista, right-click the Network icon in the System Tray (bottom right) and chose Connect to a Network.

12. Now your router's name has a lock under it or says "Security-enabled network" next to its name.

13. Double-click on the router name to connect and input the key you set in your router twice when prompted (see Figure 7.13).

14. When you are successfully connected to the WEP-enabled router, the window shows your new secure status in XP (see Figure 7.14). Vista just shows your status as Connected.

> **tip**
> My editor Rick reminded me of a trick he uses to make this process simpler, so I thought I'd pass it on. He uses copy and paste to copy the keys into a text document. Then he copies that text document to a USB thumb drive. When he wants to add a computer to his network, he just plugs the USB drive into that computer, opens the text file, then copies the key and pastes it when prompted. It saves him from having to remember or ever type the access key. Of course, if you use this method, you'll want to keep your USB thumb drive in a safe place!

> **note**
> On some routers, instead of a 64-bit or 128-bit key, you'll see a 40-bit or 104-bit key. Believe it or not, 40 bit and 64 bit are the same thing. And 104 bit is also the same as 128 bit. This is because the technology companies don't speak the same language. A 64-bit key is a 40-bit key with a (big breath here) 24-bit initialization vector. The initialization vector is the part of the key that helps scramble the information differently each time a chunk of data is sent. A 128-bit key is a 104-bit key with a 24-bit initialization vector. It's okay to go take a nap now.

7

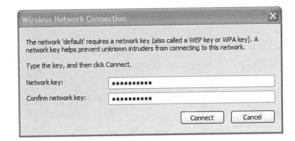

FIGURE 7.13

Double-click on your WEP-enabled wireless network and type in your WEP key twice when prompted.

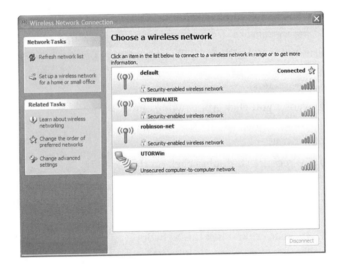

FIGURE 7.14

When you have successfully set a WEP key, Windows XP shows that you are connected to your secure router.

Turn On WPA

Wi-Fi Protected Access (WPA), or rather the second generation WPA2, is probably your best choice for wireless security. This security measure is a lot stronger than namby-pamby WEP. In fact WPA came along because businesses needed a tougher measure than WEP to keep network snoops out. Lingo alert: WPA2 is also known as 802.11i.

Then the experts discovered WPA was hackable too. So WPA2 was developed.

In turn they discovered WPA2 is hackable too, although not easily and not by just anyone.

While this may seem like a losing battle, it turns out that to hack WPA2, you need a big honking computer and a lot of determination. So the bottom line is: if you have missile launch codes on your home network in your house, worry about this. If not, your prom photos are safe.

Table 7.2   Router Security Measures

Router Security Feature	Defends Against...	Vulnerable to...	Tips
WEP	Snooping neighbors	Any geek who has the time to find a publicly available hacking tool and read up on how. The FBI cracked a WEP connection in 3 minutes at a conference in 2005	Skip it if you have access to WPA or WPA2
WPA	Casual hackers	Determined hackers with time on their hands	Unless you are defending business secrets, WPA is fine to use on your home network
WPA2 (802.11i)	Almost everyone	The Government and the military, and those who have access to super-computers	Effective use of a complex WPA2 passphrase with no recognizable words and a mix of numbers, upper- and lowercase characters and punctuation makes it almost impenetrable

Similarly to WEP, WPA uses a code at each end of the wireless connection; however, it's in the form of a phrase (see Figure 7.15). When you set up WPA, it asks you for a *passphrase*, an easy-to-understand sentence or series of words such as "Andy's cats are called Biff and Boo," which is not only a good passphrase because it's hard to guess, but it's also true.

Here's how to turn on WPA. First, you hold its hand and tell it that it's beautiful. (Oops, recycled joke.)

7

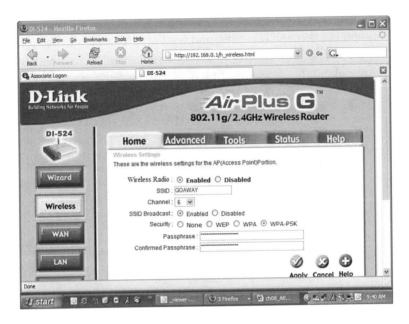

FIGURE 7.15

To enable WPA on your router, choose WPA-PSK and enter a passphrase you can remember. Try to make it funny because there's not enough humor in home computer security.

Here are the step-by step instructions:

1. Access your router's settings by typing its IP address in your web browser. (I told you I'd refer to this a lot.)

2. Once again I'm using a D-Link router for this example. If your router is a different brand, follow along because the steps are similar. From the Home tab, click the Wireless button on the left.

3. Next to Security choose the WPA-PSK radio button.

4. Two passphrase boxes appear. Type in a passphrase you can remember, such as "Sausages are delicious" or "pet goats mow lawns." Have fun here; just be sure to remember what you typed in.

5. Click Apply. The router restarts.

6. After your router is restarted, you'll need to reconnect. Double-click on the wireless icon on the bottom right of your Windows XP screen

note On a Linksys router you may see the version of WPA and WPA2 used on home networks referred to as PSK Personal and PSK2 Personal.

and choose View Wireless Networks. Now you'll see your router's name with a lock under it. Click the name to connect and enter the WPA passphrase you created twice as necessary.

7. In Vista, reconnect by clicking on the Network icon on the System Tray and choosing Connect to a Network. Locate the access point you just secured, which will now show "Security enabled network" next to its name (see Figure 7.16). Click on it and input the WPA passphrase you set in your router. You should then be able to connect.

tip If it won't connect in Vista and shows as "The settings saved on this computer for the network do not match the requirements of the network," then right-click on it, choose Properties, and then enter the type. Choose either WPA2-Personal or WPA-Personal in Security Type, depending on which you set up. In Encryption Type, choose the one that matches your router's setup. You probably had the opportunity to select either TKIP or AES in the router settings. (The router geeks don't make this easy, have you noticed?)

FIGURE 7.16

The Windows Vista connection screen shows the Cyberwalker2 access point is protected by security, but it doesn't tell you which type. This keeps the bad guys guessing.

note The same passphrase is used for all wireless computers (and other wireless devices) that connect to your Wi-Fi router, so remember you might have to configure the other computers in your home if they use wireless.

7

MAC Address Filtering: Keep Out the Scottish

The third option to secure your Wi-Fi network is to use *MAC address filtering*. When it is engaged, it means that no Scottish people can access your wireless network. Of course, they are not the only ones shut out. Everyone else is, too, whether they wear kilts or not.

Here's how it works. Every networked device is assigned a MAC address by its manufacturer when it is made (see Figure 7.17). The MAC address is a unique identifier that consists of a series of codes separated by dashes. It looks something like `00-90-96-96-5C-3E`.

No two MAC addresses are ever the same, which is useful because the MAC address can be used like an identity card to control access to your network.

This is called MAC address filtering. You can set your router to allow only certain MAC addresses to connect to it wirelessly. Two major steps are involved in this process. First you have to gather up all the MAC addresses on the computers you want to allow to connect. Then you'll have to enter these into your router.

How to Locate Your MAC Address

First off, your computer does not have a MAC address. It's your network card that does.

Some computers have two network cards: one that's for wired connections and one that uses Wi-Fi. So a computer will have a different MAC address depending on which network card it uses to connect to the network.

The MAC address can be found written directly on the network card, but since that is sometimes concealed inside a computer, it's impractical to use this method to find your MAC address.

> **tip** If a friend comes over with his laptop and wants to connect to your WPA-protected wireless network, you can simply give him the passphrase. All he needs to do is try to connect to the router and enter it when prompted by his computer.

> **tip** A MAC address has nothing to do with Macintosh computer from Apple. It's a unique registration code that every network-enabled device is given when it is manufactured. For the intrepid among you, MAC stands for Media Access Control.

> **caution** MAC addresses can be spoofed, meaning a computer can fake its MAC address when representing it to the network. The problem is that the spoofer has to know an allowable MAC address first.

> **tip** If you ever use an external adapter to connect your TV or printer to your network, an easy way to find its MAC address is by flipping the device upside down. It's usually written on the bottom.

FIGURE 7.17

Devices such as routers and network adapters that connect computers to a network each have their own unique MAC address. The MAC address for a piece of gear is usually found on a sticker on the bottom of the device, like it is on this Belkin router.

The best way to determine a computer's MAC address is to access it on the computer. Here's how to do it on various operating systems.

Windows Vista

To locate your MAC address on a Vista computer, follow these steps:

1. Click the Windows button, and type **cmd** in the Search box.

2. When it appears, right-click on it and choose Run As Administrator and then click Continue on the UAC warning. A black box will appear.

3. At the C:\> prompt, type `ipconfig /all`. You'll see the network information listed for each network adapter on the computer and this includes the MAC address, which is identified as Physical Address in the listing. If the computer can connect via both a wireless and a wired connection, it has two network adapters and each has its own MAC address.

Windows XP

To locate your MAC address on an XP computer, follow these steps:

1. Click the Start button, and then choose Run.

2. Type **cmd** and click OK. A black box appears.

7

3. At the C:\> prompt, type **ipconfig /all** (see Figure 7.18). You'll see the network information listed for each network adapter on the computer and this includes the MAC address, which is identified as Physical Address in the listing. If the computer can connect via both a wireless and a wired connection, it has two network adapters and each has its own MAC address.

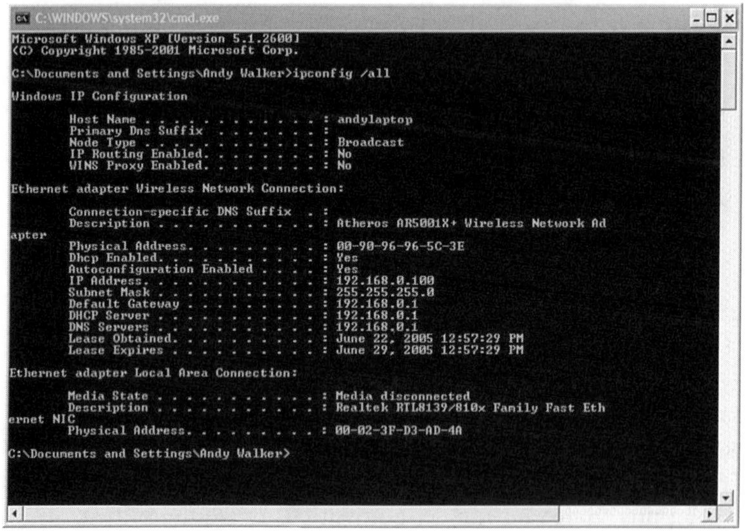

FIGURE 7.18

The MAC address for your computer's network adapters can be found using the ipconfig */all command in a DOS box in Windows XP and Windows Vista.*

Windows 95, 98, and Me

To locate your MAC address on a Windows 95, 98, or Me computer, follow these steps:

1. Click the Start menu and choose Run.

2. Type **winipcfg**. A grey box appears with all network settings, including the MAC address.

Mac OS X

To locate your MAC address on a Macintosh, follow these steps:

1. Open the Applications folder on your hard drive.

2. In the Applications folder, double-click on the Network Utility.

3. Under Info, choose the network card from the drop-down menu that you want to allow access to your network. Below this you'll see an entry for Hardware Address. This is the network card's MAC address (see Figure 7.19).

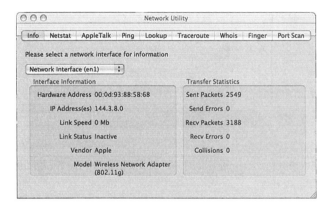

FIGURE 7.19
The MAC address on your Mac can be found using the Network Utility program.

How to Filter by MAC Address

After you have collected the MAC addresses you want to allow on your network (wired computers should be included in your list), follow these steps to engage filtering:

1. Open your router's settings page using your web browser and look for MAC address filtering, which will likely be in the Advanced area of the menus.

2. In a D-Link router, click the Advanced tab and then the Filters button on the left.

3. Under the Filter area, click on the MAC Filters radio button to select it.

4. MAC Filters settings appear. Choose Only Allow Computers with MAC Addresses Listed Below to Access the Network (see Figure 7.20).

7

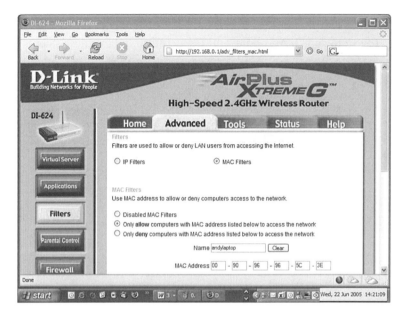

FIGURE 7.20

MAC address filtering is a common setting on most routers. It's found under the Advanced tab on this D-Link router.

Detecting a Visit from a Wireless Snoop

Most routers have a function that logs information about each computer that has connected to it.

What you are looking for is the DHCP log. DHCP is short for Dynamic Host Configuration Protocol. It sounds complicated, but it's not really. You can think of DHCP like a restaurant hostess. She guides you to a table where you will eat a meal. That table has a number and the wait-staff use that number to identify your table and to keep track of what dishes ordered from the kitchen belong to what tables. It's a temporary assignment. When you leave, someone else gets that table.

DHCP does something similar. When a computer joins a network, it needs an Internet address called an Internet Protocol (IP) address so that information it asks for (such as email or a web page) gets sent to the right place. This IP address is called an internal IP address because the address is only used inside the home network.

To the Internet, a home router looks like one computer because it has one public IP; however, it can be the keeper of several computers and it manages all their needs using these internal IP addresses assigned by DHCP.

Inside your router is a log of DHCP clients. This is a list of people who have visited the network and used an internal IP address. To see who's been visiting, all you need to do is locate the log and read through it.

On a D-Link router's Home screen, click the Status tab, and then click Log on the left menu. The log shows a computer's visit to the network and lists its name, the time of the first access, and the IP address assigned by your router (see Figure 7.21).

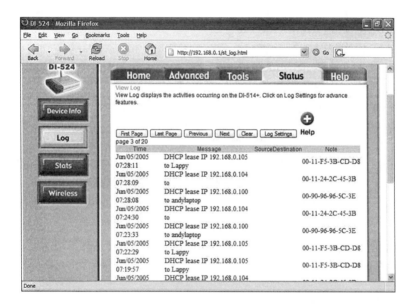

FIGURE 7.21

This is a log of visitors to a D-Link wireless router. It's my router, so you can see visits by my computer, noted as andylaptop. Notice the visitor called Lappy, who is an uninvited guest—probably one of the guys who lives downstairs from me.

You'll see that it also lists the visiting computer's MAC address. No two MAC addresses are the same, so this is a unique way to know if a computer has been on your network. Of course, to verify this you'd need to get your hands on the computer's network card to compare its MAC address to the one in your router's log.

caution A savvy visitor to a wireless network can easily hide his tracks by logging on to your router (if the manufacturer's initial settings have not been changed) and clearing the log.

I'm Under Attack! What to Do If You Discover a Wireless Network Snoop?

caution If nobody uses the wireless function on the router in your home, you should turn this feature off.

So you've discovered that someone is accessing your wireless network. Don't panic! Chances are the snoop is just a harmless bandwidth bandit. However, you need to decide what to do about this and other snoops.

Turn Off Wireless Access

The simplest way to stop someone from accessing your wireless router immediately is to turn wireless off.

That might be impractical in the long term; however, if you find someone on your wireless network and you want to instantly protect yourself, this is the quickest way to stop them.

In your router configuration there should be a setting to turn wireless access off. I'm going to show you how to do this on a D-Link router; however, the settings on your router are similar:

1. Start on the Home screen (see Figure 7.22) and click the Wireless button on the left side. You'll see the router's wireless settings.

2. Here you'll see a setting that says Wireless Radio and an option to turn it on or off.

Of course, if someone in your home has a wireless laptop, this can cause a problem because he won't be able to wirelessly access the Internet any more.

Activate Security Measures

With your wireless settings turned off, you have denied access to the snoop. The next step is to engage one of the security measures I talked about earlier in the chapter. Choose WEP, WPA, WPA2, or employ MAC address filtering. Then turn wireless back on.

Assess the Damage

Look at your router log to see if the snoop has been on your network before. This is not an absolutely reliable way of determining if a particular snoop is a threat, but it might give you some evidence to see if he is a regular visitor to your network.

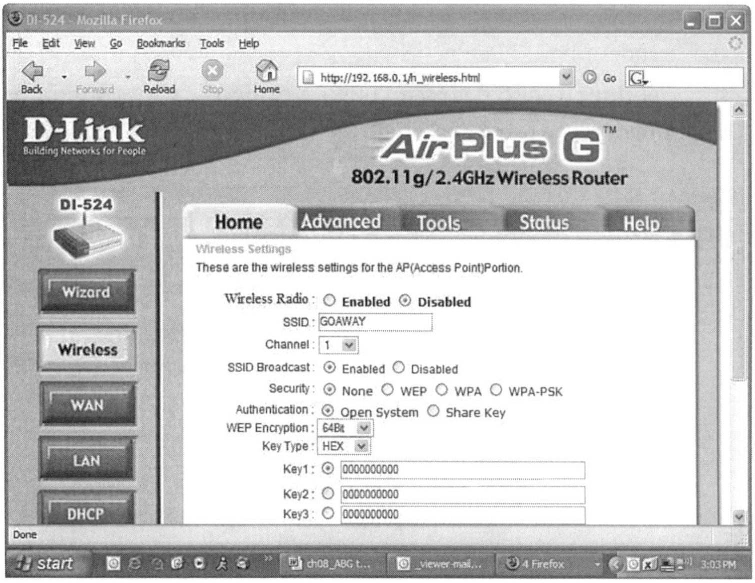

FIGURE 7.22

To turn off wireless access to your router, look for an on/off switch in your router's control panel.

There is no way to tell for sure if the snoop is a bandwidth bandit, wardriver, or wireless hacker. If in doubt, you might want to change any passwords or sensitive accounts you keep stored on your computer. The only way to be sure that nothing has been left behind by the hacker is to scrub your hard drive and start fresh.

→ See **p. 271** to learn how to do wipe your hard drive and reinstall Windows.

However, not every snoop is out to steal your identity or wrong you in some malicious way. How you proceed is up to you.

If you feel that your personal data has been compromised, go change your passwords, alert your bank, and keep an eye on your bank accounts. You might also

tip

If you think home networks are about as difficult to manage as your ex-spouse, I recommend Network Magic, a utility designed to make home network management easier to deal with. This includes tracking and dealing with network intruders (see Figure 7.23). Get Network Magic from www.networkmagic.com. There's a free version as well as a premium version with more features, which costs $29.99 to $49.99 depending on how many computers are on your network. To better manage your ex-spouse, get Ex-Magic. You wish! But you can try this web site: http://www.successfulstepfamilies.com/view/116.

7

want to change account numbers, account passwords, and identity documents the snooper might have accessed.

It's important to also do a scan of your computer with your antivirus program and antispyware programs to ensure that your system is clean of any threats.

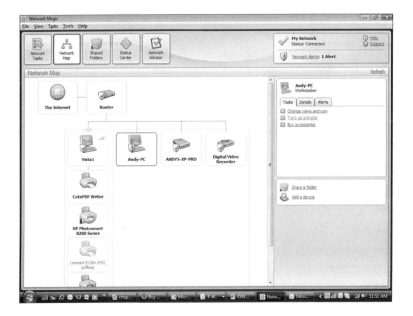

FIGURE 7.23
Network Magic makes managing your home network a snap, plus it has a really fun intruder detection tool.

Wireless Security Workup: Quick Tactics and Some That Take a Little More Time

Even though it takes more than 10 minutes, you should definitely turn on WEP, WPA, WPA2, or enable MAC address filtering as a first line of defense, as outlined on **p. 200**.

There are also some quickie steps that minimize the threat posed by a wireless network snoop. The following procedures shouldn't take you more than 10 minutes each to implement.

10-Minute Tactic: Change the Router's User ID and Password

When you first set up your wireless router, it has a default password to access its settings. This is set up by the manufacturer. I talk about this earlier in the chapter. See **p. 196** for a list.

It's important that you change this because it's easy for a snoop to determine which brand of router you have and then log in to its settings. The default user IDs and passwords for each manufacturer are commonly known.

tip If you cannot access your router's settings page because you have forgotten either your WEP or WPA settings or the router's user ID and password, you can reset it. To do this, locate the Reset pinhole feature on the back or underside of the router. Push a pin or paper clip into it and hold it in for 10 seconds. This resets the router to the factory settings, wiping out any customizations you have made, and turns off any security features.

Savvy snoops can log in to the router's settings to cover their tracks. They'll locate the router's log and clear it. Malicious snoops might commandeer it by changing the password, locking you out.

To change the router's log-in info, follow these steps:

1. Access your router's settings page with your web browser.

2. Seek out the password update screen. You might find it in the Options or Administration area of your router's settings. In D-Link routers it can be found by clicking the Tools tab and then the Admin button to the left of that screen (see Figure 7.24).

3. Enter a new password that will be hard for anyone to guess. A good password should be longer than six characters and include a combination of lower- and uppercase letters and a couple of numbers thrown in for good measure.

10-Minute Tactic: Change Your Default SSID

When you connect to your wireless network with a wireless computer, you look for a router identifier that it broadcasts called an SSID. That's short for Service Set Identifier. That's the name of the Wi-Fi network. Table 7.2 lists the factory-set SSIDs in various brands of routers. It's a sampling and not exhaustive because every now and then companies decide to change it on some models. I guess that's how some engineering geeks get their jollies.

7

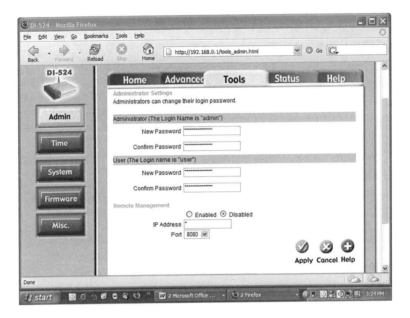

FIGURE 7.24

The router password can be updated in a D-Link router in the Admin area under the Tools tab.

Table 7.3   Factory Set SSIDs

Router brand	Default SSID
Linksys	linksys
D-Link	default
Netgear	NETGEAR
3Com	comcomcom
Belkin	WLAN or Belkin54g
SMC	WLAN or wireless

It's a good idea to change the default SSID because it demonstrates to anyone who's looking that the owner of the network has taken measures to customize the router settings beyond the factory settings. The subtext is "I know what I am doing on this router, don't mess with me."

Leaving the SSID as the factory default (see Figure 7.25) is like putting a dog cookie in your lap. You'll attract sudden and voracious interest in a place where you don't really want it.

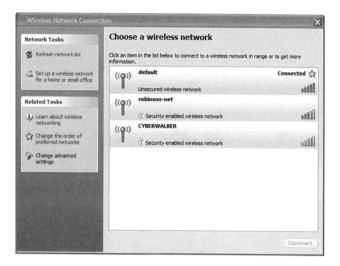

FIGURE 7.25

The D-Link router detected here is still named with the factory set SSID: default.

The SSID can be reset as follows:

1. Log into your router's settings using your web browser or, on Vista, browse to it via the Network off the Start menu.

2. Locate the wireless settings. In a D-link router, click the Home tab and then click Wireless on the right. The SSID can be changed on this page (see Figure 7.26).

3. Type in a new and unique SSID, but don't reveal any personal information such as your address or name. You can mix in numbers and letters. Try to use as many of the 32 allowable characters as possible. Think like a hacker. LUV AND KISSES is probably going to attract a lot less interest than MY FAT WALLET.

10-Minute Tactic: Turn On the Windows Firewall

One of the best ways to defend your computer against unwanted wireless intruders inside your network is to turn on the built-in Windows firewall. This is an electronic fence that sits between your computer and your network and ultimately the outside world. A firewall watches what computers attempt to connect to the computer it

> **tip** My brother Simon uses the scary sounding VIRUSVAULT as his customized SSID. Of course, this could work either way: Although it might scare bandwidth bandits off, it could also make wireless hackers curious.

defends and stops rogue computers that have no business making contact. Think of it like a really big kid that protects you from having your ice cream stolen.

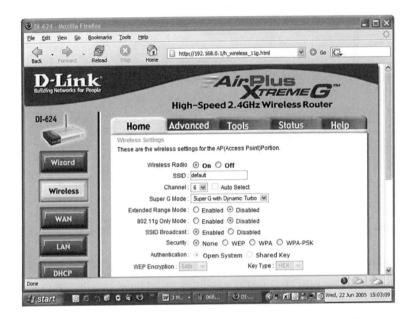

FIGURE 7.26

It's a good idea to change the SSID (the router's name) when you first set it up. Here you can spot the D-Link router because its SSID is still set with the factory setting: default.

By now your Windows XP computer should have Service Pack 2 (SP2) installed. If it does, Windows firewall is turned on automatically. The firewall is also turned on by default in Windows Vista. Here's how to check.

In Windows XP:

1. Click the Start button, choose Control Panel, and then choose Security Center.

2. Click the Windows Firewall link at the bottom of the window.

3. Click the On (recommended) button and click OK (see Figure 7.27).

In Windows Vista:

1. Click the Windows button, type **Firewall** in the search box, and click Windows Firewall when it appears in the menu.

2. In the Windows Firewall dialog it will say either "Windows Firewall is on" or "Windows Firewall is off."

3. To turn it on, click on the Change Settings link. Click Continue on the UAC warning, choose "On (recommended)," and click OK to turn the firewall on.

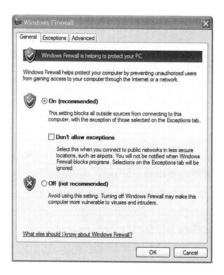

FIGURE 7.27

Turn on your Windows Firewall for an added level of protection inside your network.

If you don't have Service Pack 2 installed on Windows XP, you can turn on the firewall by doing the following:

1. Click Start, click Run, type `control.exe netconnections`, and then click OK. (You can get at the Network Connections through the Network and Internet Connections link in Control Panel, too.)

2. Right-click the connection on which you would like to enable the Windows Firewall (called Internet Connection Firewall in XP), and then click Properties.

3. On the Advanced tab, click the box to select the option to Protect My Computer or Network.

> **tip** You can tell if you have Windows XP's Service Pack 2 installed by clicking Start, Control Panel, Performance and Maintenance, and then System. (If XP's Control Panel is set to Classic View, you'll see System in the list on the Control Panel.) If SP2 is installed, it is listed in the System window on the General tab under the heading System.

If you have already installed Service Pack 2 (SP2) for Windows XP, the firewall has been turned on automatically.

10-Minute Tactic: Turn Off UPnP

A common feature on most home network routers is something called *UPnP*, or *Universal Plug and Play*. It's a powerful yet insecure technology that allows a computer to open inbound ports through the home network router to which it is attached.

> **caution** If you already use a software firewall on your computer, there's no need to turn on Windows Firewall as it's redundant and might slow things down. That would be like putting two security checkpoints on the UFO hanger at Area 51.

This means that your computer can open an electronic door in the router's firewall so that computers on the outside can get in.

The feature was designed to make it easy to use peer-to-peer file sharing, instant messaging, and other interactive computer-to-computer connections. The problem is that while this feature is supposed to make your life easier—saving you the headache of messing with router ports—it also opens up a huge security hole.

Why? Because any program on your computer—including malware—can use UPnP to open an inbound hole in your firewall without your knowledge. A virus, for example, could use the technique to download and install more malware, or allow remote access to your computer from the Internet.

So what to do? Unless you really need to enable peer-to-peer programs or instant messenger programs, simply disable the router's UPnP option.

Here's how to turn off UPnP on a D-Link router:

1. Access your router's control panel using the technique explained earlier in this chapter.
2. Click the Tools tab, and then click the Misc button on the left.
3. Look for the UPNP Settings option and choose Disable.
4. At the bottom, click Apply. The router will restart.

10-Minute Tactic: Turn Off Your Router When Not in Use

If you don't use the wireless feature on your router, turn it off. There is usually a switch in your router's settings that enables you to do this. On D-Link routers, for example, it can be found in the router settings by clicking the Home tab and then clicking the Wireless button on the left (see Figure 7.28).

If you want to be extra cautious—like a stiletto-wearing supermodel in a busy dog park—you should power down your router when you're away or asleep. If you choose this conservative approach, remember that any network-reliant computer or device will not be able to access the Internet. For example, your antivirus signatures will not be able to update automatically.

Wireless radio is turned off.

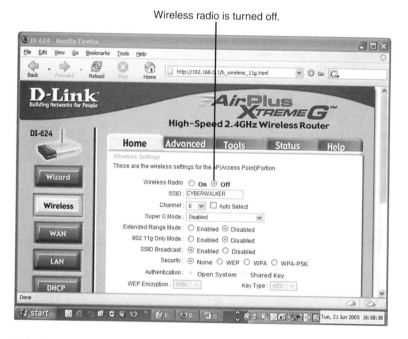

FIGURE 7.28

Turn wireless access on your router off if all the computers on your network are connected using wires to the router. The setting shown is on a D-Link router.

10-Minute Tactics: Vista Network and Sharing Settings

If you use Windows Vista, it's worth spending a few minutes to tweak the Network and Sharing Center (see Figure 7.29) to suit your situation.

This is most applicable for people who have computers that are connected to a home network router, which can share the Internet connection with other systems in your home.

Start by opening the Network and Sharing Center on Windows Vista. Click the Windows button. Then type **Sharing** in

caution When you edit the networking and sharing settings on a Vista computer, they impact only the Vista machine they are changed on, not the whole network. So be sure to review the settings on each Vista computer on your home network.

7

the search bar. When Network and Sharing Center appears on the Start menu, click it to open it.

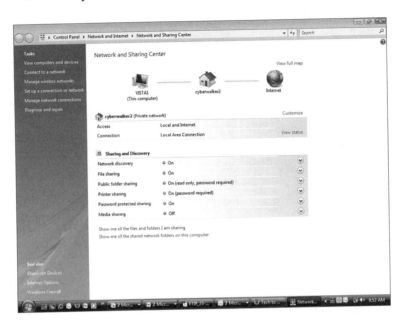

FIGURE 7.29
Spending a few minutes to review and tweak the Network and Sharing Center on Vista to your tastes and needs.

Here are some options you should review and tweak.

Private vs. Public

If your Vista computer is connected to a home network router and you want to be able to share files, printers, or media content with other computers on the network, then use the Private setting. Here's how: Click the word Customize on the right side of the Network and Sharing Center window, below the image of the globe. Select Private, if it is not selected, and click Next. On the UAC warning click Continue.

Network Discovery

On the main Network and Sharing Center screen, set Network Discovery to on if you want to engage in any file-sharing activities between computers on your home network.

> **tip** Laptop tip: The Public setting turns off sharing settings off. Use it when you are on a public wireless network with a laptop.

Set it to off if you never share files on your home network. It allows your computer to be easily detected by other computers on the network.

> **tip** Laptop tip: Set Network Discovery to off on your laptop when you connect to a public wireless access point, like at a coffee shop or airport.

File Sharing

This setting allows your files and folders to be accessed by other computers on the network (including intruders). If it's turned off, all access attempts will be denied by other computers attempting to access shared files. If you don't engage in file sharing on your home network, turn it off.

> **tip** Laptop tip: Turn file sharing off when you connect to a public wireless access point, like at a coffee shop or airport.

Public Folder Sharing

Public folders is a new feature in Vista that allows you to put files into a folder at c:\Users\Public for easy sharing.

Turn Public Folder Sharing off if you never share files. Also turn it off if you are connected to a public wireless network.

> **tip** Laptop tip: Turn Public Folder Sharing off when you connect to a public wireless access point unless the files in your public folder are free for the taking.

Printer Sharing

Printer Sharing allows you to share printers attached to your computer with others on your home network.

> **tip** Laptop tip: Turn printer sharing off when you are connected to a public wireless network.

Password-Protected Sharing

Password Protected Sharing is generally a very good idea because it forces anyone who wants to access files on your system to enter a User ID and password to access files on your system.

It should be set to on for the best security if you use file-sharing features in Windows Vista.

Media Sharing

The Media Sharing setting makes media libraries available through Windows Media Player to other computers on your

> **tip** Laptop tip: Turn Media Sharing off when you are mobile and connected to a network away from home.

7

network. Best to turn it off unless you want to share your music and movies with others on your secure home network.

Table 7.4   Recommended Vista Network and Sharing Center Settings

Network and Sharing Center settings	Vista Computer Configuration			
	Connected to a home router with WEP or WPA turned on	Connected to a home router with WEP or WPA turned off	Connected to a wireless public router	No router, but connected directly to high speed modem
Public vs. Private	Private	Public	Public	Doesn't matter, although Public is the most secure
Network Discovery	On	Off	Off	Off
File Sharing	On	Off	Off	Off
Public Folder Sharing	On	Off, but turn on as needed	Off	Off
Printer Sharing	On	On, but a network intruder could potentially print to it	Off	Off
Password-Protected Sharing	Off, for convenience, but on for better local security	On	On	On
Media Sharing	On, if you want to share your media with other computers on your network	On, if you use it, but intruders could access your media. Off if you don't	Off	Off

Time-Intensive Tactic: Be Careful with File Sharing

When you're on a network you have the ability to share folders and files with other computers on the network.

This allows you to play your ABBA music collection stored on the computer upstairs on your laptop in the kitchen.

Here's how you share a folder:

Windows XP: Right-click on the folder, choose Properties, and click the Sharing tab. You'll need to name the shared folder something unique. This is called a *share name* (see Figure 7.30).

Windows Vista: Right-click on the folder, choose Properties, and click the Sharing tab. Click the Share button. In the empty drop-down menu, click the down arrow on the right and choose an account to share the file with or choose Everyone and click Add. Then click the Share button at the bottom of the dialog box. Next click Continue button on the UAC warning that appears. This may take a few minutes to process so be patient.

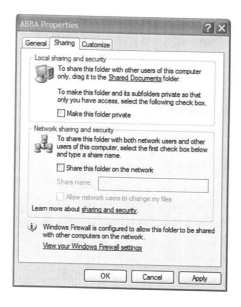

FIGURE 7.30

To share a folder on Windows XP, right-click on the folder, choose Properties, and then the Sharing tab, and enter a share name.

Anyone connected to the network can access your shared folders across the network by browsing the Network Neighborhood ("Network" on the Start menu in Vista) and locating your computer.

You can also do it as follows:

In XP, click Start, Run, and type in your computer's private IP address and the share name like this \\192.168.0.100\ABBA.

Then click OK.

In Vista, click the Windows button and in the search bar type **Run.** Then click Run in the Start menu when it appears to open it. In the Run dialog type the share name as in the preceding example and click OK.

Although this is a great way to share data, it can also pose a big privacy and security problem. If a wireless network snooper connects to your network, he has access to your shared folders. And if the folder contains a file that lists your banking passwords, you're probably not going to Aruba on holiday this year.

At the risk of sounding like a man whose dentures have fallen out of reach, the best way to stop a bad person from accessing your shared files is to stop them from accessing the network.

Turn on WEP, WPA, or use MAC address filtering to stop them. See **p. 200** to learn more about these procedures.

 You'll know a folder is being shared because its icon (the little picture that represents the file) has a hand cradling it.

If you want to turn file sharing off, follow the steps for your computer.

> **tip** If you want to understand Vista networking and file sharing in depth, pick up a copy of my book *Windows Vista Help Desk*. It also covers how to share files from a Vista PC to either an XP computer or a Mac.

> **tip** To figure out which version of Windows you have, click the Start button on the bottom-left side of your screen (and then Settings on some versions of Windows), then Control Panel, and double-click the System icon. The General tab displays which version of Windows you are using.
>
> If there isn't the word Start on the button, but instead there's the Windows logo on a round button, your computer uses Windows Vista. To determine which version of Vista (there are five), click the Windows button, type **System** in the search box on the Start menu, and then click System when it appears. Your version of Windows Vista will be displayed under the heading "Windows edition."

Windows 98/Me

In Windows 98/Me, file sharing can be turned off in the Windows Control Panel using the Network applet. Follow these steps:

1. Click on the Start button, and click Settings, Control Panel. Double-click on the Network icon.

2. When the Network box appears, click on the File and Print Sharing button on the Configuration tab.

3. If file sharing is on, check marks are in the check boxes next to I Want to Give Others Access to My Files and I Want to Be Able to Allow Others to Print to My Printer. To turn file sharing off, click on those boxes to uncheck them. Click OK.

Windows XP Home

In Windows XP Home Edition, a function called Simple File Sharing is turned on by default. This is useful because if a file is purposely shared, anyone on the network can access it. If that's your spouse, this is probably a good thing. If that's the 15-year-old kid with the Kill All Humans T-shirt from down the street, it's probably not so good.

To protect yourself, you need to set a password for the Guest account on your computer, following these steps:

1. Click the Start button, and then Run, and then type **cmd**. (In older versions of Windows, type **command** instead.) Click OK.

2. A black box appears. Now figure out a password—maybe *angryrabbits*.

3. At the C:\> prompt, type **net user guest angryrabbits**

4. If you don't want your password to be angryrabbits, type something else instead. The password happyrabbits is just as good.

5. Press the Enter key. The system responds with "The Command Completed Successfully" (see Figure 7.31).

6. The password for the Guest is now set. Close the window. Now if anyone tries to access a shared folder, they are asked for a password.

FIGURE 7.31

Change the Guest user's password in the DOS emulator in Windows.

Windows XP Professional

If you have a Windows XP Professional system and you choose not to protect your wireless network with WEP, WPA, or MAC address filtering, you'll want to turn Simple File Sharing off, using these steps:

1. Click Start, Control Panel, Appearance and Themes, and choose Folder Options.

2. Click on the View tab, scroll down to the bottom, and uncheck the option that says Use Simple File Sharing (Recommended) (see Figure 7.32).

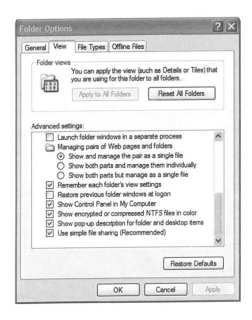

FIGURE 7.32

Turn off simple file sharing in Windows XP Professional if you are not going to use it.

3. When you right-click on a folder to share it, choose the Sharing and Security option. Then choose the Sharing tab to configure sharing options.

4. By choosing the Security tab you can also manually edit read/write permissions for individual users who have access to your computers. Just be forewarned: It's easy to get confused by these permissions and misconfigure them, so tread lightly and chew a big stick of gum. Don't mess with this stuff too much if you're new to it. A misstep with permissions can lock you out of a file or folder. If that's your late grandma's secret fabulous cookie recipe, you'll have to rely on the Keebler elves for your cookie needs.

Windows Vista

In Windows Vista, file sharing can be turned off in the Network and Sharing Center. Follow these steps:

1. Click on the Windows button, and type **Sharing** in the Search bar.

2. When the Network and Sharing Center item appears in the Start, menu click it.

3. Look for the File Sharing option under Sharing and Discovery section halfway down the window. Click the down arrow next to File Sharing. It will reveal the file-sharing settings. Choose Turn off File Sharing and click Apply.

4. Confirm by clicking Continue in the UAC dialog box.

> **tip** If you need to keep simple file sharing turned on but you only want to share folders with specific people (such as your spouse), here's a trick. When you right-click on a folder to share it, you'll need to assign it a share name. This is the name that appears on the network when it is browsed. To hide the shared folder, add a dollar sign to the end of the share name, bagelrecipe$, for instance. This way, only people who know the share name are able to access it. It does not appear when someone browses the Network Neighborhood.

The Absolute Minimum

- A home router is an appliance that connects home computers together by creating a network and sharing an Internet connection among them.

- Most routers are wirelessly enabled. This technology is called Wi-Fi.

- Straight out of the box, Wi-Fi has no security features turned on.

- Anyone can connect to a Wi-Fi network if it's not configured to be secure.

- Wireless network snoops come in three types: bandwidth bandits, wardrivers, and wireless hackers.

- Bandwidth bandits are people who just want a free Internet connection.

- Wardrivers catalog open wireless networks and share them with bandwidth bandits.

- You have to worry about wireless hackers who are malicious network snoops, but fortunately, these types of snoops are rare.

- Three ways to lock out wireless network snoops are WEP, WPA, and MAC address filtering.
- WPA is the easiest and most convenient wireless security mechanism.
- Turn off the UPnP feature in your router.
- Changing the factory settings of your router makes you look like less of a target.
- Turning off file sharing and turning on the Windows Firewall adds additional layers of security.
- If you use Windows Vista, review the network and security settings.

Hardcore Help for Safe and Secure Computing

Damage Control—How to Remove Viruses and Spyware Infections

I f you haven't been paying attention to Internet security on your PC (or as much as you probably should have), your computer is probably infected with something unpalatable. And you're here to get rid of it. No judgment here. It is the eventuality that many people face. The hard lessons get learned in a crisis. And this chapter is here to bail you out.

Of course, if you've been following the advice in this book, you could be here simply for some amusement. What would it be like if my computer was infected with something nasty? What misery would I have to subject myself to? This chapter could be like the fire extinguisher in the kitchen. Its presence is comforting, but it'll never get used, you hope.

If it really is time to pull the pin and aim the hose, let's get to it. The rest of you can get out the marshmallows.

8

Evasive Action: Quick Steps You Can Take to Halt the Infection

The fastest route to removing a virus or spyware infection from your computer is to understand what it is, and then remove it with an effective tool. Intelligence is everything.

Now you may be in one of three places if your system is infected:

1. You have an antivirus or antispyware program on your system that has thrown an alert that your system is infected with something.

2. Your system is behaving oddly, and you have no antivirus or antispyware product on the system. Or you got a call from your Internet provider saying your system is infected and doing bad things across the Internet to others.

3. Your system is behaving oddly, and you have an antivirus or antispyware product on the system, but it has failed you.

Disconnect the Internet and Evaluate

In the first minutes after discovering (or suspecting) an infection, the very first step to take is to disconnect the Internet from your system. This buys you time. That's because malware sends spam, attacks other computers on the Internet, spreads itself, and invades your privacy.

And it will also fight for its life by repairing itself and downloading new infections.

In doing so, it may attempt to stop you (or your antivirus or antispyware program) from using the Internet. And it may try to stop you from taking evasive action by blocking administrative actions on your system, like access to the Windows registry or the System Restore utility.

You need to cut off its lifeline and allow yourself time to think.

So physically unplug your Internet modem or router from the back of the computer or switch off the wireless connection if that's what you use to connect to the Internet.

The network cable (see Figure 8.1) will be on the back of a desktop system. It looks like a thick cable with a fat square head (like a fat North American telephone jack). This could also be the case on your laptop, except the cable may connect to a jack in the side.

8

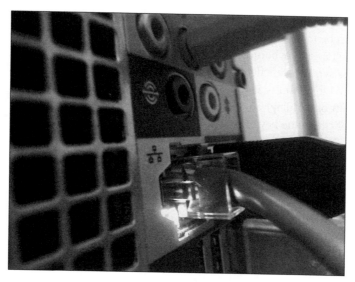

FIGURE 8.1

Look for a connected network cable on the back (shown) of your desktop computer or side of your laptop and unplug it to disconnect the Internet.

If you use a wireless connection, you'll need to slide a switch for your wireless network radio to off. It will be on the front or side (see Figure 8.2) of your laptop. In some cases you'll find it beneath the screen.

Wireless connection switch

FIGURE 8.2

Look for a slider or switch on the front or side of your laptop to turn the wireless connection off.

8

In some machines, the wireless connection can be toggled off using a function key on the laptop keyboard. You may see a wireless symbol stenciled in blue. To use it you need to push the Fn button (near your Shift or Ctrl key) at the same time as the stenciled blue key.

It's possible your Internet connection comes through a USB adapter, too. That will have to be unplugged. If you use a dial-up connection, unplug the phone wire from your system.

caution If you're not sure, simply power off your Internet modem or router. However, this will cause a bit of a problem because if other computers in the house use the connection through a router (a connection box that shares the Internet), they will all be disconnected.

Inventory Your Tools and Their Status

The next step is to figure out what security tools you have at your disposal to help solve the problem. Ask yourself these questions:

1. **Do I have an antivirus AND an antispyware program installed?**
   Optimally, protected systems have both an antivirus and one or more antispyware programs installed. When they are active and protecting your system they'll be found in the System Tray in the bottom-right side of your screen. You can also see the status of your antivirus program in the Security Center. This can be found in Windows XP (if you have Service Pack 2 or 3 installed) by clicking Start, then Control Panel, and double-clicking Security Center.

   In Vista, open the Security Center by clicking the Windows button on the bottom left and then type **security center** in the search box. Then click Security Center when it appears on the Start menu. It'll list the status of your antivirus program under the Malware Protection section (see Figure 8.3). There is also a link in this section you can click to show your spyware tools that are installed and their status. In XP, antispyware applications are not listed in the Security Center. In Vista there's also an option under Malware Protection that shows you the status of your antispyware and other anti-malware tools.

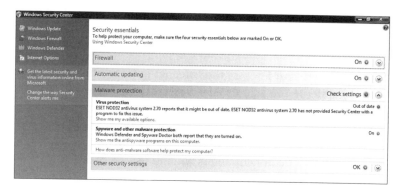

FIGURE 8.3

The Malware Protection section of the Security Center will show you the status of your antivirus and antispyware tools (if you have any).

> **Action**: If you don't have an antivirus and antispyware product on your system, you'll need to get these tools immediately. In the sidebar below (called Infection Fighters), I outline free and pay products you'll need and where to get them on the Internet. You can go and download them after you get reconnected to the Internet, in the section entitled "Jump into Safe Mode" on **p. 243**.

2. **Are those programs up to date with the latest virus signatures?** If the signatures on your security tools are out of date, the first step would be to bring them up to date. Most brand-name security tools look for signatures on the Internet (from the program's maker) and download them daily or on demand. If you have an antivirus product that you bought a few years ago and you haven't been keeping up with the annual fee to keep the product current, your system got infected because it wasn't downloading daily updates to defend itself properly.

> **Action**: Your security products need to have the latest signatures and updates installed to be effective. We'll do this in the section called "Search and Destroy: Techniques to Target the Infection and Remove It," later in this chapter. At that point you'll be reconnected safely to the Internet.

3. **Do you have two or more antispyware programs?** In my experience, no one single antispyware product can defeat or remove all spyware infections, though the antispyware companies will tell you different. It's useful to install more than one.

8

Action: Consult the sidebar to source two or more antispyware tools. I also cover this topic in depth in Chapter 2, "Spyware: Overrun By Advertisers, Hijackers, and Opportunists."

4. **Where can I access the Internet quickly other than on the infected system?** You will also need access to the Internet. I know I said disconnect from the Internet, so that may sound confusing. Because your system is infected, it's not a good idea to use it because some infections are so clever that they can stop your attempts to connect to Internet sites that can help and download new components or infections that cause further problems.

Action: Make sure you have Internet access through another computer. Go next door to a neighbor. Use the computer at work. Or preferably use another system in the house that is still connected to the Internet. If none of these options are available, we'll work around that shortly.

INFECTION FIGHTERS

It's important that you have the weapons to fight a computer infection. You'll be using one up-to-date antivirus product and two or more antispyware products.

Here are some free and pay products I recommend and the websites where you can get them:

Recommended Antivirus Programs (pick one)

- Grisoft AVG Free Edition from free.grisoft.com **FREE!**
- Avast! from www.avast.com **FREE!**
- TrendMicro from www.trendmicro.com **$$$**
- F-Secure Internet Security from www.fsecure.com **$$$**

Recommended Antispyware Products (pick two or three)

- Microsoft Windows Defender from www.microsoft.com/defender **FREE!**
- Spybot Search & Destroy from www.safer-networking.net **FREE!**
- AdAware from www.lavasoft.com **FREE!**
- Webroot Spy Sweeper from www.webroot.com **$$$**
- PC Tools Spyware Doctor from www.pctools.com **$$$**

Gather Information

The fastest way to effectively remove an infection, no matter where you are at with it, is to understand it first. If you have an antivirus or antispyware program that's up to date with the latest signatures, run it now. If you have the option do a deep scan (some might call it "full scan"), make sure you do that, too.

tip If you don't have the name of an infection yet, just keep notes on what you've noticed so far including error messages, weird behavior, and the like. You can use these clues to search for more information in an effort to determine what's happening on your system.

Note that the infection may have found a way to disable your antivirus or antispyware product. If so, go to the next section and put your system in Safe Mode with Networking and update these scanners before running a scan.

If your security tools detect an infection, make a note of what it finds. Write it down. Also take notes of any error messages you might have seen or erratic or odd behavior.

All this information is going to be helpful in understanding what infection your system has and how to remove it.

As I said before, ideally, you still have access to the Internet on another computer someplace. You're going to want to use the Internet and figure out what's going on using the notes you've made after you've done a bit of reconnaissance.

First search Google.com (see Figure 8.4). Type in the name of the infection your antivirus and antispyware system has identified. This should lead you to a web page that will teach you more about what it is.

8

Name of the infection

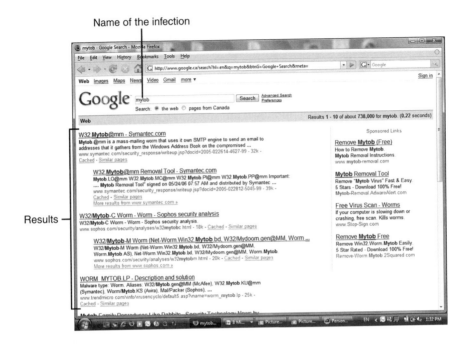

Results

FIGURE 8.4

Search Google and other Internet search engines to find out more about the infection on your system.

You might also look it up on the following websites. These are good places to start your search in your effort to figure out what infection is dogging your system.

- **Mcafee.com**—On McAfee's website you'll find a good library of risks and infections at vil.nai.com/vil/ as well as some information that will help you understand and in some cases remove infections.

- **Symantec.com**—On Symantec's website you'll find a remarkable set of tools and resources to help you with your plight. Check out the threat library on this page: www.symantec.com/norton/security_response/threatexplorer/azlisting.jsp. It features an A-Z listing of all known threats. It also offers a search feature.

> **caution** Note that the antivirus and antispyware companies don't always name the infections the same. So any given infection may be named differently by different companies, especially in the first few days after an infection is discovered.

■ **Sophos.com**—Sophos is not a well-branded consumer security company, but it does do a lot of work around business security and its tools are sometimes used by software companies to power their threat detection tools.

They have a library of threats here: www.sophos.com/security/analyses/viruses-and-spyware/.

Jump into Safe Mode

Windows can be so cumbersome that sometimes it gets in the way of removing an infection. So a good practice for infection removal is to swap into Windows Safe Mode.

Safe Mode is a diagnostic mode where only a minimum of system resources and programming are used to run Windows. No programs or drivers are loaded at startup, including infections that may have wedged themselves into the startup process.

This is an ideal environment to scan for and remove infections.

Here's how to get into Safe Mode.

1. Shut down your computer and reboot it. If Windows won't shut down or it is hung, locate the power button and hold it down for 10–20 seconds. This will cause a hard boot, meaning the system will force a shutdown and restart from scratch.

2. When the screen is blank and the machine shows signs of starting up again, start tapping the F8 key.

3. Tap the F8 key repeatedly and quickly like a woodpecker until the computer starts objecting with a series of beeps.

4. As the computer starts up it will offer you a diagnostic menu before it gets to the Windows bootup routine. If you see the Windows logo, you've missed it. Try again and be sure to start pecking the F8 key earlier.

5. If you are successful, you'll see a white menu on a black screen. In Vista, it's called Advanced Boot Options (see Figure 8.5). In XP, it's called Windows Advanced Options Menu.

caution Don't confuse the advanced boot options menu with accessing the BIOS. You may see an option to go into "set up" or "BIOS" or "CMOS" when you start. This is a whole other beast and won't help with infection removal. If you find yourself in this menu, be sure to bail out of it and be sure not to make any changes to it; otherwise, you'll find yourself in even worse peril.

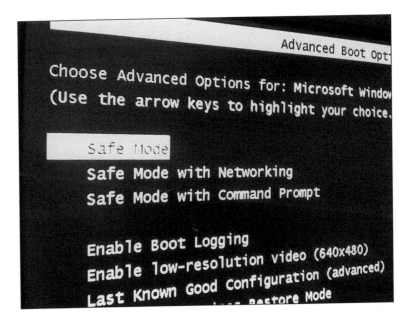

FIGURE 8.5

The Advanced Boot Options menu in Vista offers Safe Mode, the Windows version of a lifeboat.

6. On this menu, use the cursor keys, which are the up and down and left and right arrows on the right side of the keyboard. Change the section by using the down or up arrows to navigate the options. Safe Mode is the first item. You want this option if your antivirus or antispyware products are up to date and you have recently downloaded the latest virus signatures. Select it by pressing the Enter key. If you haven't had a chance to update the virus or spyware definitions on your antivirus product (or don't have these installed), choose Safe Mode with Networking. This will start Windows in diagnostic mode but also give you access to the Internet.

7. You may be asked to select a Windows installation. If you have multiple versions of Windows on your system, choose the version that is infected (although some viruses can wiggle their way into other partitions, so you'll have to check this other partition later). In most circumstances you'll only have one option.

> **tip** You should also choose Safe Mode with Networking if your computer is the only machine that you can access the Internet with. You can do your research in Safe Mode with Networking, although it's not ideal.

8. Windows will cough up a bunch of weird information as it goes into this mode. Have patience until you see the Windows logo with a login screen. Everything on screen will be larger than usual.

> **tip** If you get a bunch of error messages, click OK and ignore them. This is just programs on your system objecting because they are expecting a normal Windows boot routine. In one of my test sessions I got an Adobe warning dialog box that wouldn't go away. If this happens just leave the error message up on screen and ignore it.

9. In XP, click on the Administrator option. In Vista, click the login you use to administer the system (like one you normally use to log in, unless you have created a separate administrator login). If there's only one login option, click that.

10. If necessary, enter a password. If you don't remember entering a password, leave the password field blank and press Enter.

11. Windows will then boot in a really weird and ugly mode where everything is oversized and jaggy. You're at the right place.

12. If you have used the Safe Mode with Networking option, now is the time to reconnect your Internet connection.

Now that you are in Safe Mode, you can start the infection removal process. What follows is a series of suggestions that you can use to defeat the virus or spyware that is dogging your system.

Search and Destroy: Techniques to Target the Infection and Remove it

At this point you should be in Safe Mode with Networking, if you:

- Need to update security tool signatures
- Install extra security tools that you'll download from the Internet
- Do research because you don't have access to any other system connected to the Internet

You can use Safe Mode (without networking) if:

- You have access to another Internet-connected system to do research.
- You know what is infecting your system.
- All your security tools are installed and up to date.

If you need to switch, go back to the previous section to follow the step to switch modes.

That said, let's go infection hunting.

Replace Tools and Update Signatures

If you have an up to date antivirus program and at least two antispyware products installed, go to the next section. If not, in Safe Mode with Networking go and download what you need.

Also, be sure to run the signature update process in the security tool to make sure you have the latest malware signatures.

> **tip** Remember: There's a list earlier in this chapter of recommended tools. See the Infection Fighters sidebar on **p. 240.** You can also reference Chapter 12, "Tools of the Trade: Security Products You Should Own," for a list of security programs that I recommend. I have found that AVAST Home Edition Free is the most effective and easy-to-use antivirus program in Safe Mode. Other products may error out during installation, especially in XP.

If you don't have an antivirus product installed or need to replace it because it failed you, I recommend that here that you install AVAST! Home Edition for a few reasons:

- It has a scanner that will scan during the boot routine the next time the system restarts (see Figure 8.6).
- It works in safe mode.
- It's free.

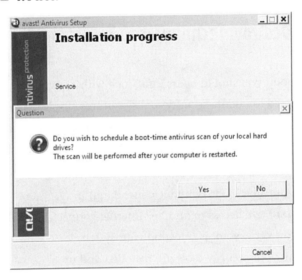

FIGURE 8.6

Install AVAST! so that it can scan your system the next time you reboot.

Scan Your System

The first thing to do is to scan your system in Safe Mode with two types of scanners:

- An up-to-date antivirus scanner
- Two or more antispyware scanners

Before you scan your system, be sure to run the signature updater tool in each program to ensure you have the latest virus and spyware signatures. To do this you'll need to be in Safe Mode with Networking and have the system reconnected to the Internet.

If you know your virus and spyware signatures are up to date, go ahead and do a deep or full scan with the program. Some will have a single scan mode. Use that if that's all there is. Others will have a quick scan and a more advanced scan. You'll want to use the deepest, most thorough scan possible.

Vista users should also use the built-in Windows Defender antispyware program. It is installed on all copies of Windows Vista. XP users can get it for free from www.microsoft.com/defender.

Defender can be found on Vista by clicking the Windows button at the bottom left and typing **defender** into the search box and then clicking Windows Defender when it appears in the Start menu above the search box. Click Scan on the menu across the top of the Defender window, and then choose Full Scan. Let the program run to completion and take any action it recommends (more on that in the next section).

caution Just a quick note about AVG. It's free for personal use if you get it from http://free.grisoft.com. There have been some rumblings that it will no longer be free. This is not the case. However, Grisoft asked users to remove version 7.5 (and gave them an option to upgrade to a paid version) and install version 8. So while a version of AVG will remain free, it appears as if the company is using some questionable tactics to influence users of the free product to upgrade to the paid version.

note Some antispyware scanners may detect some viruses or Trojan horses. Some antivirus programs will detect some spyware and adware.

tip If you choose to install AVAST!, restart your system and don't touch the F8 key (you don't want to go into Safe Mode). AVAST! will do a virus scan before it starts Windows (see Figure 8.7).

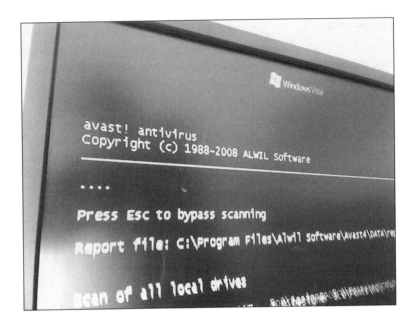

FIGURE 8.7
The free AVAST! Home Edition scans your computer before it starts Windows.

Key tasks to achieve up to this point are:

1. Do a deep or full scan with your antivirus.
2. Do a deep or full scan with two antispyware programs.
3. Make a note of any infections that are detected so that you can do further research if necessary.

Infection Found!

If any of your scanners find an infection, you'll want to quarantine the infection. This takes it off the system and puts it in the computer equivalent of a jail cell so it can do no further harm. You could also opt to simply wipe the infection from the system all together.

Quarantined items can also be submitted from the program using the Internet to the antivirus or antispyware company for analysis.

When you initiate removal of the infection, it may take your security program a couple of tries to rid the system of it entirely. The removal mechanism in the program might need to take a pass at the infection and then reboot and try a second or third time.

After the program reports that infection has been removed, do another scan with it to see if any more components of the infection are still detectable.

If that's the case, be sure that when the reboot occurs, you come back into Safe Mode (with or without Networking) each time.

Sometimes a product will detect an infection but have trouble removing it. If this is the case, you could try a different security product. If you switch antivirus products, be sure to remove the one you have before you install a replacement. Antivirus products do not play nicely with each other.

FALSE POSITIVES

Sometimes a security scanner will find an infection where none exists. This is called a false positive. Sort of like when a pregnancy test shows a woman that she's pregnant when she's not. Both can cause a bit of needless panic. For a false positive on your computer, all there is to be done is to look up the program on the Internet with the name of the infection found in it and see if there is a note that explains the false positive. For example, AVAST! found a Trojan in the freeware product called ProduKey (which digs up your License Key on Windows if you have lost it). Its author reports this false positive on his website.

System Restore

One sure-fire way to eliminate a virus is to roll your system back to the way it was the day before it was infected. Windows Me, XP, and Vista all have this feature.

In Safe Mode, go to the Start menu and locate System Restore by clicking All Programs, then Accessories, and then System Tools.

In XP: When System Restore opens, click Next. In the calendar choose the date that was a day (or two) before the infection occurred. If you're not sure, use your best guess. The restore points will be listed each with a description of why they were created. Select one. Click Next. Close all other programs if you have any open. And click Next. XP will reboot and restore the system to the restore point you selected.

In Vista: In Vista's Start menu search box, type **system restore** and click it when it appears in the menu. Click Continue on the User Account Control warning. Click Choose a Different Restore Point, and then click Next. On the Choose A Restore Point screen, click Show Restore Points Older Than Five Days. Locate the system restore point you want to roll back the system to (see Figure 8.8), select the restore point, and click Next. Then click Finish and the system will restore itself and reboot. This time allow it to boot normally and then do a final virus scan to ensure there are no infections left on the system.

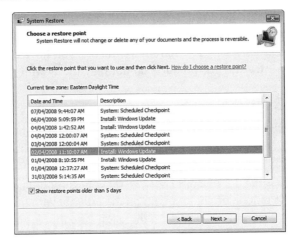

FIGURE 8.8

In System Restore (shown here in Vista), you'll see a list of restore points to which you can roll the computer back in time to get rid of an infection.

Scan and Remove with a Targeted Tool

If you have successfully identified which infection is on your system, you can target it with a specific removal tool that is available for free on the Internet. Security companies have made infection-specific tools available for free to computer users on their websites. You'll need to be in Safe Mode with networking to access these on the Internet.

> **caution** Note that some clever viruses will delete your restore points so that when you open System Restore there is nothing to restore to.

Here are several sources of those tools:

Symantec: This site provides dozens of removal tools for infections going back to 2000.
www.symantec.com/business/security_response/removaltools.jsp

McAfee: McAfee has a limited number of tools to remove common infections such as Bagle, Mydoom, and Bugbear.
http://us.mcafee.com/virusInfo/

Kaspersky: Kaspersky lists its virus removal tools by release date and by name. www.kaspersky.com/removaltools

Microsoft: Microsoft's Malicious Software Tools removes a selection of well-known infections including Blaster, Sasser and Mydoom. www.microsoft.com/security/malwareremove/

Bit Defender: Bit Defender offers a massive library of removal tools (see Figure 8.9) alphabetized by infection name. www.bitdefender.com/site/Downloads/browseFreeRemovalTool/

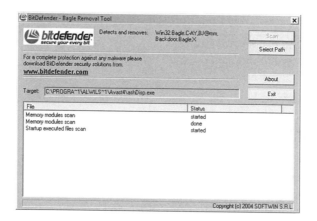

FIGURE 8.9

BitDefender.com offers dozens of free infection-removal tools like this one that removes the Bagle virus.

F-Secure: F-Secure has an extensive library of removal tools including a version of their antivirus product that can be run in DOS mode. www.f-secure.com/download-purchase/tools.shtml

To access these tools, open Internet Explorer in Safe Mode with Networking and visit the website. When you find the download link, click it and choose Run (see Figure 8.10) when the File Download—Security Warning box appears. It will download and a secondary dialog will open. Click Run on that too to execute the program.

8

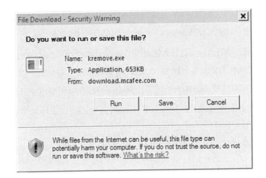

FIGURE 8.10

When you download the removal tool, click Run to execute the program and then let the tool download. You'll need to click Run a second time on another dialog box after that to execute the program.

How to Manually Remove a Virus

Viruses and spyware can be tricky little beasts. Sometimes your antivirus or antispyware applications can detect them, but not remove them, partly because the malware has its own evasion technologies and sometimes because security software just misses the mark. So what follows is how to manually remove an infection.

Do Your Research

As I said earlier in this chapter, it's important to understand the infection as best you can. Ideally you'll know the name of the infection because it's been provided by the antivirus or antispyware scanner that failed to remove it.

It's very difficult to remove an infection if you don't have that intelligence. If your antivirus or antispyware product is not picking up the name of the infection, swap those programs out for other more effective security programs. There is an extensive list of recommended free and pay security products in Chapter 12 of this book.

When you know the name of the virus or spyware that's at issue, you'll need the following information:

- Location of the infected Windows files or the location of the files that make up the malware
- Any startup files that gets triggered when Windows boots up
- Registry keys that get inserted or modified by the malware
- The name of the Windows services that get started by the malware

Companies such as Symantec and McAfee provide in-depth analysis of infections, so you will want to track that down.

Symantec has a really good list of threats and a detailed analysis of each one that includes the information above at:

www.symantec.com/norton/security_response/threatexplorer/threats.jsp

McAfee has a similar threat library (see Figure 8.11) here: http://vil.nai.com/vil/.

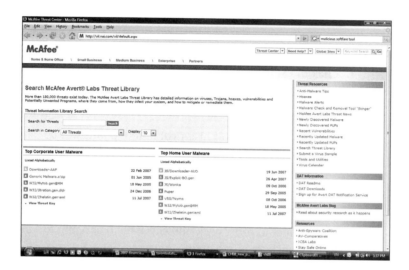

FIGURE 8.11

McAfee has a good threat library where you can look up virus specifications including file names, registry entries, and more.

Disconnect

Start by physically disconnecting your system from the Internet and your network (if applicable) so that any active virus or spyware can't communicate back to the Internet or infect other computers nearby.

For more info on this refer back to "Disconnect the Internet and Evaluate" on **p. 236** earlier in this chapter.

Back Up Data

Back up any data you are concerned about losing onto an external media source. Note that if any of your data is infected, this backup will preserve the malware, so be cautious about this and see the instruction on restoring it at the end.

Don't use backup programs that take complete snapshots of your hard drive as these will also preserve the virus or spyware infection.

Your best approach is to manually copy your data files to an external storage source such as a USB or FireWire hard drive.

Disable System Restore

Before you do any manual malware removal work, disable the System Restore feature.

Disabling System Restore in XP

1. Click the Start button, then choose Control Panel, and then System.

2. Click the System Restore tab.

3. Put a check mark in the box that says Turn Off System Restore.

4. Click OK. Note that all historical restore points will be removed, so be sure you've already tried to roll back the system using System Restore before taking this step. See **p. 249** earlier in this chapter.

5. Click Yes in the dialog box that warns you that all Restore Points will be deleted.

6. Don't forget to come back and check the box again to turn System Restore back on after you are done.

Disabling System Restore in Vista

1. Type **System** into the search bar on the Start menu and click System when it appears.

2. Click System Protection on the left.

3. Click Continue on the UAC warning.

4. Clear the check box next to your hard disk, and then click OK.

5. Click Turn System Restore Off on the dialog box that pops up (see Figure 8.12).

6. Don't forget to come back and check the box again to turn System Restore back on after you are done.

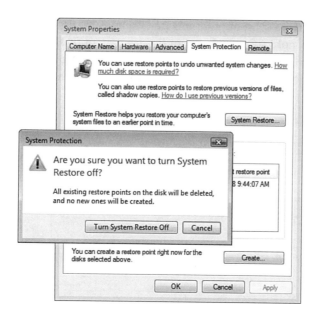

FIGURE 8.12

Turn off System Restore and let the system delete all Restore Points.

Work in Safe Mode

Restart your computer and continuously tap F8 until you get a menu that lets you select Safe Mode. Enter Safe Mode, a barebones version of Windows that doesn't load anything but necessary Windows components. It's a good place to do malware diagnosis, scanning, and removal.

Clean Out Windows Startup

The first step in a manual removal is to work with the Windows System Configuration tool, a hidden tool that helps you edit the startup routine.

> **tip** If you haven't already, you should do a scan with your antivirus and antispyware programs in Safe Mode.

1. In Vista, in the search bar of the Start menu type **msconfig** and press Enter to start the application. Click Continue on the User Account Control warning. In XP, click Start, then Run, and then type **msconfig** and click OK.

2. When the System Configuration Tool starts up, click the Startup tab.

3. You'll see a list of programs (see Figure 8.13). Uncheck any application that looks suspicious or that has been identified as part of the virus or spyware when you did your research earlier. Make a note of the information in the Startup Item column as well as the Command column and the Location column.

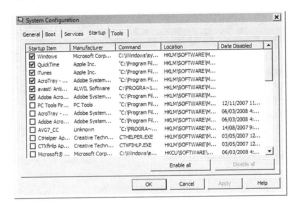

FIGURE 8.13

Turn off any programs in the Windows startup routine that are part of the virus or spyware using the System Configuration Tool.

4. The Command column provides the path to the file used to execute the application. You'll want to track the file down and remove it later.

5. The Location column will provide the location of the registry key that starts the application when Windows starts up.

6. If the information in the Command or Location columns is obscured, put your mouse on the separator until you get a cursor that looks like a plus sign with two arrows on either side. Click and drag the separator bar to expand the column so you see its contents better.

> **tip**
> Here's a handy web site that list loads of startup programs. Use it to determine what they are used for and if they are dangerous.
> http://www.pacs-portal.co.uk/startup_index.htm.

Turn Off Services

In the System Configuration Tool, also click the Services tab (see Figure 8.14). Look for rogue entries and turn those off. Be sure to click Hide All Microsoft Services to suppress system services.

This can be a bit daunting, and your success will be dependent on what you've been able to find out about the virus and how it deals with Windows services from your research.

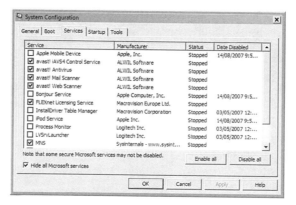

FIGURE 8.14

Turn off any Windows services that are part of the virus or spyware using the System Configuration Tool.

Clean Out the Registry

The next malware removal tactic is a key one. It's time to remove and restore any changes to the Windows Registry.

Open the registry editor as follows:

> **note** Because you are working in Safe mode, most Windows Services and the programs in the Startup routine are not running, so that's why safe mode is a good place to do this work.

1. In Windows XP, click Start, then Run, and type **regedit** and click OK. In Windows Vista, click the Windows button and type **regedit** in the search box and press Enter.

2. The registry editor will open so that you can access and edit registry settings.

3. Use the data you have gathered in your research to find the rogue registry entries and delete them. Here's a sample registry entry you might find in the Location column in the Startup tab of System Configuration:

   HKLM\Software\Microsoft\Windows\CurrentVersion\Run

4. To find it, you'd start the Registry Editor and click the arrow next to HKEY_LOCAL_MACHINE (HKLM), then click Software, then Microsoft, and so on down to the registry key in question (see Figure 8.15).

5. To delete the key, right-click and choose Delete.

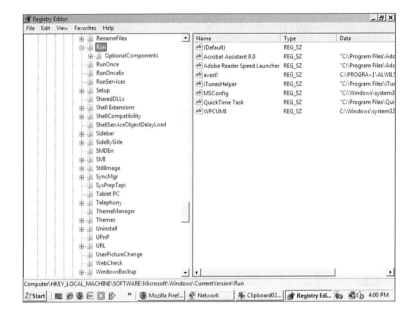

FIGURE 8.15

Use the Registry Editor tool to find registry entries being used by malware and delete or modify them.

Disable Malware that Runs as a Windows Service

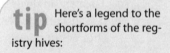

tip Here's a legend to the shortforms of the registry hives:

HKLM – HKEY_LOCAL_MACHINE
HKCR – HKEY_CLASS_ROOT
HKCU – HKEY_CURRENT_USER
HKU – HKEY_USERS
HKCC – HKEY_CURRENT_CONFIG

If you discover through your research that the malware runs components as a Windows service, disable the service (and in the next step) delete the source file of the service if applicable. You can locate the file that starts the service in the Properties tab under "Path to executable."

Disabling Malware Running as a Service in Vista

1. Go to Control Panel and double-click Administrative Tools.

2. Double-click Services.

3. Locate the service, right-click it and choose Properties, and then under Startup Type, choose Disabled (see Figure 8.16).

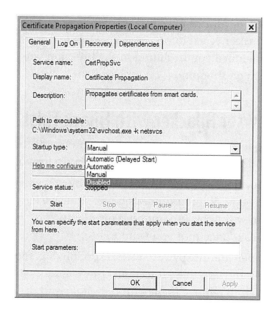

FIGURE 8.16

Disable any malware that runs as a Windows service.

Disabling Malware Running as a Service in XP

1. Go to Control Panel and click Administrative Tasks.
2. Double-click Services.
3. Look for the service you want to stop or eliminate and right-click it.
4. Choose Properties and then in the Startup Type pull-down menu, choose Disabled and click OK.

Delete Files and Folders Related to the Malware

Finally, go on a search-and-destroy mission and delete any files or folders created or used by the malware that you have discovered through your research or through working through the steps above.

Restart and Check

When you are done, restart your system and boot into Windows normally. Check

> **tip**
> If you have a hard time deleting a stubborn file, use the MoveOnBoot utility to mark and file and have it deleted on reboot. Get it from: http://www.snapfiles.com/get/moveonboot.html

that the system runs as expected. Turn System Restore back on and carry out any other tasks needed to restore the system to normal. If your antivirus or antispyware failed you (resulting in the infection you just removed), now is good time to go shopping for a replacement.

Remove a Browser Hijacker with Hijack This!

Browser hijackers, as you may recall, are programs that take over your web browser and force you to use a specific webpage as your home page.

Why do they do that? Because they make money when you click links on the forced web page. So programmers go to extensive lengths to not only infect your system with their program but also to stop you from changing the home page back to a page that you want to use.

Some commercial antispyware tools, especially PC Tools Spyware Doctor, do a nice job of removing these infections. However, sometimes you'll have to take steps yourself to remove them with a digital crowbar. The crowbar in question is a free program called HijackThis (see Figure 8.17), a program written by a clever Dutchman called Merijn Bellekom. He has since sold it to TrendMicro and is now available for free (as it always was) from TrendMicro's website at www.trendsecure.com.

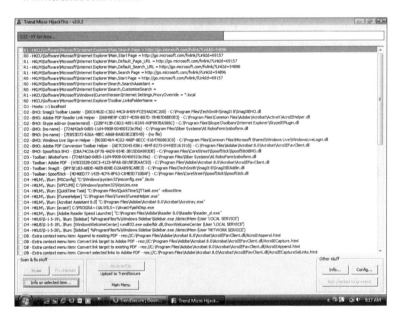

FIGURE 8.17

HijackThis is a good, but complicated, tool that helps you remove a browser hijacker from your computer.

That said, here's a piece of bad news. HijackThis is about as do-it-yourself as a 747 jet. It's not a tool that beginners should use on their own. That's because you can really bung things up if you make a wrong move. Let me say that again:

You + HijackThis + cavalier attitude = computer goes BOOM!

> **caution** So big neon caution here: Your best bet is to find an expert to help. But if you want to do it yourself, in the next few pages, I'll show you how to use HijackThis effectively to rid your system of the infection.

HijackThis is like that pull catch in your car that opens the hood. Anyone can use it, but it exposes inner workings that can be intimidating, and if you blindly mess around in there, you can get a limb caught in the fan belt.

The program shows you the settings that relate to the guts of Internet Explorer, other web browsers, items that activate during the Windows startup, and other key system settings. It can also remove those settings. The problem here is finding the right items to remove. That takes a trained eye and a steady mouse finger.

Installing and Using HijackThis

To start, download the HijackThis installer from www.trendsecure.com.

I used the installer made available on the TrendSecure.com website. When it has finished downloading to your computer, double-click the installer and let it set itself up. This won't take very long.

To run it, double-click the HijackThis icon in XP. In Vista you'll need to employ an additional step. Right-click the HijackThis icon and choose Run As Administrator.

This gives the program access to administrator-only areas of Vista.

If you attempt to run the program and you get a message that says "HijackThis is already running," you'll need to shut it down in memory. This seems to be a glitch in Vista.

1. To kill it off, use what geeks call the three-finger salute: hold down the Ctrl key and Alt key at the same time and tap the Del key.

2. Then click Start Task Manager from the list. Windows Task Manager will open.

3. Click the Process tab and find HijackThis.exe in the list of programs running in memory (see Figure 8.18). Select it and click the End Process button. Next, click the End Process button in the dialog box that appears.

4. Get out of the Windows Task Manager and right click the HijackThis icon and choose Run as Administrator. You'll see a User Account Control warning. Click Allow.

The HijackThis should start just fine.

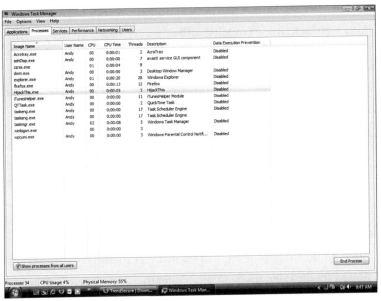

FIGURE 8.18

A glitch in Vista leaves HijackThis in memory when you shut it down.

Recruit a HijackThis Expert

HijackThis is a very advanced tool and it's really **not** designed for beginners. Nevertheless there are lots of people out there willing to help you to diagnose a spyware problem with it. You just have to find one. So, here's how to get an expert to help you.

Close Internet Explorer and any other browsers that are running. Start HijackThis, (remember to Run as Administrator in Vista) and follow these steps carefully:

1. In the opening menu of HijackThis, you'll see an option called Do a System Scan and Save a Logfile. Choose it. This scans places deep inside Windows where browser hijackers might have put entries. Then it creates a log of these in Notepad.

8

2. Ask for help by posting your log on a web forum where HijackThis experts hang out. Be sure to cut and paste it into your forum post with your request for help. There's a good list of web forums with experts that will help you diagnose your HijackThis log at www.merijn.org/forums.html. There's also a very good Malware Removal forum at Spywareinfo.com (see Figure 8.19).

FIGURE 8.19

The Malware Removal discussion area in the forums at SpywareInfo.com is a good place to post your request for analysis of your HijackThis log.

3. The expert diagnoses your log and walks you through procedures on how to fix the problem using HijackThis and other tools and techniques they'll explain.

4. Ask for the expert's mailing address and send them a box of chocolate cookies. Geeks like cookies.

Do-It-Yourself HijackThis

If you're the kind of person who likes to land the 747 yourself—and really, who doesn't?—you're going to need a few days and an in-depth step-by-step do-it-yourself process to learn HijackThis.

However, how about a quickie course that should both fix most ornery snags that most antispyware programs can't fix and at the same time get your feet wet with HijackThis?

Check the Memory First

At the top of your HijackThis log you see a series of programs listed as Running Processes (see Figure 8.20). This is what is in your computer's memory at the time of the scan.

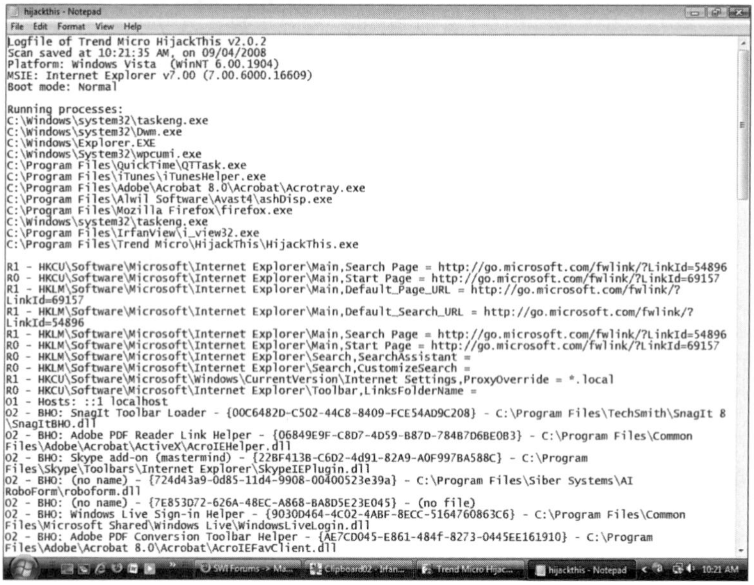

FIGURE 8.20

At the top of the HijackThis log is a list of processes running in your computer's memory.

You may see some obvious spyware program running. I helped out one guy who had a nasty spyware infection. Here are five of the 10 things that were running in his system's memory. Pop quiz! Can you guess which program is spyware?

1. C:\WINDOWS\system32\winlogon.exe

2. C:\WINDOWS\system32\svchost.exe

3. C:\PROGRA~1\Grisoft\AVGFRE~1\avgcc.exe

4. C:\DOCUME~1\s1\LOCALS~1\Temp\nsu1C.tmp\ns1E.tmp

5. C:\Documents and Settings\s1\My Documents\Porn stars.exe

If you answered 4 *and* 5, you're right! Number 4 is a giveaway because it an obscure gobbledygook program name with a **.tmp** extension. Very suspicious! Sometimes spyware programs randomize the names of the program they launch to evade detection from antispyware programs.

Item 5 is pretty obvious, too. In this sample case, two of these with slight variations to their names were running in memory. Actually, these files had longer names that mentioned actual actors and described the act they were acting, so to speak. I cleansed it for you to keep this book out of the Human Sexuality section of the bookstore.

So check your HijackThis log for suspicious entries and then do the three-finger salute again: Hold down the Control and Alt keys and tap the Del key.

The Windows Task Manager will open. If you click on the Processes tab, you'll see all the programs running in memory. Scroll through them and try to figure out which ones are spyware.

To help, check out www.processlibrary.com. You can enter the names of the files you see on that site and it tells you whether it's a legitimate program or spyware. It won't have an answer for everything, though. What it's best for is to help you make a short list of the suspicious programs. Then you can investigate each one.

Use Google.com to help search for program names and be sure to enter them between sets of quotes if there are spaces in the name, as follows:

```
"porn stars.exe "
```

This tells Google to search for the whole name as a phrase and not pieces of it.

Here Spyware, Spyware. It's Time to Die

With the memory cleansed, you can get down to the business of killing spyware in the system.

Open HijackThis, click the Scan button, and look at the list of entries (see Figure 8.21).

8

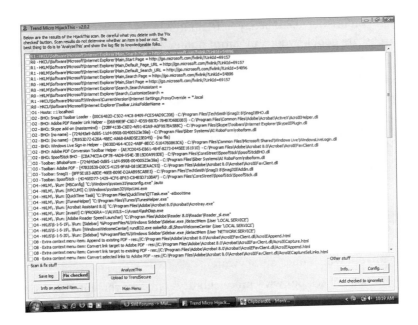

FIGURE 8.21

HijackThis generates a series of entries from the Windows Registry where spyware might be hiding.

There are lots of entries and they all look like they could be items on a Chinese food menu. But if you study them, you'll start to see stuff you recognize. Let's go through some notable entries you will likely encounter.

■ **R0, R1, R2, R3—IE Start and Search Page**—These are addresses of the web pages Internet Explorer uses for the home page and the default search page. If anything looks funky here and you see web addresses you don't recognize on the right side of each item, the entry is probably a hijack. Check off the boxes to the left of these and click the Fix Checked button. This wipes out the settings. Congrats, you have just killed your first spyware with HijackThis. I think you are clever! But wait, we are not done.

■ **F0, F1, F2, F3—Autoloading Programs from INI Files**—These are autoloading programs from old versions of Windows. F0 references are always bad. Nuke 'em. F1 items are usually old programs. If you run old Windows programs, you will probably recognize these. Do research on these if you're unsure.

- **N1, N2, N3, N4—Netscape/Mozilla Start and Search Page**—These are Netscape and Mozilla (Firefox) web browser settings for their start and search pages. This looks like the following:

N1 - Netscape 4: user_pref("browser.startup.homepage", "www.google.com");
➥(C:\Program Files\Netscape\Users\default\prefs.js)

These browser settings are usually OK. Malware called Lop.com hijacks these, though. If you don't recognize the web addresses, BBQ them.

- **O1—HOSTS File Redirections**—These are HOSTS file redirects. What that means is the web address on the right will be redirected to the numerical Internet address (called an IP address) on the left when you type it into your web browser. For example

O1 - Hosts: 199.181.132.250 google.com

In this example, if you typed in Google.com into your web browser, it would be redirected to Disney.com (because that 199 number is an ABC/Disney-related IP address). Unless you put these in your HOSTS file yourself, these are bad. The only one that belongs there is

127.0.0.1 localhost

- **O2—Browser Helper Objects**—These are called Browser Helper Objects or BHOs. They are programs that install into Internet Explorer that can add new features. They look like the following:

O2 - BHO: AcroIEHlprObj Class - {06849E9F-C8D7-4D59-B87D-784B7D6BE0B3}
➥ - C:\Program Files\Adobe\Acrobat 5.0\Reader\ActiveX\
➥AcroIEHelper.ocx

For example, you'll see the Google Toolbar here if you have it installed. Of course, BHOs can also be spyware.

If you see something that looks odd or unfamiliar, it could be spyware. Again, it's worth searching Google.com for entries to learn more about them before you nuke them.

- **O3—IE Toolbars**—These items reference Internet Explorer toolbars and look similar to this example:

8

```
O3 - Toolbar: Yahoo! Companion - {EF99BD32-C1FB-11D2-892F-0090271D4F88}
➡ - C:\Program Files\Yahoo!\Companion\Installs\cpn0\ycomp5_5_5_0.dll
```

> If there's an odd toolbar at the top of IE that appears and wasn't there
> before, chances you'll find it listed as an O3 entry. Torch it.

- ■ **O4—Autoloading Programs from Registry or Startup Group**—These
  entries reference programs that load automatically when Windows
  starts. They look like the following:

```
O4 - HKCU\..\Run: [msnmsgr] "C:\Program Files\MSN Messenger\
➡msnmsgr.exe " /background
```

> This is where many spyware programs get started. Killing them off here
> stops them from loading when Windows restarts. Tread carefully here.

Besides these entries listed, there are loads more esoteric entries that could
hide spyware references. Learning them all requires a university course, time,
and patience.

For a full complement of entries and what they do, check out this really good
reference page: www.bleepingcomputer.com/forums/tutorial42.html.

If you have the time and the inclination, you can learn tons more about the
workings of HijackThis and can make a study of all the critical entries it finds.

I also recommend visiting this web page to learn more about using
HijackThis: www.spywareinfo.com/articles/hijacked/

Decimate the Little Suckers with CWShredder

Another free program, also owned by Trend Micro these days, is called
CWShredder (see Figure 8.22), and it might also be able to help you with your
browser hijack. It finds and destroys traces of CoolWebSearch, a name given
to a wide range of browser hijackers. It's available for free from www.inter-
mute.com/spysubtract/cwshredder_download.html.

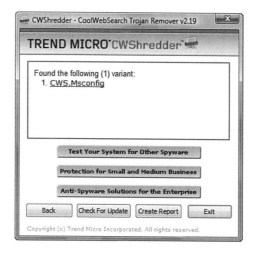

FIGURE 8.22

CWShredder is a free program that helps defeat CoolWebSearch browser hijackers. This is one I found on my Vista machine.

It's a small file, so it won't take long to download. Before you run it, be sure to close Internet Explorer and Windows Media Player, if they are open.

Now run CWShredder. You'll see four buttons at the bottom of the initial window. Click Scan Only if you want to see if there are any CoolWebSearch hijacks on your system. Click Fix-> if you want to search for infections and clean them.

> **note** CWShredder was first written by Merijn Bellekom, author of HijackThis. He handed it over to Intermute, makers of the antispyware program SpySubtract PRO, in October 2004. The company, which was bought by Trend Micro in May 2005, is responsible for updating it and continues to make it freely available.

The Absolute Minimum

- When you discover a virus or other infection immediately disconnect your computer from the Internet and assess and check to see what security tools you have. Find time to breath and don't panic.
- Do your malware removal work in Safe Mode with Networking and install or update security tools.
- Rescan and remove infections in Safe Mode.

8

- Plan B: Manually remove a virus by understanding it through research on the Net. Removing it infection elements from the startup area, from the Windows registry, from Windows services and also destroy actual files related to the malware.

- Use HijackThis and CWShredder to remove browser hijackers.

- Seek help on the web by posting your HijackThis log to a forum visited by people that can offer advice.

Ground Up Security—Wipe Your Hard Drive and Build a Secure Windows PC from the Ground Up

S ometimes a computer is just so infested with viruses, spyware, and other bits of computer unhappiness that it's easier to just wipe your hard drive clean and start from scratch, rather than start a prolonged search-and-destroy mission. This is especially true if you're not really sure what you're looking for. This chapter explains how to wipe an XP or Vista computer clean, reinstall Windows, and build a more secure computer from the ground up.

Light the Fuse and Stand Back

Let's say you live in a house that keeps the rain out just fine, but it's not very pleasant to live in because it's fallen into slumlord disrepair. Mice crawl behind the walls. Roaches snack on your toast crumbs. The neighbors steal your garden tools through a broken window. And the mailbox is jammed full of furnace-cleaning flyers and pizza delivery menus. What do you do?

Well, you can call in the exterminator, patch the windows, threaten the post-man, and stop eating toast. It's going to be expensive, inconvenient, and take a lot of time. Plus there's no guarantee that your defensive efforts are going to turn the house into a Barbie Dream Home.

Maybe what you need to do is drop a wheelbarrow full of TNT down the base-ment stairs, light a match, and run. When the smoke clears you can rebuild the house from the ground up.

That's what we're going to do to your computer in this chapter. We're going to scrub the hard drive clean and start fresh.

Let's Get Started

You're going to need some tools to get that proverbial TNT down the stairs in order to rebuild again. Here's what you'll need:

For Windows XP:

- Windows XP install CD or system recovery CD
- Windows XP Service Pack 2 (XP SP2) or Service Pack 3 (XP SP3)
- XP driver files for all your crucial hardware
- Install CDs/DVDs or program setup files and license keys for all your programs
- Internet service setup disk and/or settings

For Windows Vista:

- Windows Vista install DVD or Vista system recovery CD
- Windows Vista Service Pack 1 (Vista SP1)
- Vista driver files for all your crucial hardware
- Install CDs/DVDs or program setup files and license keys for all your programs
- Internet service setup disk and/or settings

Let's go through the tools one by one.

Installation or System Recovery Disc

You need one of the following to reformat and reinstall:

- **Windows XP CD or Windows Vista DVD**—This is a disc provided by your computer manufacturer that contains the installation files for Windows XP or Windows Vista. You might also have bought this from a retail store. Think of it as a house kit you buy from a prefab builder—it has all the plans, materials, and instructions to build a do-it-yourself house.

■ **Recovery CD**—Some computer makers provide a recovery CD or DVD. This is a disc that, when installed, wipes your XP or Vista system clean for you and puts the computer back to the way it was the day it was bought. Think of this as the original blueprints from a brand-name builder who first built your house years ago. Recovery discs for computer companies such as Dell, HP, and Gateway often contain a customized version of Windows along with drivers specific to their proprietary hardware.

> **caution** It's important to note that recovery disc and Windows installation discs are *not* interchangeable. If you purchased a system from HP and it came with a recovery disc, use that. Or you could instead use a store-bought version of Windows to do your reinstall, but you'll have to do a bit more legwork to also get the correct drivers for your system from HP. The recovery disc may also restore with bonus programs that came with the computer.

Make sure you also have the Windows product key. That's the license code on the Windows disc's sleeve or packaging. The Windows installation process will ask for this. If you don't have the key, you won't be able to complete the installation.

If you have lost your product key for Windows XP, Vista, or Microsoft Office, you should be able to recover it from your computer (before reformatting) by using a free program. Try Produkey from www.nirsoft.net/utils/product_cd_key_viewer.html or RockXP, available from www.snapfiles.com/get/rockxp.html.

> **caution** Instead of giving you a recovery disc, some PC makers put the Windows installation files on your hard drive. You need to check with your computer maker if this is the case. There should be an option to restore the system to its original configuration when you start it. If not, look up your computer make and model on the manufacturer's website to find out how to restore the system without a disc.

Windows Service Packs

Microsoft has a history of shipping Windows to the public with loads of bugs in the programming. It's part of the reason why each new version of Windows can be so flaky and frustrating on its initial release.

The company remedies this in two ways. First, as bugs are found it issues patches or fixes through the Windows Update feature (via the Internet) to repair them on the fly.

They also issue mega fix-it packs every year or two. These are called Service Packs that aggregate all the known bugs and fixes into one giant repair kit. In the lifetime of an operating system you'll usually see two and sometimes more service packs.

Microsoft issued two service packs for Windows XP in the first four years of its existence. The second one, called XP SP2, is famous because it plugged a lot of the security flaws in Windows XP. In early 2008, Microsoft scheduled a third service pack (SP3) for Windows XP. SP3 aggregates all fixes found in SP1 and SP2 plus some new fixes that will extend the life of Windows XP.

A year after Windows Vista was launched, Microsoft issued Vista SP1. It won't be the last for the much-criticized, beleaguered operating system.

Vista SP1 makes Vista more stable and less prone to freeze-ups. It also gives older programs and hardware better performance on the new operating system and adds to the number of drivers available for Vista.

Windows XP SP2: The Mother of All Service Packs

If your Windows XP installation CD or XP recovery CD was acquired in mid-2004 or before, you also need a copy of Windows XP SP2 (see Figure 9.1). SP2 is short for Service Pack 2. It's an uber-update to Windows XP provided free by Microsoft. It has major fixes in it that patch many critical security holes in XP.

How to get it: You may have a disc for this or you may simply want to get it as a download from Microsoft.com after the reinstallation of Windows XP. (It's quite big so hopefully you're not using dial-up Internet.) Microsoft once offered a free disc with XP SP2 on it. It's since been discontinued.

FIGURE 9.1
The Windows XP Service Pack 2 can be downloaded from the Microsoft.com website.

XP SP3: Even More Fixes

To extend the life of Windows XP, Microsoft issued SP3 in May 2008. It is now available for download from Microsoft.com via the Windows Update feature on Windows XP.

It's worth installing for several reasons:

It boosts performance up to 10% faster than Windows XP SP2.

If automatic updates are set to on, your system will get it automatically.

How to get it: Download it using the Windows Update utility found on the Start menu or visit http://windowsupdate.microsoft.com. You'd do this after a reinstallation.

> **tip** If you have a recovery CD or Windows XP installation CD made in 2005 or later, SP2 is a part of the installation programming. Versions of the Windows XP CD that have SP2 integrated into them are marked as such. XP will continue to be available beyond the release of Vista, so you may see install discs with SP3 built in too.

> **note** Think of XP SP2 as a renovations crew that updates the original floor plan and fixes all the original design flaws of a home. XP SP3 is another crew that fixes flaws that XP SP2 missed or even created.

Windows Vista SP1: Microsoft's Repair Job

To improve the performance of Windows Vista, Microsoft released the first service pack (SP1) for the much-criticized new operating system in March in 2008. It is available for download from Microsoft.com via the Windows Update feature on Windows Vista. If automatic updates on your system are set to on, your system will get it automatically.

How to get it: You can download Vista SP1 using Windows Update. You'd do this after a reinstallation.

Collect Your Drivers

Drivers are files that contain little pieces of programming that help Windows XP and Windows Vista communicate with various parts of your computer. These include your motherboard (the big main circuit board inside your computer), video adapter (which runs the monitor), network card, and so on.

If you are using a recovery disk from the manufacturer, you won't need most of these because they are built into the CD or DVD. You just need the drivers for any computer parts that were added since you bought the computer.

> **tip** You might think of drivers as servants. You tell them what to do and they go deal directly with the appliances. In a new house, you don't really need servants because you operate the appliances yourself. But for the sake of the analogy, let's pretend we're related to Paris Hilton and we can't live without a maid, a chauffeur (a driver!), and a cook.

You can usually download drivers from your computer maker's website or from the manufacturer of the add-on part (such as a mouse, video card, or network card). You should always look to see if the maker of a particular piece of hardware offers a newer driver than the one that came with your piece of equipment. If you can find a newer driver, use it instead.

Installation Discs for Your Programs

When you wipe your hard drive clean, all your programs are deleted, so you need the programs' installation discs for programs such as Microsoft Office, Adobe Photoshop, FileMaker, and so on, to restore them to your system after the fresh Windows installation. Be sure to have their license keys handy, too.

If the programs were downloaded, you need a copy of their installation files and license codes, if applicable, on a blank CD, DVD, or other external storage device, such as a USB key or external hard drive.

An external hard drive plugs into your computer (with a USB or a FireWire connector) and acts as additional storage space. It's a good place to keep installation files and backups of your data. External hard drives cost US $150 and up.

A USB key is a similar device except it has no moving parts and is about the size of your thumb (see Figure 9.2). They cost a few dollars for a small one (512MB) and $100 to $200 for a large-capacity USB drive that holds more than 32GB.

FIGURE 9.2

A USB key is a thumb-sized storage device that can be used like a high-capacity floppy disk to store files and programs.

Also make sure you have the installation CD and registration key for your antivirus, antispyware, and firewall programs. If you don't have any of these programs, I'll provide you with some places on the Web to get freebies a little later in this chapter.

note You can think of your programs like furniture and appliances. They serve a specific task and they make a house functional.

Internet Service Software and Settings

If you use a high-speed Internet service from your telephone company or cable TV company, make sure you have your installation disk handy (assuming your ISP provides such a disk). You also need your username and password, if applicable, and any other settings provided by your Internet provider.

note Antivirus, firewall, and antispyware programs are like the security guard, video surveillance, and alarm systems in a mansion.

tip Your network settings and installation disks bring the outside world of the Internet into your computer. In a house, this is like cable TV and phone line service.

If you use dial-up networking to connect to the Internet (where you use a modem to dial a phone number to connect to the Internet), make sure you know the phone number you need your modem to dial, your username, and your password.

Above all, keep the tech support number for your Internet service handy. If you are inexperienced with configuring your Internet service, you probably need to talk to the company's tech support people to get back online.

Step 1: Download Drivers and Software You Need for the Reinstall

The first job at hand is to go get the drivers you need for your computer from the Internet. These files allow Windows to communicate with the various parts of your computer such as the motherboard, hard drives, and peripheral devices such as printers, mouse devices, and keyboards.

Got a Recovery CD? That's Good News!

If you have a recovery disk from your computer maker, you already have pretty much all the drivers you need to proceed because they are built into the CD or DVD.

One caveat: If you have added parts to your computer, such as a better video card, a printer, or a new mouse, download drivers for all of these products from the part maker's website, unless you have the original installation CDs for the add-ons handy.

> **tip** INF files are information files that are simple text instructions that outline an installation process. You can open them with Notepad and see which files are copied, which Registry items are set, and beyond. They can also be used to restart an installation process. Simply right-click an INF file and select Install.

Retail Copy of Windows? There's Some Work to Do

If you're installing from a Windows XP or Vista disc you bought from a retail store, you need to ensure you have at hand important drivers for your system, or you might not be able to finish your installation. The most important ones you need to ensure you have are discussed next.

Motherboard or Chipset Drivers

The motherboard is the major circuit board inside your computer. The Windows installation disc has drivers for major motherboard makers. Often, however, you'll have better system performance if you get the drivers directly from the computer maker or motherboard maker. Depending on who manufactured your motherboard, these drivers are referred to as motherboard drivers or chipset drivers.

These driver packages include INF files, network adapter drivers, and integrated video drivers, if your system uses a video adapter that is built into the motherboard. The best way to get these is by looking up your make and model on your computer maker's website.

If the computer maker is not helpful (this is often the case) and you are not sure what motherboard you have in your system, you should be able to find this information by opening your computer case and looking for the information printed on the board itself (unless you have a laptop and then this is not possible, at least not without voiding your warranty).

To download an updated version of your motherboard driver, follow these steps:

1. Determine the motherboard make and model by looking at the printing on the motherboard, and then look for the motherboard manufacturer's website. Google.com can be helpful here.

2. Find the Support or Download section on the manufacturer's website, and locate your motherboard model.

3. Download the system/chipset drivers (sometimes known as INF drivers).

4. Download the Ethernet/LAN drivers, if your Ethernet adapter is on the motherboard. An Ethernet port is sometimes called a network adapter.

5. Download the video/graphics drivers, if your monitor plugs directly into the motherboard, and not into a separate card.

6. Download drivers for your hard drive controllers (designated as SATA or IDE drivers). You probably won't need them for your installation, but it's better to be safe.

> **tip** Once upon a time, computer motherboards were purely circuit boards. Everything else, such as network cards, sound cards, and even mouse devices, attached to them separately using special slots called ISA, and later, PCI slots. For cost and efficiency (to the end user), motherboard makers started integrating many of the extras onto the motherboard. Today it's common to see these features built in as part of the motherboard. Also, many add-ons are now plugged into AGP, Serial ATA (SATA), or PCI-Express slots.

Ethernet Drivers

The Ethernet port is where you plug your network cable in. If it is on a separate adapter card (sometimes called a network interface card or NIC), you can determine the name and model number of the card by following these steps:

> **tip** Don't be confused here by the various buzzwords used to refer to your network card. The device to which you connect your high-speed Internet cable is variously called a network interface card (NIC), a network adapter, or an Ethernet port. You might also hear it called a local area network (LAN) card or adapter. It's all the same. Sometimes this is integrated into the motherboard and sometimes it's connected via a special slot called a PCI slot.

In Windows XP:

1. Click Start, Control Panel.

2. Click System.

3. Click the Hardware tab and select Device Manager.

4. Click the + sign beside Network Adapters and look for the make, model, and manufacturer (see Figure 9.3).

In Windows Vista:

1. Click the Windows button (XP users know it as the Start button).

2. In the Search box, type **device manager**.

3. When the screen dims, click Continue on the UAC security warning.

4. In the Device Manager, click the + sign beside Network Adapters and look for the make, model, and manufacturer.

Use Google.com to find the device's driver on the Internet. Search using the make, model, or manufacturer or visit the manufacturer's website.

tip If any of this hardware talk is making your head hurt, don't worry; you're not alone. Although there are many people out there who live and breathe this stuff, there are far more of you out there who want to stay as far away from the inner workings of your PCs as humanly possible. That said, a little casual knowledge about these technologies can save you lots of time and money when your PC is on the fritz. Unfortunately, there's no way I can cover everything there is to know about PC upgrading and repair. For that, I recommend you pick up a copy of Que's *Build It. Fix It. Own It—A Beginner's Guide to Building and Upgrading a PC.* It's an excellent counterpart to my book and will answer all of those hardware questions that just go beyond the scope of this book.

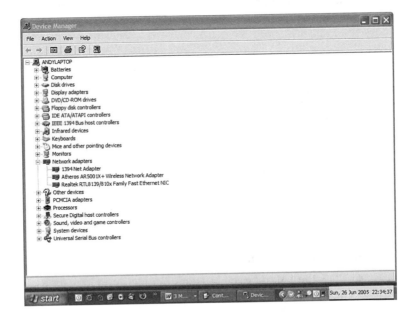

FIGURE 9.3
You can find the make and model of your computer parts in the System applet in Control Panel. The network adapter is shown here on Windows XP.

Video Drivers

If the video adapter, which makes the computer screen display stuff, is on a separate card, you can determine what graphics card you have by opening up the Device Manager (as you did for the video card above) and clicking the + sign beside Display Adapters. You can also do this as follows:

In Windows XP:

1. Right-click on any unused space on the Windows desktop.
2. Choose Properties.
3. Click on the Settings tab.
4. Click the Advanced button.
5. Choose the Adapter tab.

In Windows Vista:

1. Right-click on any unused space on the Windows desktop.
2. Choose Personalize.
3. Click Display Settings.
4. Click the Advanced Settings button.
5. Choose the Adapter tab.

Security Software

Your new system needs an antivirus program, an antispyware program, and a firewall to round out your defenses. If you don't already have these on CD or DVD, make sure you download all of them. If you're looking for free programs, I recommend the following:

- **Antivirus**—Your best bet for a free antivirus program is AVG Free Edition from free.grisoft.com (note that the address is different from www.grisoft.com, where you only get a 30-day trial). Alternatively, look at Avast! from www.avast.com.

- **Antispyware**—When it comes to antispyware programs, no one program does a perfect job. You need two programs to catch all the infections. For XP users, I recommend Windows Defender from www.microsoft.com/defender as your primary program. Spybot Search & Destroy from www.safer-networking.org and Ad-Aware SE from www.lavasoft.com are good second choices. Windows Defender comes built into Windows Vista. Add Spybot for extra security. For people who have older Windows versions, I recommend both Spybot and

9

Ad-Aware. All three programs are free. If you want to use a commercial antispyware product as one of your two antispyware defenses, I recommend Webroot Spy Sweeper (www.webroot.com) or PC Tools Spyware Doctor (www.pctools.com).

tip Before you go any further, save all of the driver files and program files you need for the reinstallation process to a USB key or burn them to a blank CD or DVD. Keep this in a safe place.

■ **Firewall**—I discuss the merits of software versus hardware firewalls in Chapter 4, "Hackers: There's a Man in My Machine." If you do not have a home network router (a device that shares your Internet connection with several computers in your home), I recommend a software firewall that keeps bad people and some viruses and worms on the Internet out of your computer. Alternatively, Windows XP has a basic built-in firewall you can use. The built-in firewall on Windows Vista is even better because it filters two-way traffic. If you'd like to use a free firewall program instead, download Firewall Plus from www.pctools.com or Zone Alarm Free from www.zonealarm.com.

Mozilla Firefox Web Browser

Take a few minutes to download a copy of the most recent version of Mozilla's Firefox web browser. Avoiding Microsoft's Internet Explorer web browser and using Firefox with Windows XP or Vista goes a long way toward reducing your security risks. Download it free from www.getfirefox.com.

On Windows Vista, Microsoft's Internet Explorer 7 is drastically improved over its predecessor. However, my preference is still to use Firefox on Vista.

tip Think of this as removing all the family pictures, personal effects, and Niagara Falls souvenir snow domes from the house before the wreckers come.

Step 2: Back Up!

It's time to back up your important data because you're about to wipe your hard drive clean. Are you rolling your eyes? I hate backups, too. But all you have to do is find your critical data files: that novel you have been working on, your family photos, and maybe your email files. You don't need to back up every file on the sys-

tip For more advanced users: If you have a home network, you can always save your data to another computer on the network. Just be sure you back up across a wired connection because a wireless connection is slower and can sometimes be flaky.

tem, just the data that is irreplaceable, like those cute pictures of your spouse with that enthusiastic herd of goats.

You have to save all of the files you want to keep on external media, such as a USB key, DVD, CD, or external hard drive. It's best to have a CD/DVD burner in your system, or use an external hard drive. Don't do this with floppy disks unless you have a lot of time on your hands, like if you're reading this in prison.

tip In this section and in the next you'll see a reference to [*username*]. This is your User ID that you use to log in to Windows. For example, when Windows boots up I type in Andy to get into Windows. In Vista all your files are stored in `C:\Users\[`*username*`]\` or in my case `C:\Users\Andy\`.

9

If you're organized, you have probably saved the majority of your data in the My Documents folder in XP.

Make sure you save all subfolders in this folder to your external media. If you're disorganized like me (I found my sandals under the vanity in the bathroom the other day), it's probably not quite that simple.

In Vista, My Documents has been renamed simply Documents and is located at `C:\Users\[`*username*`]\Documents`. However, I recommend you save all files and folders in the `C:\Users` folder.

If you have other folders on your hard disk, specifically for your photos, business files, and so forth, make sure you find and back them up, too. If you want to keep your email, don't forget to save your mailboxes, too.

The following is a series of items you should remember to back up and where you can find them on your computer. It's by no means a comprehensive list, but hopefully it will help you gather most of the important data and settings you should back up.

Outlook

Outlook 2002, 2003, and 2007 store all of data and settings, including Outlook email and Contact and Calendar information, in a big fat file called `outlook.pst`. It's usually kept in `C:\Documents and Settings\[`*username*`]\Local Settings\Application Data\Microsoft \Outlook`. When it auto-archives old emails, it stores those in a file called `archive.pst`, so be sure to back up that file, too.

note Learn more about backing up and reformatting your computer and reinstalling Windows Vista in Chapter 5 of my book *Microsoft Windows Vista Help Desk*.

Outlook Express/Windows Mail

If you use Outlook Express as your email program on Windows XP or Windows Mail on Windows Vista, you'll need to back up your emails and content by following the steps in the following sections.

> **tip** When Microsoft released Windows Vista they included a program called Windows Mail that looks very much like Outlook Express, the free email program given away with the Microsoft web browser Internet Explorer. If you're a fan of OE, you'll be happy to know that Windows Mail is actually the next version of Outlook Express, simply renamed.

Outlook Express

1. Select Tools, Options, Maintenance, and click the Store Folder button.

2. In the dialog box, you see the name of the folder that contains your mail files. Look in that folder to locate files named after your mail folders and news groups. They all have a .DBX suffix.

3. Make copies so you have a safe backup of your email.

Windows Mail

In Windows Mail, the backup process has changed substantially. Microsoft has nixed the old .DBX files that stored contained your emails in Outlook Express. Instead they created what is arguably a more complex email archive. However, it has advantages.

Every email now lives inside its own file and not in some big archive file. The advantage is that if an email is corrupted under the new system, it doesn't ruin the other 12,734 emails that you have in a .DBX file. The email files are called .EML files. Newsgroup threads are called .NWS files. And contacts, not surprisingly, are each stored in .CONTACT files.

All files for Windows Mail, including the account settings (.OEACCOUNT files!), are stored as separate files under the Windows Mail folder, usually located at `C:\Users\<username>\AppData\Local\Microsoft\Windows Mail\`.

Once again in the example, *<username>* is the Windows profile name (the name you click on when you log in to Windows Vista) of the user who owns the mail account. So, if I log in to Vista as "Andy," my Windows Mail data is kept in:

`C:\Users\Andy\AppData\Local\Microsoft\Windows Mail\`

> **tip** If you don't see the AppData folder you may need to unhide it as follows: In the Control Panel, click Appearance and Personalization, Folder Options, and click the View tab. Then scroll down to Hidden Files and Folders and click the radio button next to Show Hidden Files and Folders and click OK.

You can locate the actual folder your Windows Mail files are kept in as follows:

1. In Windows Mail, click Tools, Options, Advanced and click on the Maintenance button.

2. A dialog box will open that contains a "Cleaning Up Messages" area. Click the Store Folder button. Another dialog box will open up with the folder path to all your email data.

3. Note that to back up your contacts, be sure to copy this folder separately: `C:\Users\<username>\Contacts`.

Documents Folder

Windows XP creates a folder for you called My Documents where many people keep all their personal files and folders, as well as pictures, videos, and music among other personal files. In Vista this folder is called simply Documents.

If you are in the habit of keeping files here, back up the whole folder. You can find it in XP at `C:\Documents and Settings\<username>\My Documents`.

In Vista, it's located at `C:\Users\<username>\ Documents`.

IE Favorites and Cookies

If you keep favorites in Internet Explorer, you want to save those. Use the Import Export wizard for that and follow these steps:

1. Open IE and click the File menu.

2. Choose Import and Export to manage favorites and cookies files. There's a wizard that will walk you through the mechanism to back up and restore this data.

Firefox Favorites

Firefox bookmarks can be exported to a file as follows:

1. Open Firefox and click the Bookmarks menu and then Organize Bookmarks.

2. The Bookmark Manager opens in a new window. Click the File menu and click Export.

3. Choose a name for the bookmark file, select a location to save it, and then click Save.

Saved Games

If you play games, make sure you create a copy of your saved games. These files are located in a folder where your game is installed. Usually your game shows you the path where the files are saved.

In Vista, note that there is a new folder called *Saved Games* under `C:\Users\<username>\` for data saved by Microsoft Games.

Pictures, Music, and Videos

You might keep your pictures, music, and video files in the My Documents folder in XP or in applicable subfolders (Music, Pictures, Videos) under `C:\Users\<username>\` in Vista or you might keep them elsewhere. Either way, make sure you don't forget to back these up to a safe place.

Microsoft Office 2003 Settings

If you use Microsoft Office 2003, you can save your settings as follows:

1. On the Start menu, click on All Programs, Microsoft Office, Microsoft Office Tools.

2. Choose Microsoft Office 2003 Save My Settings Wizard.

3. When the Setting Wizard box appears, click Next, and then choose Save the Settings from This Machine and click Next again.

4. It then shows you where it will put the OPS file that contains the aggregated settings. You can store this anywhere you like.

Windows Media Player

If you use Windows Media Player 10 and have licenses for music you have bought, you want to back those up. The following sections show you how to do it.

For WMP 10

1. Open Windows Media Player and click the Tools menu. If the menus are hidden, click the down arrow at the top right of the WMP window.

2. Click Tools and then Manage Licenses.

3. Choose a location to put the license file and then click Back Up Now.

You can also see what folders your music and video files are kept in as follows:

1. Click the Tools menu in WMP10 and then Options.

2. On the Library tab, click the Monitor Folders button. The music and video folders WMP10 uses for its library are listed.

If you would also like to back up the WMP playlists you have saved, you'll find them in the C:\Documents and Settings\<user>\My Documents\My Music\Playlists folder. Note that <user> is the name of your Windows login account.

For WMP 11

In Vista, Microsoft, in its infinite wisdom, removed Windows Media Player 11's capability to back up your digital rights management (DRM)-protected music files that you purchased from a music store.

This means if you buy music from a legitimate online source, back up your files, reformat your hard drive, and reinstall Windows, you might lose the capability to play those purchased songs on your freshly installed version of Windows Vista. The caveat here is that some music stores will let you redownload the rights to reinstate your songs so that they are again playable on your system.

Since Microsoft removed the built-in music backup feature in WMP11 on Vista, it recommends using the Vista Backup wizard for music instead. To use that feature follows this procedure:

1. Click the Windows button and type **Backup** in the search box.

2. Click on the Backup and Restore Center when it appears in the Start menu. A dialog box will open.

3. Click the Back Up Files button.

4. Click Continue on the User Account Control warning.

5. Choose a location to back up your files. Do not choose the hard disk where Windows Vista is installed as all the data on that disk will be destroyed when you reformat. Instead choose to burn to a DVD, to a location on your network, or to an alternate hard drive.

6. You may see multiple locations to back up from. Select whichever ones contain the files you want to back up. In most cases, you'll simply want to back up from your C: drive, but select other drives if there are files on those you want to back up too.

7. Click Next. Choose the type of files you want to back up. (Notice that Music is one of the options.)

8. Click Next again. On the final screen you'll be able to set a schedule. Click the button Save Settings and Start Backup.

Other Odds and Ends

In addition to the items previously listed, there are a number of other items that you likely want to save. Of course, no list I can place here could be all-inclusive. Because every user is different, there's just no way to tell you precisely what you should back up on your computer.

My best advice: Think it through carefully and make a list. If you're not sure that you have everything, don't start the reinstall. Talk to your friends or a tech-savvy co-worker. Make sure you cover all the bases because I can tell you, there's no pain quite like the one you feel when you realize that you forgot to back up irreplaceable data. Remember how Charlie Brown would look up to the sky and scream when Lucy pulled the ball away just as he was about to kick it? It's sort of like that, only much, much worse.

Finally, here are a few other things you should nab:

- Print out a copy of your Outlook Contacts. Trust me, if something goes awry and you lose your Outlook data, you will consider a quick scamper into traffic, especially if you live and die by your Contacts list. Think about losing every email address, mailing address, cell phone number, and so on that you own. Printing the Contacts list is just some extra insurance.

- If you make software purchases online and have been emailed registration keys, make sure you print those emails so you can unlock your software after you reinstall it later. This is especially important if you download music from legal online music stores, such as iTunes or MusicMatch, as your digital license for those files is tied directly to your registration key.

- Make sure you write down all of your instant messenger buddy contact info. If you chat online and have buddies with whom you chat frequently, you can save yourself a lot of heartache if you make sure you have this information so that you can restore your buddy list later.

- Make sure you write down settings for connecting to the Internet, including phone numbers if you use dial-up and your computer name if you use broadband (cable, DSL, or satellite). You need this info to reconnect. Make sure you know your email password. This might sound silly, but most of us tell Outlook (or whatever email program we're using) to remember our password so we don't have to enter it every time we check email. It's not unheard-of to forget the password. Before you nuke your drive, make sure you remember the password because you have to enter it later to get your email.

Saving Your Windows Settings

If you've been running Windows for some time, it's likely that you've made a bevy of custom changes (display settings, printer settings, keyboard settings, and so forth). It isn't a huge deal to reset these manually after Windows is reinstalled. That said, Microsoft includes a utility for this. In XP, it's called a File and Settings Transfer Wizard. In Vista, it's called Windows Easy Transfer. The following sections show how it works:

Windows XP

1. Click the Start menu and choose All Programs, Accessories, System Tools, Files and Settings Transfer Wizard.
2. Click Next in the resulting dialog box.
3. Click the Old Computer radio button.
4. Choose how you want to save settings; you have the option of saving them to floppies, CD/DVD, or to another networked drive.
5. If you've done a good job backing up all of your personal data, you can just choose the Settings Only option. If you want to have the wizard back up your documents, too, choose Settings and Data. Just remember that Windows isn't going to be as thorough about saving your data as you can be when doing it by hand. If you save relatively few files and you trust the good folks at Microsoft to know best, go for it.
6. The wizard now gathers your settings and prompts you through the remaining steps, which vary depending on what method for saving the settings you chose in step 4.

Windows Vista

1. On the Start menu, select All Programs, Accessories, System Tools, Windows Easy Transfer (or type **Easy Transfer** in the search box on the Start menu and click it when it appears on the Start menu).

9

2. Click Continue on the User Account Control.

3. Then click Next in the resulting dialog box. Close any programs that are listed.

4. Click Start a New Transfer.

5. Then on the next screen that says "Which computer are you using now?" choose My Old Computer, because your system is not yet cleaned and reformatted.

6. After the system is wiped clean and has a fresh version of Windows Vista on it, you can come back to this point to restore the data and select My New Computer.

7. Next choose how you are going to transfer the files and settings. Your best option is to choose CD, DVD, or other Removable Media here. Choose the other options if you want to transfer data from computer to computer with a special USB cable you've bought or to a computer on your network.

8. Choose where you want to store the backed-up data. I prefer to store it on an external hard drive connected via a USB or FireWire cable because external storage is cheap, easy and safe. So for this example, click External Hard Disk or To a Network Location.

9. Click the Browse button to select the external drive. A Save As dialog box will open. You may need to click on the down arrow next to Browse Folders to expose all the drives and folders on your system so you can select the correct one.

10. After you've selected the drive, click the Save button, and then option- ally you can password-protect the backup. Click Next.

11. On the next screen you get to choose what will be backed up. Be care- ful here. You could choose the option All User Accounts, Files and Settings, or alternately My User Account, File and Settings Only, but both of these can take a long time to complete. When I selected the All User Account option on my machine the backup size was calculated to be 43.5GB.

12. Best option here, unless you have Dalai Lama patience, is to choose Advanced Options. This will allow you to pick and choose which fold- ers, drives, and data get backed up.

13. Click Next. The data transfer to your backup device will then start. To back up an external hard drive, expect this process to take from one to two minutes per gigabyte of data.

FIND MISSING FILES

If you're not sure where all of your photos or documents are or think you're missing some, do a search for them. In XP, click the Start button and select Search. You can search for all Microsoft Word files on the computer by clicking All Files and Folders and typing `*.doc` into the search window.

By changing your view mode to details using the View menu on the top of the search window, you can see all of the files and the locations where they are saved. This tells you which directories you can check for your files. You can open the directories from the search window by right-clicking on one of the files and choosing Open Containing Folder.

In Vista, click the Windows button (formerly known as the Start button) and click Search on the right side of the Start menu. When the search box opens, click the Document item across the top. Next type `*.doc` in the top right Search box. Note that Word 2007 files have use the extension .docx, so to search for those documents, type `*.docx`. The asterisk means any group of characters. You can also use a question mark (?) to denote any single character. So you could also use the filter `*.doc?`, which would find all filenames that ended with .doc or .docx.

Step 3: Pull the Plug on the Network

If you are using a high-speed broadband service to connect to the Internet (from your phone company or cable TV service, for example), it's time to turn it off.

Unplug the network cable from the back of your computer (see Figure 9.4). If you are using an old-school dial-up modem, unplug the telephone cable from your computer.

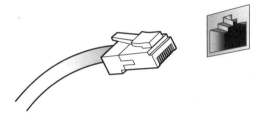

FIGURE 9.4

Disconnect the network cable from your Ethernet adapter on the back of your PC.

If you're connected via your wireless network, turn the Wi-Fi switch to off or disable your wireless connection in Windows.

In XP, click Start, go to Connect To: and Show All Connections, and then right-click on the wireless connection to disable it.

In Vista, click the Windows button, then Connect To, and then find the wireless network in the list and click Disconnect, and on the Are You Sure You Want to...? screen, click Disconnect again. (And try not to swear at it.)

In short, disconnect from the network entirely.

Step 4: Set Your Boot Sequence

One important thing to check here before you call in the wreckers is to see if you can boot the computer from a CD or DVD. When a computer starts up, it reads files on the hard drive and that gets the operating system running in memory. But you can also get it to start up without checking the hard drive by booting from a bootable CD or DVD.

In the case of an operating system installation, this is necessary because you don't want to be using files on the hard drive that you are going to wipe clean. This would be like ordering the demolition of a house while you are still inside making a curry.

That said, here's how to configure your CD or DVD drive to boot the system:

1. Reboot your computer, and look for the option to go into your computer's BIOS. Sometimes it's called Setup. The instructions for which key you should press to enter the BIOS should flash on screen quickly during startup. Often it's the DEL key or a function key such as F2.

2. If you see your computer manufacturer's logo when the computer boots up, you might have to press the Esc key to see information that tells you how to access the BIOS.

3. After you know which key to press, restart the computer, and press the appropriate key. You enter the BIOS settings.

4. You see a raw-looking screen with lots of weird settings. It looks like technology out of a 1980s submarine movie.

5. In the BIOS, use the cursor keys to go over to the BOOT menu. If there isn't one, look for an option in one of the menus that reads Boot Disk Priority, Boot Sequence, or something like that (see Figure 9.5). BIOSes from different manufacturers are slightly different, so it's impossible for me to tell you exactly how yours works.

tip

If you are uncertain which key to tap to access the BIOS, check with your computer maker's support area on its website. Or you could just use this handy-dandy little cheat sheet I've provided here:

BIOS Manufacturer	BIOS Access Key
AMI BIOS	Delete
Phoenix BIOS	F2
Award BIOS	Delete or Ctrl+Alt+Del
MR BIOS	Esc

And if that doesn't help, don't despair. I've also listed brands of computers and their BIOS access keys on my website at http://www.cyberwalker.com/article/28.

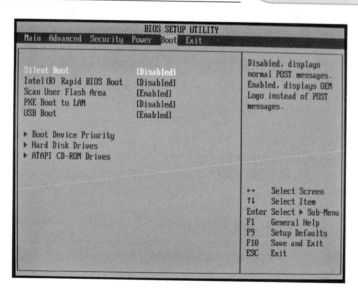

FIGURE 9.5

Locate the BOOT menu in your computer's BIOS, and then locate the menu that allows you to change the order of the bootable drives.

6. In many cases, the computer is set to boot from the floppy first, then the hard drive, and finally the CD. You want to move the CD to the top of the list. Some BIOSes allow you to choose each item separately and set its priority. Others make you move items up and down the list.

7. Read the instructions on the screen, typically found on the right side of the screen. It tells you what keys to use to rearrange the list (see Figure 9.6). Then look for the option to save. It's often F10, but not always. Save and exit.

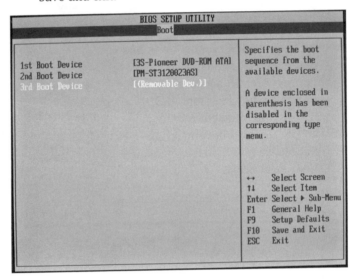

FIGURE 9.6
Change the order of the bootable drives in BIOS so the CD or DVD drive boots first.

8. After the BIOS is configured to boot from your CD or DVD drive, place your Windows XP or Vista install CD or DVD or your system recovery disk into the CD/DVD drive and restart the computer.

Step 5: Start the Installation

Now you're ready to wipe the hard drive clean. This is called *reformatting*. The process destroys all the data on the primary partition on the hard drive. That's what you probably know as your C: drive.

The key tool to use here is one of three items:

- Windows XP CD
- Windows Vista DVD
- System Restore disk for XP or Vista

Each one is very different from the other, so I'm going to split the steps for each situation out into different sets of steps here.

Go to one of the three following instruction sets:

- Step 5a: Using a System Recovery CD/DVD. This section starts immediately after this one.
- Step 5b: Using a Windows XP CD. This section starts on **p. 296**.
- Step 5c: Using a Windows Vista DVD. This section starts on **p. 304**.

caution Be extra careful when tinkering with your system's BIOS! If you think Windows can be ornery, you haven't seen anything yet. Because the BIOS is the heart of your computer, it's a very powerful and dangerous item. Don't toggle options on and off unless you know what they do, and for the sake of all that's good and wholesome in the world, don't save your changes unless you're absolutely certain you know what you're doing. Changing the boot order sequence is a simple task, but toying with some of the other settings is kind of like opening the hood of your car and randomly heaving bits in the lake. It can be fun at the time, but you'll find yourself helpless and stranded later.

Step 5a: Using a System Recovery CD/DVD

Place the System Recovery CD in your CD/DVD drive and then restart the system allow the system to boot from it.

When the system restarts, files are read from the disc, the system boots, and the reinstall process will start.

caution Using a copy of a Windows XP installation CD or a Windows Vista DVD or using a recovery disk from a different brand of computer does not work. You either get an error or the system ignores the CD/DVD and tries to go to the hard drive to boot up.

Follow the instructions as they appear on your screen. This process is different for each brand of computer because it's customized by the computer maker. It should, nevertheless, be fairly straightforward and mostly automated, prompting you for input when needed.

This will destroy all the data on your C: drive, so be sure that you have backed up all the data and have all the program installation disks handy (or the ability to download them again) so that you can reinstall when Windows is restored. When you are finished, your system will be in the exact state you got it from the manufacturer, with all Windows files and drivers already in place as well as any programs the manufacturer may have included with your system.

If everything is working, skip ahead to "Step 7: Install Protection Against Malware," on **p. 317**.

Step 5b: Using a Windows XP CD

If you're using a Windows XP CD, put it in your CD/DVD drive and restart the computer.

When the computer restarts, it'll boot from the CD (assuming you have followed the advice in Step 4 about setting up your BIOS to boot from the CD/DVD drive).

You will be prompted to Press Any Key to Boot from CD. Note that there is no Any key. Press whichever key you fancy. However, the Enter key will do as well as the [key.

You'll see a blue screen, but don't panic. This isn't the typical Windows blue screen of death (as geeks are fond of calling it) that you see when the computer crashes. It's the Windows Setup screen. You won't see much for a while—just a blue screen with a white bar at the bottom. The white bar lists all of the things that the Windows Setup process is loading.

When these are all loaded, you see a screen that says Welcome to Setup near the top (see Figure 9.7). Just below it is an instruction that says To Set Up Windows XP Now, press Enter. Ignore the items below this instruction and press Enter. The bottom of the screen reads Please Wait. So wait. Maybe go floss your teeth because you can never floss enough.

Eventually the End User Licensing Agreement (EULA) appears on your screen. This is where you click away all your rights. A lawyer would tell you that at this point you should read really carefully because not only is it a legal contract between you and Microsoft, but it's also really interesting. I'll leave it up to you. I hold my nose and press F8.

The setup program then searches for previously installed copies of Windows. A screen appears (see Figure 9.8) offering to repair previously installed copies of Windows. Ignore this offer and press the Esc key to continue installing a fresh copy of Windows XP.

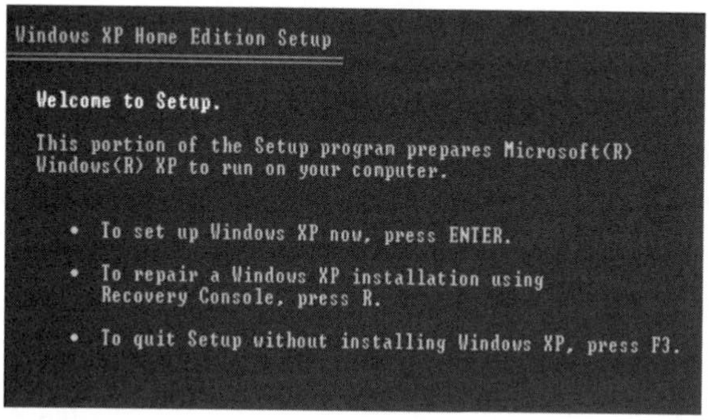

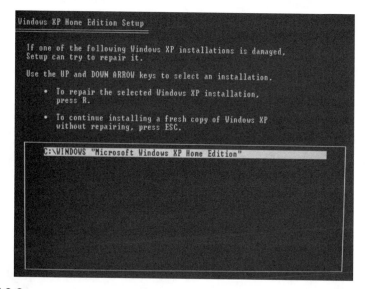

FIGURE 9.7

When you first boot from the Windows XP CD, you see a blue setup screen like this one.

FIGURE 9.8

Ignore the very nice offer to repair a previously installed copy of Windows XP.

Destroy the Partition

The next screen shows you the partitions on your computer (see Figure 9.9). A hard drive can be subdivided into sections called *partitions*. Each of these partitions is assigned a drive letter. So if your computer had a hard drive that was divided into three partitions and your system had a CD-ROM drive, it would look like this:

- **C: drive**—Your primary partition where Windows is installed
- **D: drive**—Your CD-ROM drive
- **E: drive**—Your second hard drive partition
- **F: drive**—Your third hard drive partition

Most hard drives only have one partition, and it is listed on this screen.

If you have more than one partition, your current Windows installation is generally the first one. Drive letters are listed on this screen, too. You generally want to choose the C: drive.

note Think of partitions as individual storage bins. Hard drives can be a single bin or can contain multiple bins. Some users divide their drives into several partitions for storing different kinds of data (operating system on one partition, data files on another). Some users create more than one partition because they're really big geeks who want to run Windows XP on one partition and say, Linux, on another partition. In the end, just be sure that you install your new version of Windows in the correct partition and all will be right with the world.

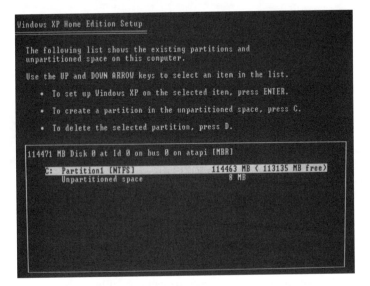

FIGURE 9.9

The installation screen lists the partitions on your hard drive.

Because you want to do a thorough job of this reinstallation, first you want to delete the selected partition. Press the D key. You see a confirmation screen. This might make you a little nauseated. I poise my finger over the Enter key at this point and close my eyes tightly. It helps.

So press Enter.

Just for good measure, the screen asks you if you're sure one more time. Don't chicken out. Unless you have good reason, go ahead and delete the partition. Press L (see Figure 9.10).

> **caution** Have you backed up your data? This would be a good point to press F3 and quit the installation process if you have forgotten to back up something important. In computer terms, this is where the dry cleaner says, "Are you sure you want to clean this dress, Miss Lewinsky?" After this point, there's no turning back.

Get it? D-Enter-L? D-E-L? Yes, even Microsoft has a sense of humor.

So do it. This bit is where you push the big red button that drops the big demolition ball into the house. At this point, all the data on the C: drive is gone. Poof! Just for fun, pretend to cough and wave away the dust. Mime can be a fun part of Windows demolition.

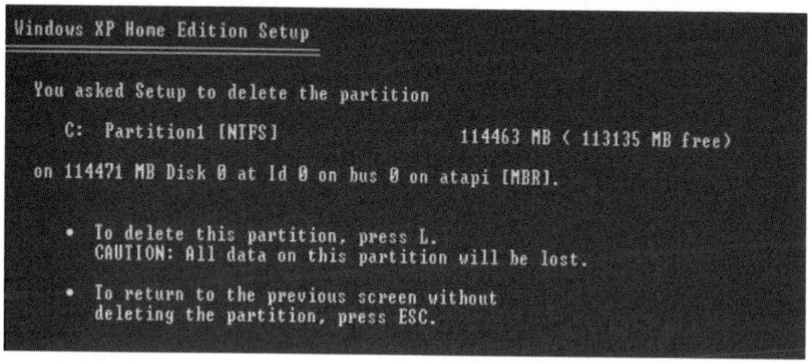

```
Windows XP Home Edition Setup

  You asked Setup to delete the partition

    C: Partition1 [NTFS]                    114463 MB ( 113135 MB free)

  on 114471 MB Disk 0 at Id 0 on bus 0 on atapi [MBR].

      •  To delete this partition, press L.
         CAUTION: All data on this partition will be lost.

      •  To return to the previous screen without
         deleting the partition, press ESC.
```

FIGURE 9.10

Press D, press Enter, and then on the next screen press L. You'll DELete the partition.

The process now takes you back to a previous screen showing the partitions, but the partition that was previously listed now appears as unpartitioned space. This is like the smoking hole where the house used to be.

If you want to reinstall Windows onto a single big partition, select Unpartitioned Space and press Enter. You can think of this as space to put a foundation for your house. If you subdivided your land into several partitions, you'd have lots to build several smaller houses.

9

If you want to create smaller partitions, choose C, and tell the installer program how big a partition you want (in megabytes). Don't make these partitions too small—make sure they are at least 10GB. Repeat until all your unpartitioned space is used up.

If you're uncertain, you can delete and add partitions as many times as you want. By the way, 8MB are always listed as unpartitioned. Ignore this, like you would a cat licking your hair from the back of the couch.

After you are done divvying up the hard drive, select the first partition and press Enter. The next screen tells you to format the drive using NTFS (see Figure 9.11).

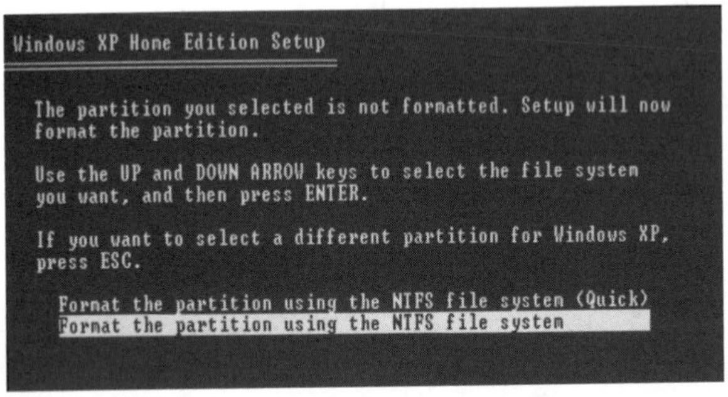

note Some people subdivide their hard drives into partitions because they want to install various operating systems. Others do it because they like to keep one partition for Windows and programs and another for data.

tip Because of a weird piece of computer math, there are actually 1024MB in 1GB. So if you make your partition 10GB, be sure to use 10240MB as your partition size.

```
Windows XP Home Edition Setup

    The partition you selected is not formatted. Setup will now
    format the partition.

    Use the UP and DOWN ARROW keys to select the file system
    you want, and then press ENTER.

    If you want to select a different partition for Windows XP,
    press ESC.

        Format the partition using the NTFS file system (Quick)
        Format the partition using the NTFS file system
```

FIGURE 9.11

Choose to format using the NTFS file system, but don't cut corners by using the quick mode.

You have a quick option and a regular option. You're welcome to use the quick format option and save some time, but I like to do it right and choose the regular option. It'll take a bit longer, but it erases the drive. Go find something to do while the hard drive is formatting (see Figure 9.12). I bet there are dishes in the sink. Every time I look at the sink, I think, "I wish I had time to clean those up." This would be that time.

note NTFS is the file system Windows XP likes to use. A file system is a way of organizing data on a hard drive. It stands for NT File System. NT is an old business version of Windows. If you think of a dozen eggs as data, the egg carton would be the file system.

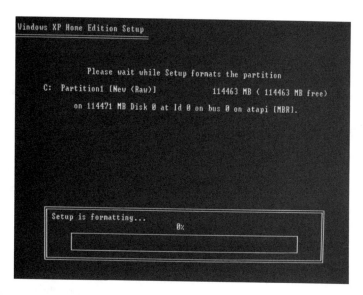

9

FIGURE 9.12

The formatting process takes a while, but shows its progress along the way. Note that staring at it or yelling won't make it go any faster.

The formatting process takes a while, but it is worth it. Do not turn the computer off during the process, no matter what, because half-formatting a drive and stopping it in the process is like half-pooper-scooping the lawn. It still can't be used for sunbathing.

caution While your drive is formatting and you're off bathing the cat, patrolling the lawn for dog bombs, or moussing your pompadour, you should be very, very careful to not let anyone—especially children—in the room with your computer. A sudden power loss during drive formatting leaves your drive in an ugly, unrecoverable state. And we all know how much children enjoy power buttons. In fact, years ago a cover for power buttons called a Molly Guard was invented to protect power switches from little hands after the daughter (Molly) of a programmer shut down a few machines. So close and lock your office door, or if your computer is in the living area of the home, lock the children outside with a tent and a packed lunch. If you have pets, particularly cats who like to walk on the keyboard or lounge near your power strip, you're just asking for trouble. I recommend temporary detention of any furry creatures in another part of the house.

When the formatting process is complete, your computer does a bit more work on the drive, and then automatically restarts. Do not press any keys during the reboot process no matter how tempting it is.

> **caution** If you realize at this point that there's data you forgot to back up, I'm sorry to say, it's too late. Like a toilet paper tube in a hamster cage, that data is munched.

A Fresh Copy of Windows XP

The good news at this point is that the hard part is done. Now you get to build your new house. Yep, it's time to install a fresh, squeaky clean version of Windows. Hooray! This is a good time to dance around your office chair and make victorious chicken noises.

> **note** If you have a mouse plugged into the system, it should be working again at this point. If for some reason it isn't, look at the onscreen options you need to change. Each one has an underlined letter in the selection. You can choose the option by pressing the Alt key and the designated underlined letter.

The beginning of the Windows installation is largely automatic. Sit back and allow the computer to gather information about your system, set things up, and start installing components. You see a status bar at the bottom right reading Setup Will Complete in Approximately xxx Minutes. Keep an eye on this. If it freezes for too long, you might have to press the reset button and start this portion again, but in general, let the reinstall process do its thing.

The first time you need to do anything is when the setup program asks you which language and regional settings you'll be using on the computer. The standard choice should be U.S.-based English. If you need to change this, click Customize. If you need to add other input options, click Details. Unless you have any special language requirements, you can just click the Next button.

The next screen asks you to personalize your software with a name and organization. Put in something appropriate and click Next.

Input the License Key and Finish Up

The next screen asks you for your installation key, sometimes called a *product key*. You'll find this on back of your Windows XP CD sleeve or on a sticker found on your computer case (in some instances). Type the installation key in and click Next. The key is not case-sensitive, but it must otherwise be typed exactly as it appears.

USING AN UPGRADE VERSION OF WINDOWS XP

If you are using a version of Windows XP marked Upgrade to reinstall your system, you should have a copy of an older version of Windows on CD on hand. At some point during the installation, the Windows installer asks you to insert the old Windows CD into your computer to validate that you are eligible to use the upgrade. If you don't have this, you won't be able to continue the installation.

You are then asked to choose a name for your computer. By default, a seemingly random near-gibberish name already appears in the box. It's better to choose a name that you will remember. If you connect your computer to a home network, this name is used to identify the computer. You can change this later, by the way. So if you name your computer Liza-Minnelli and later change your mind, it's no big deal.

One thing you might keep in mind here is that some cable Internet companies use your computer name to validate your Internet access. So if you have a cable Internet connection and you do not use a home Internet router, you should name your computer in this process the same name as you had when you first set it up so you don't bung up the Internet reconnection process.

If you can't remember or aren't sure of your computer name, name it whatever you want and if you have trouble connecting to the Internet later, call your Internet service to resolve this issue.

When you have chosen a name, click Next.

Now make sure your date and time settings are correct. Then click Next. The install process goes into automatic mode again for a few minutes as it sets up networking.

The next screen asks you if you want to use typical or custom settings for your networking setup. Choose Typical install and click Next. The setup process configures your network, registers components, and saves your settings.

When this process is complete, your computer restarts. Again, don't press any keys during the reboot process. When it reboots, you see a message noting that Windows is about to automatically adjust your screen resolution. Click OK. Your desktop is automatically resized. If you can see the dialog box at the top, click OK. If not, don't worry. Just wait. It will fix itself. You can readjust these display settings later.

The Windows XP installation process is now complete. Have a sandwich, you deserve it. I like peanut butter and jelly.

9

ACTIVATE LIKE YOU HAVE NEVER ACTIVATED BEFORE

Microsoft has gotten clever with its antipiracy measures. The company introduced a new scheme to stop you from buying a copy of its software and installing it on all the computers within a half-mile radius of your home, which is what we all used to do.

Now when you install Windows XP, Microsoft makes you activate your copy within 30 days of installation or it stops working. Office XP, Office 2003, and Office 2007 also require activation. They get gimped (you can't save or change a document) after 50 launches without activation. Activation works like this: The system takes an inventory of all the components in the computer and generates a numeric identifier that is like a digital thumbprint. It sends the thumbprint to a Microsoft server on the Internet and this is paired with the license you typed in from the back of the XP CD.

When you install the same CD on another machine, Microsoft checks the new machine's thumbprint against its database and if it the thumbprint doesn't match, the activation is rejected and the software stops working or gets gimped after the grace period.

There's a certain amount of tolerance in the system. You can activate two copies before the axe falls. And if you change a couple of parts in your computer, which changes that thumbprint, the activation process doesn't choke. But if you swap out your motherboard, add new RAM, and add a new video card, you might have a problem. If this is the case, it can be rectified with a call to Microsoft.

Step 5c: Using a Windows Vista DVD

In this section, I'm going to take you through the destruction of Windows Vista partition and the installation of a fresh copy of Windows Vista.

You have a choice in your approach here:

- ■ **Option 1**—Insert the install disc and start the reinstall and reformat from the Windows desktop (see Figure 9.13).
- ■ **Option 2**—Boot from the Vista install disc, and then reformat and reinstall without booting into your existing Windows installation.

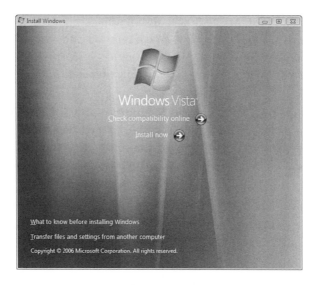

FIGURE 9.13

You can reinstall Vista from your DVD directly from desktop (shown) or by booting from the DVD directly.

The pros and cons to both options are shown in Table 9.1.

Table 9.1   Booting from Vista DVD vs. Installing from Desktop

Type of Reinstall	Pros	Cons
Booting from Vista DVD	Destroys partitions completely. You can create and size partitions.	Requires BIOS edit to make optical drive bootable.
Installing Vista from desktop	No messing with the BIOS. Preserves the previous installation of Windows in a folder called Windows.old. You can update Vista installation files via the Web before Vista installation.	Not all data is wiped. You cannot destroy partition(s).

I am going to show you how to install using both methods; however, the desktop process is the easiest way to do a reinstall and reformat. If you're with me on that, skip over to "Install Vista from the Desktop," on **p. 306**, which shows you how to boot from the DVD after making edits in the BIOS to your startup routine.

If you'd like to install Vista by booting from the CD/DVD drive, you'll first need to make an edit to a BIOS setting so that the optical drive is bootable, as I mentioned earlier in this chapter. If you've done that, let's proceed. If not, go back and set that up. Instructions can be found later in this chapter in "Set Your Boot Sequence."

1. Pop the Windows Vista disc is into your DVD drive. Restart the system.

2. The disc will boot your system into the reformat and reinstall routine, after a long stall where you look at a grainy screen that looks like blue underwater curtains.

3. The first screen will ask for your installation language, time and currency format, and keyboard input method. The defaults are fine unless you specifically want other settings. Click Next, then Install Now.

4. Now skip ahead to "Installing a Fresh Copy of Windows Vista," later in this chapter.

Install Vista from the Desktop

If you've opted to skip the booting from the Vista install disk and want the kinder gentler routine whereby you install from the desktop, here's what you need to know:

1. From the Windows Vista Desktop, pop the DVD in your optical drive. It should auto-start. Or it may throw open a box that asks you to Run Setup. If so, choose that option. If it doesn't, click the Windows button, and then click computer and double-click your DVD drive. The User Account Control screen will kick in here, so click Allow. The Setup file will run and get the process going.

> **caution** If you have multiple optical drives, make sure the Vista DVD is in the right one when you boot. If the DVD isn't read and the system boots into Windows via the hard drive instead, it could be a sign of a damaged Vista install disc. If you are using a backup copy that you burned yourself, make sure the drive is compatible with the DVD media. Sometimes copies don't work—it's best to use the original install DVD.

2. When the pretty Vista installation Windows opens up, click Install Now.

3. If your Internet connection is working, choose "Go online to get the latest updates for installation (recommended)" In the next window. The Vista installer will search online for updates and download them for the installation. It will also grab drivers and any OS fixes, which will save you from grabbing them later.

4. When it's done, follow the instructions in the next section.

Installing a Fresh Copy of Windows Vista

This is where the boot-via-DVD routine and the desktop installation routine previously outlined converge.

Let's proceed:

1. You'll see a screen that prompts you to enter your product key. This can be found on a label on the packaging or the sleeve that the Windows Vista disc came in.

2. You may also want to choose Automatically Activate Windows When I'm Online. The software will need to verify that your key is legitimate using the activation wizard within 30 days of installation.

3. Next is the license agreement. Some lawyer at Microsoft wrote this. Most people don't read it, but I'll leave that up to you. Because it's a contract between you and Microsoft, you should eyeball it carefully.

4. If you accept the agreement, click the "I accept..." box, and then click Next.

5. The next screen gives you the options Upgrade or Custom. Choose Custom because we want to wipe the hard drive clean.

> **tip**
> If you don't have your Vista product key, you can abort the reinstall at this point and go back and retrieve the Vista product key from your previous Windows installation. Simply take the DVD out and reboot the system and go back into Windows Vista as normal. Then fetch a free program called ProduKey. Download it for free from http://www.nirsoft.net/utils/product_cd_key_viewer.html, and then use it to recover your product key and start the whole reinstall process again.

MICROSOFT KNOWS IF YOU'RE NAUGHTY OR NICE

Keep in mind that you can only legally use a product key on one computer, although there is leeway in the software for use on two machines. If your machine rejects it, someone else might have used the key on their computer. Did you "loan" out your software? Did your kids? Does your housekeeper do Windows?

"Borrowing" product keys from other discs won't necessarily work, and using a product key on a retail installation disc from a disc that came with your computer (called an OEM or Original Equipment Manufacturer version) won't work either.

If that's not the case, you can call Microsoft and plead your case. Microsoft's contact page with local customer service phone numbers for all countries around the world can be found here: http://www.microsoft.com/worldwide/

Sometimes, if it's a reasonable request, and there's no evidence of piracy, Microsoft will reset the key so you can use it for your reinstall.

6. On the next screen, you'll see a choice of drive locations where a fresh copy of Windows can be installed (see Figure 9.14). Your current installation of Windows Vista will likely be on the largest disk, marked Disk 0.

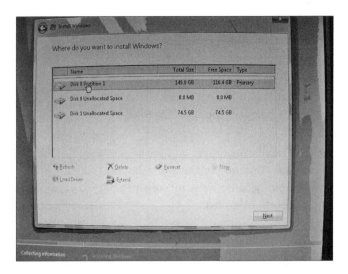

FIGURE 9.14

A list of storage locations where Vista can be potentially installed will appear. Usually you'll want to install it to Disk 0 on Partition 1.

7. If there are multiple disks listed—for example, Disk 0, Disk 1, and Disk 2—each one of those is a unique physical drive.

8. If each disk has partitions like this:

```
Disk 0 Partition 1 (C:)
Disk 0 Partition 2 (E:)
Disk 0 Partition 3 (F:)
```

That means the disk has been carved up as partitions, meaning that each partition appears to Windows as drive C:, E:, and F: (drive D: is not shown because it is usually your CD or DVD drive). If your manufacturer has put restore information on a partition on your hard drive, you might see a small partition, or the partition may be numbered starting at 2, as in the following:

```
Disk 0 Partition 2 (C:)
Disk 0 Partition 3 (E:)
```

This could indicate that Partition 1 is hidden from view on purpose by your manufacturer so that you don't overwrite the restoration data.

Your boot partition, where you will put Vista, should be the lower-numbered partition on Disk 0 that has the largest space.

HOW TO CREATE MULTIPLE PARTITIONS

If you booted from the Vista DVD, you'll have an option here to delete a partition and create one or more new ones. If you want to ensure that any data on the previous installation is annihilated like chocolate in a sorority house, choose the partition and click Delete.

When it's gone, the partition will show the space as "Unallocated." You will need to create a new partition by selecting the partition that has unallocated space, clicking New, and then specifying the size of the new partition in the Size box provided.

If you want two or more partitions on the disk, size it smaller than its maximum space and create a second with the remaining unallocated space. One partition could be used as your C: drive to house Windows, and a second one could be used for data (and assigned another drive letter, such as D: or E:).

9. When you select the partition and click Next, a message might warn you that a copy of Windows already exists on the partition. If it does,

this is a good sign. It means you are about to overwrite your existing copy of Windows. My preference, though, is to delete the partition to destroy all the previous data and then create a fresh blank partition in its place for the new installation of Vista. This will only be possible if you booted from the DVD. The desktop reinstall procedure does not offer this option.

10. After you have either chosen a partition or deleted and re-created one, click Next. If you have chosen to overwrite the partition, you will see a warning message that says, "The partition you selected contains a previous Windows installation" (see Figure 9.15).

note Unless you delete the Windows partition first and create a new one, the Vista installation process will save your previous Windows installation in a folder called Windows.old.

caution If you have any external hard drives, you might want to unplug them for this process and click the Refresh command so that only the hard drives inside the system show up.

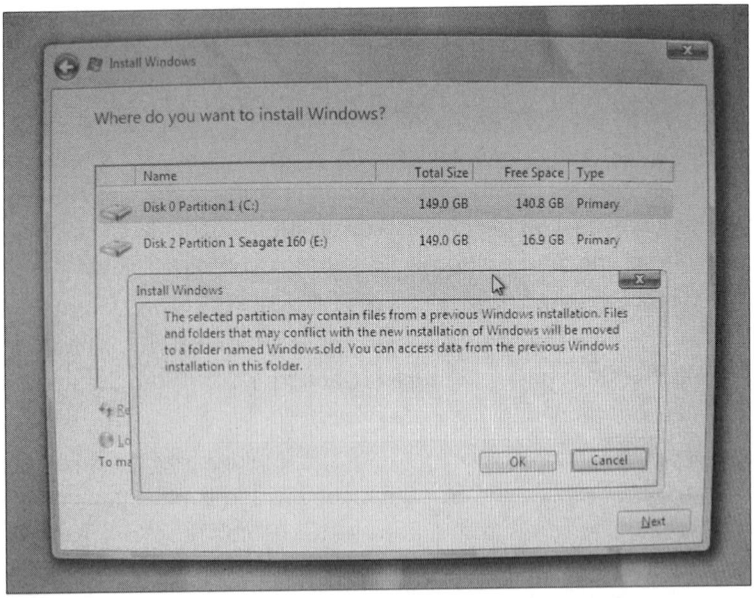

FIGURE 9.15
Vista detects the old Windows installation and warns you that it will wipe the partition but keep the old stuff just in case.

11. It will also note that, if you are upgrading from XP to Vista, your folders called Windows, Documents and Settings, and Program Files will be moved into a folder called Windows.old. Click OK to confirm. The install DVD will then wipe the partition clean and install a fresh copy of Vista while preserving the Windows.old file.

> **caution** Whatever you do, don't reboot the system yourself during this process; otherwise, you could corrupt the installation. In that event, you'll have to boot from the Vista installation disc and start the whole thing again.

12. During this process, the screen will show a list of the tasks it is doing. Then the system will reboot a couple more times until you get an almost-finished Vista installation.

13. While the machine does this work, you can walk away from it and let it do its business. It's a good time to surface and let the family or room-mate know you're OK. If the kids are around, you have enough time to de-lint them; however, remind your spouse that there is not enough time to mow the lawn or paint the garage door. Plan on a 15- to 30-minute break.

14. You're on the final leg of the process when you get a screen that asks you to choose the country that you live in and a keyboard layout (if you boot from the DVD, you will have done this off the top). Make your choices and click Next.

Finish the Vista Install

You're almost done. Only a few more tasks before you get your system up and running and can boot to your desktop back and then start the task of restoring all your data.

Create an Admin Account

Next up, you'll be asked to enter a user-name and choose an optional password. This will be the administrator account you'll use for all system-level changes, fixes, and updates.

Microsoft recommends against making this your primary login. Instead, create a standard user account for day-to-day use and

> **tip** If you're wondering if you need a password on your administrator account, here's a tip. If you live alone and rarely let your computer come into contact with other humans, don't bother. Otherwise, make sure you do, especially if you have naughty children or super-naturally smart pets.

reserve the administrator account for maintenance, backups, and other system administration duties. It's a good idea because if you come into contact with a nasty piece of malware as a limited user, it won't get very far.

> **note** This username you create will also be the name of your user folder under `C:\Users`.

That said, it is not very practical if you're always mucking around in the system as an administrator. But if you don't twiddle with the system every day, it might be a strategy you want to use. Frankly, though, I think it's a bit cumbersome and I don't practice it myself.

Either way, go ahead and create an admin account here and choose one of the offensively happy icons Microsoft suggests you use to distinguish the account (see Figure 9.16). The good news is you can change it later to whatever you like—maybe a picture of a slice of cheddar or a smiling chicken.

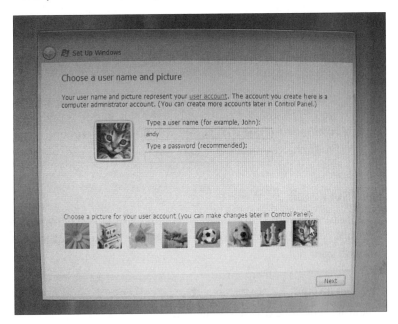

FIGURE 9.16

Choose a username and an icon. Later you can customize it. For now, match your mood and be the constipated kitten.

Name Your Computer

On the screen that follows, you'll be asked to name your computer. Choose a name without spaces or these special characters:

`" / \ [ ] : ; ¦ < > + = , ? "`

And keep it short, under 15 characters. This name will be used to identify your computer on your home network, if you have one. Amusing or clever computer names can be fun.

I knew an admin who called his computers John, Paul, George, and Ringo.

You could also try Batiste, Newbold, Eaton, and Zinni.

Recognize the reference? They're the names of the retired generals who called for Donald Rumsfeld's ouster in mid-2006.

Who knew that home IT could be so politically savvy?

If you're more practical, something like AndyDell3000 might be useful—it identifies my Dell Dimension 3000 on my network. However, this kind of naming scheme gives away personal information to anyone who tunes into your wireless network (if you don't turn on wireless security settings) because computer names are browseable—that, plus there's no comedy in it.

Turn on Security

On the next screen, Vista asks how it should protect your system. This is a vast improvement over the original Windows XP, which has no security functions during a reinstall. Microsoft gives you three options in security setup, as described next.

Use Recommended Settings

Choose this option, and you'll turn on the following features:

- **Windows automatic updating**—Fixes and highly recommended updates will be auto-downloaded to your system and installed.

- **Enhanced spyware protection**—The built-in antispyware program called Windows Defender will be enabled and will automatically remove severe and high-alert spyware and adware infections that are known to compromise your security or damage your system.

- **Automatic driver updates**—Vista automatically checks the Internet for a new driver when a new piece of hardware is installed.

Unless you have a good solid reason not to, I'd urge you to choose Use Recommended Settings.

Install Important Updates Only

This option turns on Microsoft Updates so you get the latest fixes and high-priority updates automatically. It doesn't turn on antispyware mechanisms or enable automatic Windows problem reporting.

Ask Me Later

This procrastinator setting is not recommended, unless you're determined to spend time configuring security to your liking later. Even if this is the case, I'd turn on everything now and turn off stuff later when you go to customize your security settings manually.

Finish Up

Finally, set the system time and date and your time zone. And that's it. After a bit more processing, Windows Vista will start up all squeaky clean. The work is still not done, however. There is a lot of post-installation work still ahead that you need to complete. That's what I'll cover next.

Step 6: Reinstall Your Drivers

If you've reinstalled Windows XP or Vista from a recovery CD or DVD, you can generally skip this step altogether, as all of the drivers for your system are loaded at the same time Windows is reinstalled from this disc. You should only need to reinstall drivers for hardware you installed yourself, as an add-on to your system.

Windows XP and Vista both do a nice job of allowing your system to work right after an installation, by using generic hardware drivers. You might be able to use the generic drivers (the ones that come with Windows) without ever noticing anything is wrong, but it's always best to install the drivers designed specifically for your computer's components.

You can find a list of all of the drivers that need to be updated before you finish this whole process.

Windows XP

1. Click the Start button.
2. Move your cursor over to the My Computer icon and right-click on it.
3. Choose Properties.
4. Select the Hardware tab and click on Device Manager.

Windows Vista

1. Click the Windows button.

2. Move your cursor over to the Computer icon and right-click on it.

3. Choose Properties.

4. Click Device Manager in the left margin.

5. Click Continue on the User Account Control screen. The Device Manager window will open.

In the Device Manager, you will see a list of hardware installed inside or connected to your computer.

In most cases, all parts and peripherals should be working normally. Items that aren't yet working appear with a yellow question mark in XP beside them. In Vista you'll see a yellow triangle containing an exclamation mark next to devices that are not working properly.

Often you'll see these under the Other Devices category (see Figure 9.17).

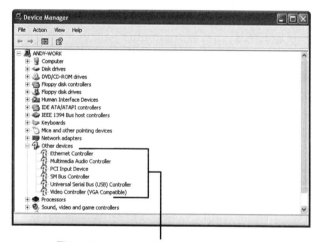

These devices need properly installed drivers

FIGURE 9.17

Drivers not installed properly are marked with yellow question marks in the Device Manager in XP.

Install drivers for all of these, but let's get to the critical ones first.

Begin by looking for the motherboard drivers in the list. If you have an installation CD for your motherboard, insert it into your CD/DVD drive and run the installation program. If not, pull out your CD with the previously downloaded drivers, and start installing.

Install the system/chipset drivers first. These are the foundation for your system. Then install the Ethernet drivers for your network adapter, if it is on the motherboard.

caution Be aware that some motherboard manufacturers make variations of their motherboards with different components on them. So, don't just install everything that's on the installer CD. Some drivers are not applicable. Be selective.

If your video or audio adapters are on the motherboard (meaning you don't have separate audio and video cards), install drivers for them, too. You should also install drivers for your USB controllers, if these are available. In fact, if you have the motherboard installer CD, you can safely install all of the drivers for components that appear on your motherboard at this point.

If your network adapter isn't on the motherboard but is on a separate card, reinstall the drivers for it now. Don't plug the network cable in just yet. Video and sound card drivers can be installed as well, if you have them. But because they're not essential to the rest of the process, you can always fix these later, after your system is fully up and running again.

Use System Restore Before Installing Drivers

Drivers can be sticky little critters. Sometimes they just don't work, so keep these troubleshooting tips handy when installing a new driver.

As a precaution, you might want to set a System Restore point before you install a new driver. This feature was first included in Windows Me and is available in XP and Vista. It allows you to roll the system back in time to the state it was in before something went wrong.

Windows XP

1. Click Start, All Programs, Accessories, and finally System Tools.

2. Click System Restore to start it and choose Create a Restore Point and name it something such as Installation of Video Driver, and then click Create.

3. If you install the driver and it bungs the system, you can go back to System Restore, choose the restore point you created, and roll the system back to the way it was before everything exploded.

Windows Vista

1. Click the Windows button and type **system** in the Search box.

2. Click System when it appears in the Start menu above the search box.

3. Click System Protection on the left side of the System Properties box when it appears.

4. Click Continue on the User Account Control.

5. Click the Create button

6. In the dialog box that opens, type in a name for your restore point. Click the Create button.

7. The system will create a restore point with that name.

> **note** To revert the system to that restore point, use the System Restore program. Access it by typing **System Restore** in the Start menu's search bar.

Step 7: Install Protection Against Malware

If you've already read the rest of this book, you know what that viruses and spyware are digitally toxic to your computer. What you might not know is that an unprotected XP computer can be infected within minutes of being connected to the Internet after a Windows reinstallation. Vista is less vulnerable thanks to the User Account Control, but it still needs to be protected. So you need to have some security software in place before you reconnect either operating system.

INFECTED IN SECONDS

My colleague, Sean Carruthers, who has good hair and a better music collection, maintains his mom's computer. One day he reinstalled Windows XP on her system and hooked it up to her high-speed Internet connection. The machine was attacked by eight worms within three minutes of being connected. The computer got so hamstered up in those first few minutes that he had to yank the Internet connection, reformat the drive, and start again, this time installing McAfee's antivirus product before connecting the network cable again.

So before you go any further, you should install antivirus software, a firewall, and antispyware software on your Windows XP or Vista system as follows.

Install an Antivirus Program

If you already have an antivirus program, install it as you did on your previous Windows installation and be sure to update its virus signatures. These are updates from the software publisher that recognize viruses that are inbound to your computer and nab them.

If you don't have an antivirus program, install AVG Free Edition. It's available free from http://free.grisoft.com (see Figure 9.18). It updates its virus signatures once a day and scans inbound email as well. It also works on both XP and Vista.

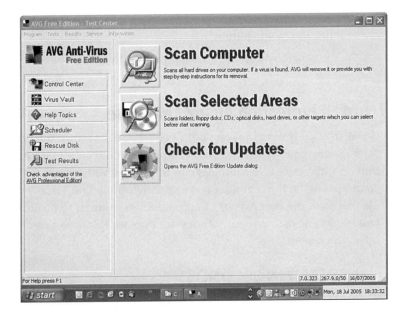

FIGURE 9.18

AVG Free Edition is a very good antivirus program that can be used free of charge by individuals.

To learn more about antivirus software, see Chapter 1, "Viruses: Attack of the Malicious Programs."

Install an Antispyware Program

Spyware and its nasty sister adware are worse than the virus problem because

> **tip** Some antivirus programs offer to run a virus scan before they install. In general you can skip this during a Windows reinstallation process, unless you're installing from a questionable copy of the Windows CD/DVD. If you're installing from a legitimate CD/DVD, there's no need to scan at this point.

there are many more types and variations of spyware and adware than there are viruses. Spyware sneaks onto your computer and records and sometimes steals information about you. Adware watches your computer behavior and then shows you ads.

The best defense in my experience is to install at least two antispyware programs because one won't catch all of it.

Windows Defender is a free antispyware product that comes preinstalled on Windows Vista. Windows XP users can also get it for free by downloading it from www.microsoft.com/defender/.

> **tip** Here's a bonus antispyware tip. While using two or three free antispyware products together is a good low-cost defense, you can do equally well with two if you spend a bit of money. Buy one reputable commercial antispyware product and a freebie product together. Two commercial products that get consistently high marks are PC Tools Spyware Doctor and Webroot Spy Sweeper. I use both of these (on different machines) in concert with Spybot and Windows Defender.

There are two other free antispyware product that, if installed, will help augment spyware defense on your XP or Vista system. They include:

- Spybot Search & Destroy from www.safer-networking.net
- Ad-Aware SE from www.lavasoft.com

If you run an older copy of Windows, install both of the listed programs. Windows Defender won't run on older versions of Windows.

To learn more about antispyware software, see Chapter 2, "Spyware: Overrun by Advertisers, Hijackers, and Opportunists."

Install a Firewall

You should also use a firewall, a program that protects your computer from intruders on the Internet from accessing your computer. Think of it as a large cinderblock wall between your computer and the outside world, with a beefy security guard that raises the gate only when you invite someone in. Firewalls only let data in if you initiate contact with the data source first, such as when you fetch your email or a web page, for example. A firewall also stops worms, which are network-traveling viruses that infect exposed computers.

You have several choices when it comes to a firewall. I talk about these at length in Chapter 4. However, here's a quick summary.

   Hardware Firewall: If you have a home network where you share your broadband Internet connection from the phone or cable company, you probably have a home network router. This little junction box has a built-in mechanism called Network Address Translation (NAT) that hides your computers attached to it from the Internet. This works as a basic firewall to keep intruders out.

For most people, this is sufficient protection. It's also simple because it's a physical barrier between your computer and the Internet. It's also the least intrusive technology because it doesn't need any software installed on your computer to work.

Third-Party Software Firewall: If you don't have a home network router with a built-in firewall, you might want to install a software firewall from a third-party publisher. I recommend two free products:

- ZoneAlarm from www.zonealarm.com
- PC Tools Firewall Plus from www.pctools.com (see Figure 9.19)

Both inspect inbound and outbound data traffic to and from your computer. Inbound data inspection is important because it stops hackers and worms. Outbound data inspection stops unauthorized programs from sending data out to the Internet without your knowledge. Trojan horses, viruses, and spyware would all be stopped by outbound data inspection.

Windows Firewall: The simplest approach is to use the Windows Firewall, a built-in software firewall integrated into Windows XP. It is turned on for you in Vista. In XP, it is turned on when you install your service packs using Windows Update.

tip If you are asked to activate or register your antivirus or antispyware program at this point during the reinstall, choose the option to do this later. You will also be prompted to update your virus and spyware signatures. Hold off on this; you'll do that later when you reconnect to the Internet.

caution If you use a third-party firewall, XP and Vista will both automatically disable the Windows firewall. (If not, access the Security Center in Control Panel to turn it off manually.) Running two firewalls does not double up protection on the system. It may instead impair system performance.

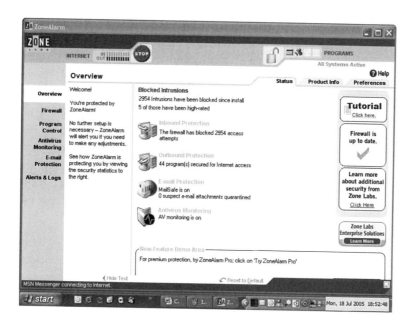

FIGURE 9.19

Zone Labs offers a free version of ZoneAlarm, a software firewall that protects your computer from hackers, viruses, worms, and spyware.

Step 8: Install Firefox

The Microsoft Internet Explorer web browser has a nasty history of being very insecure. If you surf the Web with it in its uncustomized, unpatched state, your computer will be extremely vulnerable to all kinds of malware. It is about as safe as wrangling a guard dog wearing pepperoni pants.

I have been showing you how to secure Microsoft Internet Explorer because there is no way of living without it. Some websites (such as the Windows Update site, for example) just won't work with alternate browsers.

However, it's wise to access most websites with a different browser. The one that has gained the most popularity in recent years is Mozilla Firefox, a free web browser available from www.getfirefox.com.

My dear friend and TV colleague, Leo Laporte (www.twit.tv), has been promoting the benefits of switching browsers since Firefox first appeared on the scene, and if you've heard about it before, it's probably in large part due to his influence. And for good reason: It is a lot more secure than Internet Explorer because it does not support VBScript or ActiveX, which are technologies used by malware to hitchhike onto your computer. It also avoids Microsoft's Java virtual machine, a piece of programming that enables programs written in the Java language to run on Windows. Firefox isn't without its own flaws, but it is innately more secure than Internet Explorer 6.

IE 7 which is now available for Windows XP and comes with Windows Vista is drastically improved from a security perspective. That said I think Firefox still has the edge and I prefer it. Try both and make up your own mind.

Earlier I asked you to download Firefox's installation program. I hope you did because we're going to install it now. If you didn't, this step can be done after you reconnect to the Internet.

When you have the installer program, double-click on its icon, and when the program launches, click Next (see Figure 9.20). Click the dot beside the I Agree option for the license agreement, and click Next. Choose the standard installation, and click Next twice. Then click Finish.

FIGURE 9.20

Use Mozilla Firefox as your web browser to avoid the security flaws in Internet Explorer.

Step 9: Configure Your Networking

Now it's time to reconnect the Internet. Here's how, using the most common types of Internet connections.

> **Home Network:** If you have a home network, it's time to reconnect your network cable or turn your wireless back on. You should be able to reconnect instantly.
>
> **DSL:** If you have a Digital Subscriber Line (DSL) available through your telephone company, install the software provided, and enter your username and password in the appropriate places. Then connect your Ethernet cable to your DSL modem.
>
> **Cable Internet:** If you use cable Internet, consider getting a broadband home router, if you don't use one already. Cable Internet makes your entire neighborhood one big local network. So a router gives you extra protection against bad things circulating in your neighborhood. If not, your software firewall (installed earlier) protects you. After either of these protections is in place, reconnect your network cable.
>
> **Other Broadband:** If you have wireless broadband or use some other technology to access a broadband connection, turn it back on, plug it back in, or reactivate it as necessary.

Dial-up

If you use a dial-up connection with your phone line to connect to the Internet, reinstall the connection software provided to you by your Internet provider, if any was provided. Otherwise, follow these steps:

In Windows XP:

1. Click Start and select Control Panel.
2. Select Network and Internet Connections.
3. Click Setup or Change Your Internet Connection (see Figure 9.21).
4. Choose Add and then Dial Up to Private Network, and follow the setup process, entering all of the information for your Internet provider.
5. Reconnect your modem to the phone line.

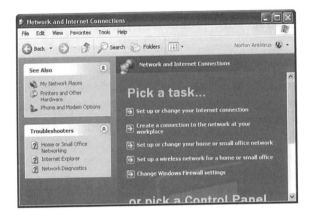

FIGURE 9.21
Set up your dial-up modem in Network and Internet Connections in Control Panel.

In Windows Vista:

1. Click the Windows button and type **Network and Sharing** and click Network and Sharing Center when it appears in the Start Menu.

> **tip** If you don't see Network and Internet Connections in Control Panel, click the Switch to Category View on the left side of the window.

2. On the left side of the Network and Share Center, click Setup a Connection or Network.

3. Choose Set-up a Dial Up Connection and click Next.

4. Follow the setup process, entering all of the information for your Internet provider.

5. Reconnect your modem to the phone line.

Step 10: Install Security Fixes and Service Packs

Now that you are able to connect to the Internet, go to Windows Update and download any necessary security updates and service packs.

Note that you'll want to install all security fixes including service packs on both Windows XP and Windows Vista.

Windows XP latest service pack (as of 2008) is Service Pack 3. For Vista you'll want Service Pack 1 (SP1), however service packs beyond SP1 may be available by the time you read this if its 2009 or beyond.

You may have to install Service Pack 2 on XP before installing Service Pack 3.

Windows Update in XP

To use Windows Update in XP:

1. Click Start.

2. Select All Programs and click on Windows Update.

3. Internet Explorer launches and takes you to the update site.

tip You can also get to the Windows Update website by opening Internet Explorer and typing **http://windows update.microsoft.com**. Note that it won't work using Firefox.

At this point, your firewall software might pop up an alert asking your permission to connect to the Internet. Of course, you want to say yes. As Internet Explorer connects to the update site, you might also get a security warning. If so, click OK (see Figure 9.22).

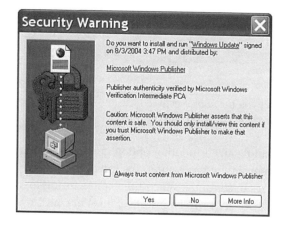

FIGURE 9.22

When Windows Update loads, you might get a security warning because it uses ActiveX technology.

After the page loads, you have to choose between Express and Custom install modes (see Figure 9.23). To install only the most important updates, click on the Express Install option. If you want to update other software and hardware that's non-essential, choose the Custom Install option. But don't worry about it too much, as you can come back to this at any time.

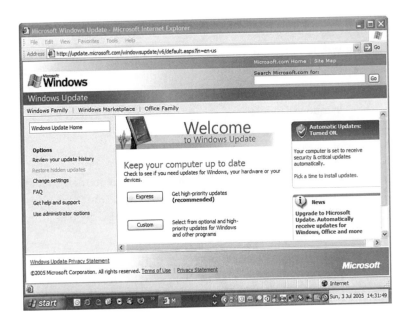

FIGURE 9.23

Windows Update gives you the choice between Custom and Express updates. Only the most important updates are downloaded if you choose the Express option.

After choosing your installation option, a message might pop up warning you that any information you send to the Internet may be viewable by others. If it does, click Yes to continue. When the Express Install menu appears, it lists a number of items that will be installed, most of which are security updates.

Click the Install button. An End User License Agreement appears; click I Accept to continue, and then sit back while your updates download and install (see Figure 9.24).

When this process is complete, the installation program asks you if it can restart your computer. Go ahead and wait for the computer to reboot.

After your computer has rebooted, go to Windows Update again to make sure there aren't any further updates that need to be downloaded. Sometimes installing one update makes another available on Windows Update. Repeat this step until your system is up to date and no more updates are available for download.

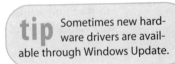
tip Sometimes new hardware drivers are available through Windows Update.

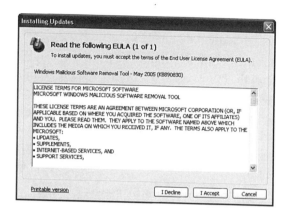

FIGURE 9.24

You are asked to agree to the End User License Agreement again when running Windows Updates. Then the updates begin to download.

Windows Update in Vista

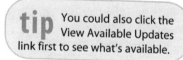

tip You could also click the View Available Updates link first to see what's available.

To access Windows Update in Vista:

1. Click the Windows button on the bottom-right side of your screen.
2. Type **Windows Update** in the search box.
3. Click Windows Update when it appears in the Start menu above the Search box.
4. You can click Check for Updates on the left, although the system should simply show you what updates are available automatically.
5. Click the Install Updates button to initiate the download.
6. The download could take a while, so it's a good time to take a break. A reboot will likely be required when the process is done.
7. Repeat this process until Windows Update reports that no more updates are available.

Windows Validation in XP

To download non-critical updates for Windows and other Microsoft freebies, you will have to first go through the Windows validation process to ensure your copy of Windows XP is legal. Here's how to do that.

1. Use Internet Explorer browser to find the download you want on Microsoft.com.

2. Click to download the item you want and you will see a screen that says "Validation required".

3. Click the Continue button. You'll see a screen that prompts you to install the "Genuine Windows Validation Component".

4. Across the top of this screen in yellow you'll see a small bar that says "This website wants to install the following add-on: Windows Genuine Advantage from the Microsoft Corporation".

5. Click the bar and from the menu that appears choose Install ActiveX Control.

6. A Security Warning box will appear. Click the Install button on it.

7. If successful you'll be taken to the download page of the item you originally wanted to install.

8. If you have an illegal copy of Windows you will be denied access to the download.

9. To resolve this issue you'll need to replace Windows with a legal copy of Windows XP or contact Microsoft to see what's going on with your system. If you Windows license was given to you with your system but is a pirated copy Microsoft wants to know and will help you get into compliance.

Windows Validation in XP

The process for Windows validation process for Vista is very similar to the one above outlined for XP. Here's another way to do it.

1. Visit www.microsoft.com/genuine/ with the Microsoft Internet Explorer web browser.

2. On the page locate the Validate Now box and click the "Validate Windows" item.

3. On the next screen click Continue.

4. A yellow bar will open at the top of the page that says: "This website wants to install the fllowing add-ons: Windows Genuine Advantage from Microsoft Corporation.

5. Click the yellow bar and choose Install ActiveX Control from the menu that appears.

6. Click Continue on the User Account Control Box.

7. Click Install on the Security Warning box that appears next.

8. Wait for the "Validation Complete" message on the next web page to appear or take action if it fails by following the instructions that appear. If you copy of Windows Vista is illegal you will have to replace it with a legal copy.

Step 11: Configure Your Security Settings

There are several security tweaks worth adjusting in both Windows XP and Windows Vista. So let's do that.

Security Tweaks for Windows XP

After you install Service Pack 2 on Windows XP, your system will reboot and take a bit longer than usual to start up, as it has to configure a few things. During this process, you see a setup screen asking you if you'd like to turn on Automatic Updates (see Figure 9.25). This gives Windows XP the ability to detect and automatically download and install new security fixes from Microsoft. This means that as soon as Microsoft releases a fix, your computer fetches it. So it's a very good idea to turn this feature on.

To do that, click the dot beside the green security shield, and click Next. Windows XP starts up, and you see the new Security Center (see Figure 9.26).

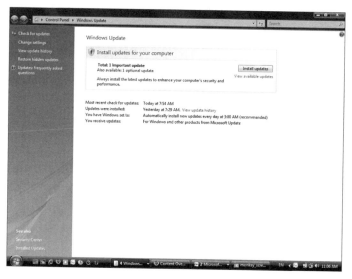

FIGURE 9.25

Turning on Automatic Updates is a key part of your security strategy.

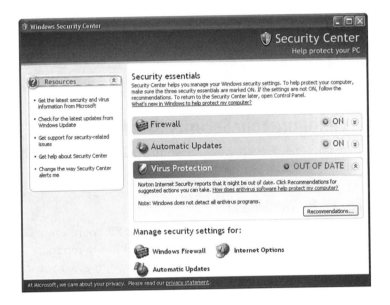

FIGURE 9.26

SP2 adds a new feature to Windows XP called Security Center. This monitors your antivirus program and your firewall, and turns on automatic updates from Microsoft.

SP2 adds a new feature to Windows XP called Security Center. This monitors your antivirus program and your firewall, and turns on automatic updates from Microsoft.

In the Security Center under the heading Manage Security Settings For, note the three icons near the bottom. They are Internet Options, Automatic Updates, and Windows Firewall. If you are having problems with your automatic updates or your firewall, you can adjust them from this panel.

Next, click on the Internet Options icon. A dialog box titled Internet Properties appears on your screen, open to the Security tab (see Figure 9.27).

> **tip** A message might pop up telling you that Windows Firewall is running. If you installed another software firewall in Step 7, you can turn off the Windows Firewall at this point (despite any admonishment that the good folks at Microsoft might dish out when you do). If you cheated a bit and didn't install a firewall program, leave Windows Firewall on.

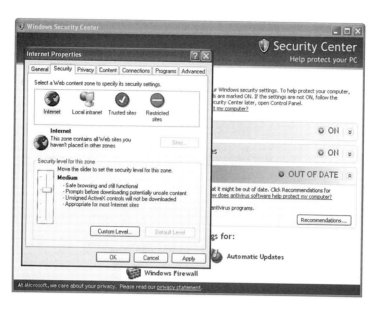

FIGURE 9.27

From the Security Center you can access your Internet Properties. These are the same settings found in Internet Explorer.

Click on the icon that says Internet. You want to create a security setting for your time on the Internet that strikes a balance between usability and safety. In general, medium is the best way to go because the high setting baby-sits almost everything you do, meaning that you'll be barraged with warnings from the firewall, asking if this application can access the Internet, if that application can act as a server, and if this one can go to the bathroom. If you're anything like the rest of us, you'll go stark raving mad and disable the firewall because it annoys you, which is a bad, bad thing. Setting the security to medium provides a solid level of security without making you want to climb out onto the roof with a rifle.

Try both security settings for a bit and surf the Internet. You'll quickly find out which suits you best. If you'd like to further tweak your settings, click Custom (see Figure 9.28) to enable or disable prompting for behaviors that are either a security risk, such as automatic scripting, or too intrusive, such as pop-up messages that ask you for permission before the browser does something. You can come back to this dialog box at any point, so don't worry if you make the wrong choice—you can change it later.

FIGURE 9.28

The Custom button in the Security table in Internet Properties can be used to customize security in Internet Explorer.

Click Custom in the Security tab to override the preset security features and customize them to your own taste. For most people, these settings seem like a menu from a Bosnian-owned Chinese food restaurant. Ideally, stick to the presets.

In this same tab, there are settings for intranet (computers on the same network as you) and a list of trusted and restricted sites. If you use an Internet service via your cable TV company to connect to the network and don't have an Internet-sharing home router, you should bump your Intranet setting up to a higher setting. Otherwise the default settings should be okay.

tip In case you're wondering, ActiveX is set of a Microsoft technologies that allow programs to download from the Web and run on your computer. An ActiveX control can trigger sounds, animations, or other programs that execute from the Web. It's that last item that is scary. If ActiveX is turned on, you might get an ActiveX control automatically downloading programming from a web page and installing malware such as a Trojan horse, spyware, or adware.

You can come back to this dialog box later to add trusted sites—websites you visit that you know are safe but that trigger too many security warnings. You might also want to restrict websites—sites that you want to be off limits for members of your family, including adult content sites, spyware-infested sites, or other scary content you want to block, such as Martha Stewart's home page. (Clip-art napkin rings kind of scare me.)

SP2 also adds a new feature under the Privacy tab to help you manage pop-up windows in Internet Explorer. You see a Block Pop-ups section at the bottom of the Privacy tab window (see Figure 9.29). Note the Settings button here. If you click this, you can enable pop-ups for trusted sites you visit that require pop-ups to work. Some sites, for example, pop open separate windows to enter site login information.

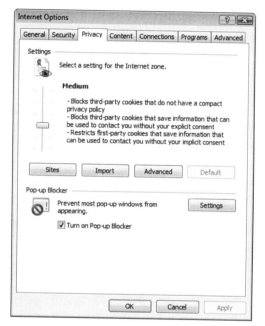

FIGURE 9.29

Service Pack 2 adds a customizable pop-up blocker to Internet Explorer.

While on the Privacy tab, reset your Privacy setting to medium-high or high. High is a good option if you want maximum security and are willing to be pestered by your computer when surfing the Internet.

Again, note the Sites button. You can use this to change cookie settings for specific websites. Cookies are little pieces of text sent to you by a website and stored by your web browser to track your movements, populate a shopping cart, and store settings such as User IDs and passwords. To learn more about cookies, see Chapter 2. At this point, you can close your Internet Properties dialog and the Security Center.

Security Tweaks for Windows Vista

When Windows Vista is installed, it is worth making a few more tweaks around security.

Start with the Security Center. Access it by typing **security center** in the search box on the Start menu. And click it when it appears.

In the Security Center you'll see four settings (see Figure 9.30). Here's what to do with each one of them:

Firewall: The Windows firewall should be turned on unless you have a third-party firewall installed.

Automatic updating: This setting looks for and downloads security fixes made available through Microsoft automatically. It should be turned on unless you like to check manually yourself on a weekly basis.

Malware Protection: This will list which antivirus product is installed (if any) and if it is up to date. Under the link that says Show Me the Anti-Spyware Programs on this Computer, it lists antispyware products that are installed and whether they are up to date. This includes Windows Defender, the built-in antispyware tool that comes with Vista.

Other Security Settings: Other alerts will show up here when Windows detects settings that are less than optimal. For example, when the User Account Control is turned off it will show here.

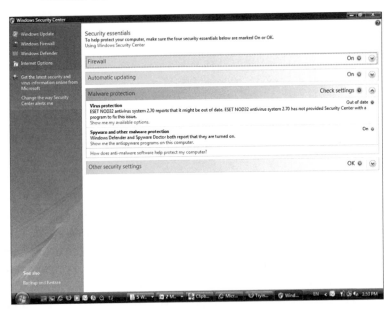

FIGURE 9.30

Check the Vista Security Center to see if anything is amiss on your system. In this example, there's an alert that the antivirus program is out of date.

Next, it's worth clicking on the Internet
Options item on the left side of the Security
Center to adjust the settings in Internet
Explorer.

A dialog box titled Internet Properties will
appears on your screen, open to the
Security tab.

> **note** There is no low setting. There's Medium, Medium high and High, which suggests Medium is actually really the low setting. Microsoft doesn't want to call it that because no one wants "low" security.

Click on the icon that says Internet. You want
to create a security setting for your time on the Internet that strikes a balance
between usability and safety. In general, Medium-high is the best way to go
because the High setting baby-sits almost everything you do on the computer.
You'll be barraged with warnings from the firewall, asking if this application
can access the Internet, if that application can act as a server, and if this one
can go to the bathroom.

If you're anything like the rest of us, you'll go stark raving mad and disable
the firewall because it annoys you, which is a bad, bad thing. Setting the security to Medium-high provides a solid level of security without making you
want to climb out onto the roof with a rifle.

Try the various security settings for a bit and surf the Internet. You'll quickly
find out which suits you best.

If you'd like to further tweak your settings, click Custom Level to enable or disable prompting for behaviors that are either a security risk, such as automatic
scripting, or too intrusive, such as pop-up messages that ask you for permission before the browser does something.

For most people, these settings will be confusing. Stick to the presets for simplicity.

Vista also has a feature (created for XP SP2) under the Privacy tab to help you
manage pop-up windows in Internet Explorer.

While on the Privacy tab, reset your Privacy setting to Medium-High or High.
High is a good option if you want maximum security and are willing to be
pestered by your computer when surfing the Internet.

Tweak User Account Control

There's one key feature in Vista that you won't see in Windows XP. It's called
User Account Control or UAC for short. UAC is a new stopgap in Vista that
helps to block malware infections from changing settings on your system.

So if you or anything else (aka malware or even legitimate software) tries to make a system setting change including: editing the registry, changing Windows settings or tweaking startup items, or even something as simple as changing the time, an alert will appear. You'll see a box asking you for permission to make a change. Simply click Continue in this box when it happens if you initiated the action.

If you didn't initiate the system change, click Cancel and do a virus or spyware scan because there is something on your system trying to do bad things.

tip If you hate UAC, you can turn it off, though I highly recommend against it. To switch it off, click the Windows button and type **msconfig** in the search box. Click msconfig when it appears in the Start menu. Click the Tools tab. Then look for Disable UAC (see Figure 9.31) and below it Enable UAC. Click Disable and then click Launch. It'll be turned off. Turn it back on by using the Enable UAC command.

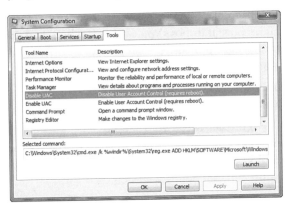

FIGURE 9.31
User Account Control can be turned off in the hidden System Configuration Utility.

Step 12: Update All of Your Security Programs and Security Signatures

After you have connected to the Internet, some of your security programs might have started updating themselves to protect you automatically against new threats.

Nonetheless, you should manually go to each security program you've installed and look for the option to update the program.

Don't forget to update the following programs:

- Antivirus program
- Antispyware program(s)
- Firewall program

tip And here's another handy tip. Try out TweakUAC, a freebie tool from www.tweakuac.com, to make UAC easier to turn on or off. It also has a "quiet" mode that disables UAC if you are logged into Vista as an administrator, but leaves UAC on for those with accounts on the system that are Standard users.

Sometimes an update of your program might trigger several further updates of the program. For any updates that require you to restart your computer, run the update process on that program again after rebooting to make sure you've caught all relevant updates. Just like it says on a shampoo bottle: Repeat as necessary.

Step 13: Activate Windows

After you're satisfied that everything is running properly, it's time to activate your copy of Windows.

In Windows XP, double-click the set of keys in the lower-right corner of the screen. A dialog box entitled Let's Activate Windows appears. You can choose to activate over the Internet or over the phone. Choose the Internet option and click Next. In Windows Vista, you'll be prompted to activate your copy of Windows Vista within 15 days.

1. To access the activation tool, click the Windows button and right-click on Computer on the right side of the Start menu.

2. Choose Properties.

3. At the bottom of the screen you'll see a link to initiate activation.

Step 14: Reinstall Your Programs

After Windows is updated, back in operation, and all the security programs are running, it's time to install all of your day-to-day programs. There is no real trick to this. If you have the original CD/DVD or copies of the install files on a backup disc, it's just a matter of reinstalling them.

caution If you've already activated your copy of Windows many times, you might be prompted to call Microsoft to activate your copy over the phone. Generally Microsoft is pretty good about giving you a code to activate your copy of Windows, unless your Windows key has been abused mercilessly. For this reason, you should never give your key to anyone. It might work okay for your friend in an emergency, but it could lead to you not being able to reinstall your operating system later.

After installation, though, you should check with the companies that publish the software you own to see if there are any fixes or patches on their websites.

Often patches or fixes are available from the support area of these websites. You can also look under the help menu of each program to see if there is a Check for Update option.

Microsoft Office Updates

If you use Microsoft Office, make sure you do look for updates or service packs. Updates for Microsoft Office on Windows Vista can be obtained through Windows Update on your computer.

In XP, you can use Microsoft Update. This is offered through Windows Update. It's an upgrade to Windows Update that checks for updates for all Microsoft products that are installed on your system when you run Windows Update.

Or you could open Internet Explorer and visit www.microsoft.com/office/ and look for the Office Updates link on that page.

Note that when you do this the Windows Genuine Advantage routine will run. This verifies that you have a legal copy of Microsoft Office. Click Continue and let it run. If it fails, follow the instructions on screen. It could be that you have yet to activate the Office installation. To do that, open Microsoft Word or one of the other components in Office and run the activation wizard, which will kick in when the application is opened (if Office has not been activated).

When this entire preamble is done, you may have to go back and start at the office.microsoft.com page again. This time you should be able to get to the scanner that will inspect your system to see what updates are necessary.

In the process you will hear a beep when it's done and a yellow bar will appear across the top of the screen that says "The previous site requires the following add-on: "Office Update Installation Engine…." Click the yellow bar. Then click the option Install ActiveX Control. Click Install on the dialog box that shows up after that. The scan will then continue.

Like Windows Updates, the Office Update site scans your computer to determine which updates you need (see Figure 9.32) and these updates can then be downloaded and installed.

You need to keep your Office CD/DVD handy when you install any fixes, as you might be prompted to put it into the computer to show that you own a copy of the software.

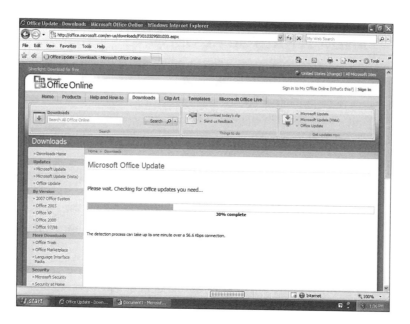

FIGURE 9.32

Be sure to check for Microsoft Office updates on the Microsoft website.

Step 15: Other Things You Can Do

If you have followed this chapter through from beginning to end, your Windows system is about as secure as it possibly can be.

Microsoft took a lot of criticism for its lax security focus in XP and has addressed much of it in Vista, although the fixes have been clumsy at times and have caused serious compatibility issues with older software and hardware.

Moving forward, you should consider adding several more tweaks to the system:

- If a new web browser becomes available from Microsoft, hold off installing it until it's several months old (if you like to be conservative). A new browser will have new flaws. It'll take three to six months for these to be revealed.

- Add an anti-spam program to your email program. I recommend Cloudmark Desktop from www.cloudmark.com.

- Consider installing the Netcraft Anti-Phishing Toolbar for both Internet Explorer and Firefox from www.netcraft.com.

9

KNOW WHAT YOU'RE OPENING

One of the stupid things Windows does is hide file extensions—the bit of the file name after the dot, such as `.doc` or `.txt`—for what it considers to be familiar or known file types. These include JPG and DOC files, but also potentially harmful files such as EXE, PIF, DAT, and COM files, all of which can execute programming that can compromise your computer.

One well-known trick hackers use is to send an email with an attachment named something like `sexygirl.jpg.exe`, which appears in most mail programs as `sexygirl.jpg` when this option is turned on. You might click on it thinking it's a naughty, yet non–security-threatening file, and wind up infecting your system.

There is an easy fix, though. In XP, double-click My Computer, choose the Tools menu from the top, and select Folder Options. Then click the View tab, and uncheck the item that reads Hide Extensions for Known File Types, if it is checked.

In Vista, click the Windows button and type `folder` into the search box. Click Folder Options when it appears in the Start menu. Then click the View tab, and uncheck the item that reads Hide Extensions for Known File Types, if it is checked and click OK.

If you make this change, you see the extensions for all files. All you have to do is make sure you always pay attention to what you're clicking on when you receive a file attachment.

The Absolute Minimum

- Be sure you have a legitimate copy of Windows XP or Vista.

- Collect all your system drivers.

- Get antivirus, antispyware, and firewall programs for your computer.

- Set your BIOS so the CD or DVD drive is the first bootable device on the system if you're reinstalling with XP. With Vista this step is not necessary if you use the Desktop installation option.

- Wipe your hard drive clean and install a fresh copy of Windows XP or Windows Vista after disconnecting from the Internet.

- Install drivers.

- Install an antivirus program, two antispyware programs, and a firewall.

- Configure your security settings.

- Install Firefox.

- Reconnect to the Internet.

- Install service packs and security fixes through Windows Update.

- Tweak security settings in Internet Explorer and the Windows Security Center.

- Add extras such as anti-spam and anti-phishing programs.

- Hold off on a new web browser from Microsoft until three to six months after it launches.

9

Ongoing Maintenance: Fend Off Future Threats!

The advice in this book is going to make your computer more secure than it ever was before. But just because your system is now malware-resistant doesn't mean it will be forever. You'll need to do a little ongoing maintenance. So in this chapter I'll show you what to do on a daily, weekly, and monthly basis to keep your computer free of computer nasties.

Note to Self: Keep Computer Secure

Let's say you've followed every tiny little detail in this book (if you have, I am very proud of you!), and you're feeling much more secure about your computer because it's much more secure.

There's still a problem, though. While you're taking your kids to soccer practice or shopping for hair products, the virus writers, spyware mavens, and hackers are remaining childless and uncoiffed because they are busy writing the next generation of Internet threats. Villains don't get many dates.

So your work isn't finished. You still need to fight the future—future threats, that is. You can do that by taking a few minutes every day or so, 30 minutes each week, and maybe an hour every month to keep abreast of emerging security issues.

To that end, here are a series of easy security maintenance tips. One little note: The frequency I recommend is just a guideline. I don't want to schedule you into oblivion. If you do most of them with any kind of reasonable frequency, you'll be ahead of the game.

Daily Routines: Walk the Dog, Feed the Kids, and Secure the Computer

Here are the tasks you should do every day to keep your computer secure. They should only take a minute or two and should become part of your routine computer maintenance.

Update Your Antivirus and Antispyware Signatures

Antivirus and antispyware programs are only as good as their signatures. You'll recall those are digital snapshots of viruses and spyware that help these programs recognize threats. Ideally, you need to check for new signatures every day. That way, if a fast, replicating virus, worm, or particularly nasty piece of spyware appears, your defenses will be able to block it when it attacks your computer.

What's handy here is that most programs automatically update signatures daily. Some programs update multiple times a day as new signatures become available. So no matter which antivirus and antispyware program you use, make sure automated updates are turned on. If you hear about a new malware outbreak in the news, be sure to manually update your antivirus or antispyware program.

Update AVG Signatures

If you are running Grisoft's AVG Anti-Virus Free Edition, you'll be pleased to know that in addition to being absolutely free, AVG virus signatures can be updated by the program daily. Here's how to ensure that this feature is turned on:

caution If you use a software firewall, it might be a good idea to manually initiate an update with your antivirus and antispyware program to see how the firewall responds. You might get a warning from the firewall that you'll have to respond to for the update to proceed. That also allows future updates to get through the firewall automatically.

1. Start AVG's Control Center by double-clicking the AVG icon in your System Tray (also called the Notification Area by Microsoft in Vista) on the bottom-right side of your screen.

2. Select the Scheduler item in the list in the main window, and then at the bottom click the Scheduled Tasks button.

3. Click on Update Plan in Basic Mode and then click the Edit Schedule button. Check the boxes next to Periodically Check for Internet Updates and If Internet Connection Is Not Available, Check When It Goes On-Line. Next to Check Daily, choose the hour when you'd like the program to check for updates (see Figure 10.1). (I like it to check for updates before I start my work day, so I set it for early in the morning.)

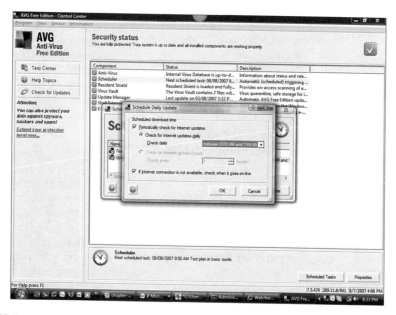

FIGURE 10.1

Set the hour in which AVG Free Edition checks for virus signatures for a time when you won't be using your computer.

4. Click OK and click Close, then close AVG Control Center.

Update Windows Defender

Windows Defender can download its spyware signatures automatically as well.

In Vista, the program is pre-installed. In Windows XP, you'll need to download and install it. Get it free from http://www.microsoft.com/spyware.

Here's how to check that this feature is turned on in both Windows XP (if you have installed it) and Windows Vista:

1. Start Windows Defender. You'll find it under All Programs in the Start menu.

2. Click the Tools menu, then Options.

3. Ensure that Automatically Scan My Computer (Recommended) is checked, and for Frequency, choose Daily. Also select an appropriate time when the system is not in use but is powered on.

4. Make sure Check for Updated Definitions Before Scanning is checked

5. Click Save. Click Continue on the User Account Control to finish.

To run a spyware signature update manually, follow these steps:

1. Start Windows Defender.

2. Click the down arrow next to the question mark on the menu across the top.

3. Choose Check for Updates.

caution Is it okay to leave your computer on all the time? Some say yes, some say no. I do because it means my security software always has a chance to check for updates. The downside is if your computer is on all the time, it's available to be attacked. Also, it burns power and is subject to being shut down rudely and unexpectedly during power outages, which is rough on your hardware. But others argue it's better to keep a computer on and warm than cycling it on and off, warming and cooling components and subjecting them to heat stress. At the end of the day, it's your call.

You should also consider whether leaving your computer on all the time is a security risk because others in your household could have access to your data if your PC is powered on and you are logged in. At the very least, log off as the computer administrator to prevent others from being able to unwittingly damage your computer.

tip Being aware of the latest computer threats is a handy habit to get into. I keep my eye on News.com's security page (click the Threats item under the News tab at http://news.com.com). I also check in with Secunia (http://secunia.com) to see what the latest security advisories are.

4. Let the update mechanism run. It downloads and installs updates if they are available.

Update Spybot Search & Destroy

Spybot can automatically download and install signatures every time you start the program. Here's how to set that up:

1. Start Spybot.

2. In Windows Vista, click Continue on the UAC warning, as necessary.

3. Click the Mode menu and choose Advanced Mode.

4. In the left margin of the main screen, near the bottom a Settings option will appear with a plus mark next to it (+).

5. Click it to reveal a list of options and scroll through them to the Settings item.

6. In the main window, scroll down to the Web Update section and select by adding a checkmark to the Download Updated Include Files If Available Online item. Optionally, add a checkmark to Search the Web for New Versions at Each Program Start to have the program check to see if there's a newer version of Spybot available.

7. When you are done, click Spybot S&D at the top left to return to the main screen.

To look for signatures manually, follow these steps. Without this step you are not as well-protected as you could be.

1. Start Spybot and click the Search for Updates button (see Figure 10.2) in the main window.

2. The updates available for download are listed.

3. Check all the items. Some will be new features available for the program, while others will be updates for the immunization database and spyware detection rules. Sometimes only Detection rule updates are available (these are the important spyware signatures).

4. At the top of the window, click the Download Updates button. A green checkmark appears after each item has been downloaded and installed.

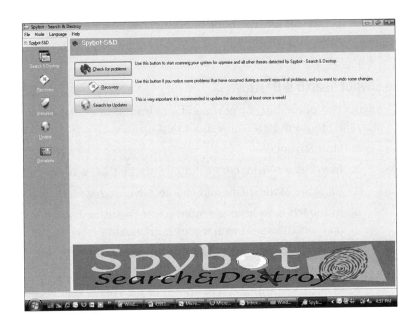

FIGURE 10.2

Be sure to check for updates in Spybot each week (and daily if you have time) or set the program to check for updates each time it starts up.

Weekly Routines: Never Be Bored on Saturday Morning

Here are the security tasks you should do once a week. They shouldn't cumulatively take more than about an hour or so.

Scan for Viruses and Spyware

Use your antivirus and both antispyware programs to do a scan of your computer once a week. Here's how to do that with the key programs suggested in this book. If you use other products, be sure to run scans with them instead.

Windows Defender

Here's how to run a system scan with Windows Defender.

1. Start Windows Defender. In XP, click Start, All Programs, Windows Defender. In Vista, click the Windows button (the button formerly called Start), and then type **Defender** in the search bar and click Windows Defender when it appears in the Start menu.

2. When Defender is running, look for the Scan menu across the top and click the down arrow next to it.

3. Choose Full Scan.

4. If you want to scan a particular set of folders or drives, click the Custom Scan on the Scan menu.

5. Select Scan Selected Drives/Folders and click the Select button. Check the drivers and folders you want scanned. Click the plus sign next to each disk to select specific subfolders.

6. Once they are selected, click OK. The dialog will close, and then click the Scan Now button to start the custom scan.

Spybot Search & Destroy

Here's how to do a spyware scan with Spybot Search & Destroy:

1. Start Spybot. In XP, click Start, All Programs, Spybot - Search & Destroy. In the resulting menu click Spybot - Search & Destroy – again to start the program.

2. In Vista, click the Windows button, type **spybot** in the Search bar, and then click on Spybot – Search & Destroy when it appears in the Start menu. You'll need to click Continue on the UAC warning to start the program.

3. Click the Check for Problems button and allow the scan to run.

4. If the software detects any spyware, it is displayed as an item to be removed under the "Problem" column.

Grisoft AVG Free Edition

Here's how to do a virus scan with AVG Free Edition:

1. Start AVG Free by double-clicking the icon in the System Tray.

2. AVG Control Center opens. Click the Test Center button on the left.

3. Click on the Scan Computer button and let the program scan your computer until it's finished.

4. If it finds anything, follow the rec-ommendations to remove the virus.

tip If AVG or any security application has a problem removing an infection, restart Windows and enter Safe mode by tapping F8 repeatedly when the computer reboots and the screen is in black and before you see the Windows logo. Choose Safe Mode from the menu that appears and enter Windows in its raw diagnostic state; then run the security program again and try to disinfect the infection. That should make virus or spyware removal easier for the program.

10

Check for Firefox Updates

The Firefox web browser is relatively new, so browser vulnerabilities are found and fixed fairly often. Some clever geek might find a security hole and alert the team at Mozilla.org to the problem. A fix is usually issued within a day or so.

note If you're wondering why I haven't suggested updating Internet Explorer, it's because those fixes are issued as part of the Windows Updates.

Be sure to check every week (or two) to make sure you take advantage of these discoveries and patch the browser with fixes. Here's how in both XP and Vista:

1. Run Firefox.

2. Click the Help menu

3. Click Check for Update (see Figure 10.3) and let the software check to see if there's an update. Be sure to install it if one is found.

To check for add-on updates in Firefox:

1. In Firefox, click the Tools menu and then Add-ons.

2. Next click the Find Updates button, and then click the Install Updates button,

3. If any updates are found, they will be installed.

4. You'll need to restart Firefox to finish.

FIGURE 10.3

Update Firefox by clicking Check for Updates on the Help menu.

Report Problems, Get Solutions

Be sure to use the Problem Reports and Solutions utility in Windows Vista (XP doesn't have this feature) weekly to report issues your system may have encountered to Microsoft and to check for solutions. Keeping your system up to date is good maintenance practice and it will also help keep your system stay secure with the latest updates for any software on the system.

tip To enable automatic updates in Firefox, click Tools, Options, Advanced. Next select the Update tab and ensure that you have checked the boxes next to Firefox, Installed Add-ons, and Search Engines. Below that choose "Automatically download and install the update". Then click OK to close the dialog box.

This includes fixes for Microsoft Office, which has been very vulnerable to malware in the past.

Here's how to do that:

1. Click the Windows button and type **Problem** into the Search bar.
2. When the item Problem Reports and Solutions appears, click it to open the utility.
3. Click the Check for New Solutions link on the left sidebar.
4. Vista will upload to Microsoft any errors (see Figure 10.4) it has found and will also retrieve any solutions Microsoft is aware of or has produced a fix for.

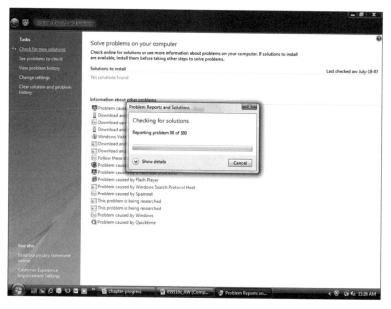

FIGURE 10.4

Look how many errors are being reported to Microsoft in the Problem Reports and Solutions.

5. Once this process is complete, look under the Solutions to Install section at the top of the main window to see if a fix is listed that you can download and install from Microsoft to solve a reported problem.

6. Below that is a section called Information About Other Problems. Look here for tips and tricks on how to solve other issues.

7. Click each item and see if there is any helpful information. You may see notifications of driver updates for devices on your system or third-party software update alerts (see Figure 10.5). Recent solutions will be marked with the word: New!

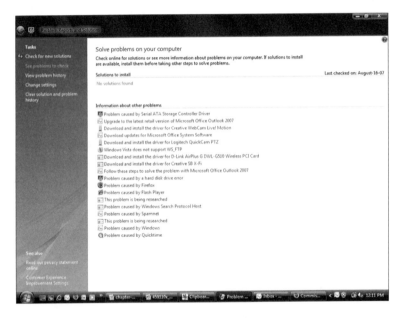

FIGURE 10.5

Click each solution to find out if there's something you can do to resolve a problem that has been reported.

Monthly Routines: Clean the Garage, Trim the Hedge, and Update Windows

These once-a-month routines can be achieved in fewer than 30 minutes each.

Windows Updates

Microsoft issues scheduled security updates on the second Tuesday of every month. When an urgent security hole is found, however, a fix is usually issued right away. If you have installed Windows XP Service Pack 2 or use Windows Vista, by default fixes are automatically downloaded and installed for you. That is unless someone has monkeyed with the settings to turn them off.

If you own XP, you have installed SP2, right? If not, please do. To learn more about Windows Updates, see **p. 271**.

Here's how to check to make sure the Automatic Updates feature is turned on so that you don't spend any time worrying about critical updates.

In Windows XP (with SP2), follow these steps:

1. Click Start, Control Panel.
2. Double-click the Security Center applet.
3. Automatic Updates should show as ON.

> **tip** It's worth invoking Windows Update manually every now and then because noncritical updates such as new Windows features, drivers, and other nonurgent updates are made available fairly often.
>
> If you have Windows XP, visit the Windows Update website (with Internet Explorer) at www.windowsupdate.com, and click the Custom button to see what fixes are available. They are accessible via the menu on the left. Look for "High Priority," "Software, Optional," or "Hardware, Optional." Click each one and scan the list of available updates.
>
> If you use Windows Vista, visiting www.windowsupdates.com with Internet Explorer will open your Windows Update utility. (It can also be opened by typing "Update" into the Search bar on the Start menu and clicking the utility when it appears.)

4. To schedule the updates check, click the Automatic Updates link at the bottom of the window.
5. Ensure that the button next to Automatic (Recommended) is selected (see Figure 10.6) and that you've chosen Every Day and a time when your computer is turned on. If you switch your computer off at night, make sure you schedule the update check for a time when the computer is on and idle. Even if you're using the computer, the check will occur quietly in the background.
6. If you are more conservative, click Download Updates for Me, But Let Me Choose When to Install Them (see the "When Updates Bite Back" sidebar).

FIGURE 10.6

Choose to download and install Windows updates automatically. If you're more conservative, choose to download the fixes and manually install them.

In Windows Vista, follow these steps:

1. Click the Windows button, type **security center** in the search box, and click Security Center when it appears in the Start menu.

2. Looking for Automatic Updating. It should show as On.

3. To schedule the updates check, click Windows Update on the sidebar on the left-hand side.

4. In the Windows Update window, click Change Settings on the left.

5. Ensure that the button next to Install Updates Automatically (Recommended) is checked and that you've chosen Every Day and a time when your computer is turned on. If you switch your computer off at night, make sure you schedule the update check for a time when the computer is on and idle. Even if you're using the computer, the check will occur quietly in the background.

6. Click OK and click Continue on the UAC warning.

caution If you are more conservative, click Download Updates But Let Me Choose Whether to Install Them (see the heading "When Updates Bite Back" on the next page).

When Updates Bite Back

Sean Carruthers, my co-host on the video podcast LabRats.tv, said to me as I wrote this chapter, "You're not going to recommend in the book that Windows updates should be set to automatically install, are you?"

tip See what updates Microsoft has issued recently at this website: http://www.microsoft.com/protect/computer/updates/bulletins/default.mspx or http://tinyurl.com/3c4wxj

Sean worries that Microsoft occasionally issues a bad fix that can cause more trouble than it fixes. So his recommendation is to set Windows to download the updates, but then notify you they are there so you can review the fix before installation. This is a good practice, but it adds a level of complexity. You not only have to review all the updates as they come in, but you also need to be tuned into what the experts are saying if a bad fix comes along.

Personally, I choose to autoinstall fixes and use the System Restore feature available in both Windows XP and Vista to roll back the system if there's a major problem. I've never had a situation, however, where an incremental patch has been a problem.

That said, Service Pack 2, the biggest and fattest security fix issued by Microsoft for Windows XP, caused huge problems. It ate my system when I first installed it. But then again, I didn't heed the very early warnings that it was temperamental at best. Hey, you can't be a pioneer without a few arrows in your back.

But it wasn't just first install jitters. A Windows XP SP2 installation went bad more recently on a Pentium III system I updated when creating a test platform for this book in the summer of 2007.

If you're confused by my SP2 waffling here, then my apologies. Let me clarify by saying that SP2 is a **very important** update and is an absolute necessity for Windows XP to be secure. I just want to make it very clear that you could encounter installation issues when you decide to put it in place. I urge you to persevere because it is one of the best things you can do to lock down Windows XP.

If you want to minimize XP SP2 installation grief then follow the helpful advice at `http://editorsdesktop.com/SP2inst.html`. The key tips are:

1. Before installing SP2, be sure to update all your installed programs with any fixes issued by their publishers. Check the software maker's web site to see if there are any free downloadable updates.

2. Uninstall any Norton products completely, especially Norton Internet Security. If you use another security suite or product uninstall that as well to avoid nasty conflicts.

3. Reboot in the sequence recommended in the article on EditorsDesktop.com mentioned above.

Check for Anti-Rootkit Updates

If you use a separate anti-rootkit application (as I outlined in Chapter 3, "Rootkits: Sneaky, Stealthy Toolboxes"), be sure to check for updates of the application so that you have the latest version on hand. Some programs have a built-in update feature. For others you simply have to visit the program's website to see if there is an update available.

For example, in AVG Anti-Rootkit Free:

1. Start the program.

2. Click the About and Update tab.

3. Note the version number of the program next to "Installed version."

4. Click the button Check for New Version.

5. A web browser will be opened to the update page on Grisoft.com.

6. Locate and click the download buttons until you get the file download. Compare the file version of the installed version of AVG Anti-Rootkit Free with the version available on the site. If it's newer, download the program, remove the old program, and install the new version.

Inspect Other Computers

Do a security check on the other computers in your home, especially if you have a home network. Even if your computer's defenses are rock solid, having a vulnerable or infected computer on your network puts all computers on your network at risk. Viruses, spyware, and other malware often can jump from computer to computer over a network connection.

Router Firmware Updates

If you have a home network router, you want to occasionally check for firmware updates to repair any bugs in the router's built-in software. The firmware is the programming inside a router that controls it. Most routers have this capability. Here's how to do it in a D-Link router:

1. Access your router's control panel by opening your web browser (I use Firefox in this example), and type in its IP address.

2. You are asked for the router's user ID and password. Enter that information and click OK.

3. In a D-Link router, click the Tools tab, and then the Firmware button on the left.

4. Make a note of the model number of your router (it's in the top-left corner in the D-Link router setup screen), and also make a note of the firmware version on the Firmware page (see Figure 10.7).

5. Right-click the link that says Click Here to Check for an Upgrade on Our Support Site and choose Open Link in New Window. This opens the D-Link site in a new browser window.

> **note** If accessing your router is new to you, I cover how to access a router's setup in great detail in Chapter 7, "Wireless Network Snoops: Lock Down Your Wi-Fi Network," starting on **p. 183**.

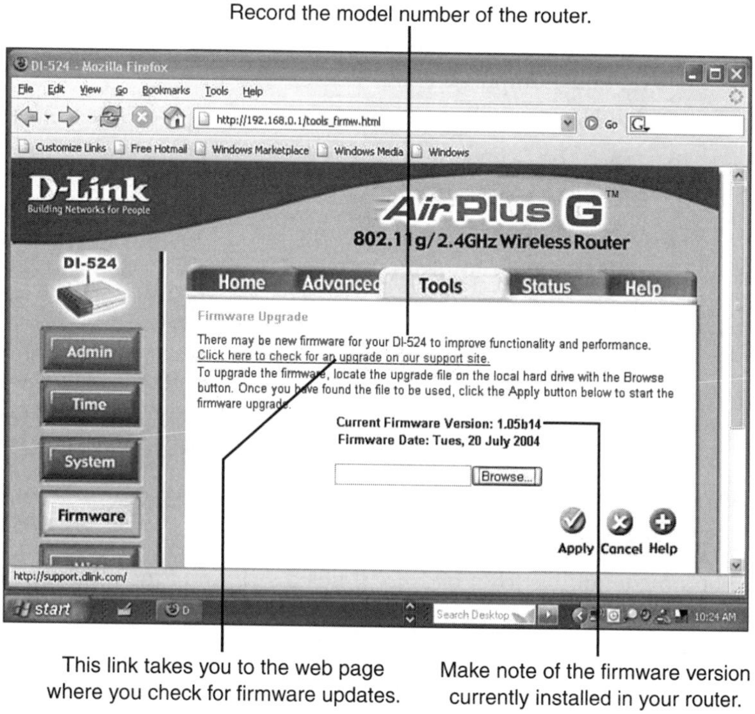

Record the model number of the router.

This link takes you to the web page where you check for firmware updates.

Make note of the firmware version currently installed in your router.

FIGURE 10.7

Locate the Firmware update page on your D-Link router. This feature allows you to update the programming inside the router.

10

6. Enter your router model number using the drop-down boxes on the site and click Go. The website should refresh with available updates.

7. Compare the firmware update version (or release date) to the firmware version or release date shown in your router. If the website's version is newer, you should download and install it.

8. Click on the Update link and choose the Save to Disk option.

9. After you have downloaded the firmware update, return to your router's setup screen, where you left off, and use the Browse button to locate the downloaded firmware file on your computer. Then click Apply.

10. When the firmware update is finished, the router restarts.

11. You have to go back into it and restore any customizations you made, including turning on WEP or WPA security, renaming the router's name (the SSID), and changing the default password.

> **caution** Do not update router firmware over a wireless connection. This is because if the connection fails during the update, it will render your router inoperative. It is okay to download the firmware file over a wireless connection, but when it comes to updating it, I recommend that you connect your computer to your router using a network cable and turn your wireless option off by right-clicking it in the System Tray (bottom right of your Windows screen) and choosing Disable.

> **tip** When you update your firmware, it is also useful to see if there is an update available for the driver that runs the wireless adapter on your computer. If you have trouble getting connected and staying connected wirelessly, it can be fixed if you update both the router firmware and the wireless adapter driver, as an old driver with new router firmware (or old firmware and a new driver) may cause problems. Learn how to update a Windows driver here: http://www.cyberwalker.com/article/449.

Patch Microsoft Office

Microsoft Office should be updated as fixes become available for it because it has a scripting language (which many macro viruses are written in). It also features the email program Outlook, which communicates with the outside world and is a popular conduit for mass-mailer worms. It should be updated as soon as bug fixes become available for it.

Here's how to update Office in Vista:

1. Click the Windows button, type **Update**, and click Windows Update from the Start menu.

> **tip** If Update Service option is not available then click Get More Updates on the main Windows Update window to enable Microsoft Updates.

2. On the left side of the Windows Update window, click Change Settings.

3. Ensure that both Recommended Updates and Update Service (if it's not there see Tip) check boxeFranks are checked. Click OK and click Continue on the UAC Alert.

4. In the main Windows Update window, click Check for Updates on the left. Let the system check for updates (this can take a minute or two). If there are updates available you'll see a "Install Updates" button. Click it to download and install the updates. Alternately, to see what updates are available click the "View available updates" link under the Install Updates button (see Figure 10.8) and selectively choose what updates you want to install then click Install.

FIGURE 10.8

Click Install Updates to download Windows fixes and Microsoft Office updates or click View Available Updates to see what's available.

5. If any Microsoft Office updates are available, they will be installed along with other updates for your system.

6. You may have to restart the system.

Here's how to update Office in XP:

1. Use the Internet Explorer web browser to visit http://office.microsoft.com.

2. Click the Office Update link.

3. Click the Continue button to run the Microsoft validation program. This validates that you have a legal copy of Microsoft Office.

4. After activation, follow the instructions to begin the download. A bar at the top of your browser will appear that reads, "The previous site might require the following ActiveX control: Office Update Installation Engine from Microsoft Corporation. Click here to install." Click the bar and choose Install ActiveX Control.

5. A box with a security warning that says "Do you want to install this software?" appears. Click the Install button.

6. A list of updates appears that are checked

7. Click the Agree and Install button. The updates begin to download. This takes a while, but after it's done the updates begin to install.

8. You need to restart the computer to enable the updates.

caution Microsoft changes the design of the site from time to time as well as the content of its site based on the operating system it detects, so if it's not "Check for updates," it'll be something similar.

tip If you fail the validation, make sure you have a legal copy of Microsoft Office installed (borrowing the disc from a friend doesn't make it legal unless the friend has uninstalled it!) and that you have run the activation routine. Do this by opening any Microsoft office program and click the Help menu and then Activate Product.

caution You may need to install the ActiveX control twice. This process is kind of finicky.

tip During the installation of the Microsoft Office updates, you might be prompted to insert your Microsoft Office CD, so keep it and your Office license key handy.

Software Updates

It's not just Windows and Office that need updating. You should check to see if there are updates available for all the programs you use on a regular basis because the fixes will close security holes that could make your software vulnerable to attack by malware. It's especially important that you check for updates for the following programs:

- Email program
- Web browser
- Any program used to communicate with the Internet
- Software firewall

Every program's update process is different, but in the Help menu there is often an option called Check for Updates that automatically checks for newer versions of most programs. If not, check with the software maker's website to see if there are any fixes or patches available. These should be available under Downloads (if there is such a section on the program maker's website) or in the product support area.

Bathe Once a Year Whether You Need It or Not and Reformat and Reinstall, Too

Once a year there's one major task you should do to ensure your computer is extremely secure. Actually, there's one major task and one minor one.

The minor one is easy. Buy an updated copy of this book ever few years because I'll keep you tuned in to new developments in security. The copy you have in your hands now is the second edition of this book.

That said, the major task you should do annually is to wipe your hard drive clean and reinstall Windows from scratch.

Wipe Your Hard Drive and Reinstall Windows

All versions of Windows are notorious for becoming unstable over time. The registry, where Windows keeps track of all of its settings, can become jam-packed with garbage and this in turn can cause sluggish behavior and crashes. That's why I strongly recommend that you reformat your hard drive to wipe it clean and reinstall Windows once a year. If you really work your computer hard (especially if you install a lot of programs), you should reformat and reinstall twice a year.

This ensures that you have the latest and greatest Windows fixes as well as the freshest versions of all your security applications. It also eliminates any residual

note The first edition of this book was published in 2005 under the title *Absolute Beginner's Guide to Security, Spam, Spyware, and Viruses.*

spyware or virus infections (should any have slipped past the defenses). If you have been visited by a hacker, the cleanse also wipes out any modifications they might have made to your computer.

To do this, simply refer to Chapter 9, "Ground Up Security: Wipe Your Hard Drive and Build a Secure Windows PC from the Ground Up", and follow the steps. It's a drastic measure, but it's extremely worthwhile. It keeps your computer as secure as it can be, and a side benefit is that it's the best way to keep your computer running as fast and efficiently as is possible. Understandably, it is an enormous pain in the yum-yum, so take your time. Try to do it over a spare weekend when the kids are at camp or tormenting their grandma at the cottage.

The Absolute Minimum

- Update your spyware and virus signatures daily or several times a week and ensure that automatic updates are turned on in these programs.
- Run Windows updates once a week or monthly at the very least.
- Run a spyware and virus scan once a week. Use a deep scan if available in the software you use.
- Run the Problem Reports utility in Vista to see if there are solutions to system problems.
- Check for Microsoft Office and Firefox updates once a month.
- Check to see if there are updates for your anti-rootkit programs.
- Update all your key programs as fixes become available.
- Be sure your firewall program's automatic updates are on.
- Help your grandma with her security and check other computers in the house, especially those on your network.
- Be sure to check for firmware updates for your home network router. These updates fix programming bugs in your router's software.
- Reformat your hard drive and reinstall Windows, all your programs, and all your security applications every year, and twice a year if you work your computer really hard.

PART

III

Tools for Maintenance and Protection

Selecting Software: Steals, Deals, and Software Duds

There's a lot of software out there in the market to help you make your computer more secure. Some of it's free, some of it's paid, and some is halfway in between. What's safe and what's not? This chapter helps you decide between the various offerings and tells you what features you should look for.

Security Software: Nothing in Life Is Free, Except Software

When it comes to security software, there are lots of choices, lots of features, and lots to worry about. After all, you're acquiring a program to protect your computer from malicious software, so you have to make sure the security software is safe and secure in the first place.

But can you do it all with free software? Yes, absolutely. I worked really hard to provide you with free software options all the way through this book.

Leo Laporte, my co-host on the TV show *Call for Help*, taught me about freeware. He has been proclaiming the merits of free software, especially free security software, for a long time. I have to say I was a little dubious at first, but Leo sold me. Freeware is often as good as payware. That said, let's look at the difference.

Payware: Software You Pay Hard-Earned Cash For

Payware is a word that I invented to define programs that you pay for. It is commercial software, the kind you see when you go to the store and buy at the checkout or download for a fee from the Internet. Typically, payware is created by a for-profit company that is in the business of publishing software.

Some payware is subscription-based. For example, antivirus programs work forever, but they stop downloading new virus signatures after a year unless an annual fee is paid. Without new signatures, it's not useful against new threats.

Advantages: Payware has a company that stands behind it. That's important when it comes to security programs because you want someone to go to in the event of a problem.

The price also includes some form of help offering (often called *support*). There is usually a phone number to call where you can reach someone (if only for a limited period of time) if you have a problem with the product or need help making it work. However, sometimes this service is not that helpful. Payware also comes with the expectation that it is spyware- and virus-free.

Disadvantages: Payware can be expensive. Although some software can be affordable, often packages will cost you $35–$65 and sometimes more. Sometimes the support offering is not very good.

Trust factor: When it comes to security software, you can generally trust payware because there's a company that stands a lot to lose if its products fail, are defective, or are not trustworthy.

Freeware: Don't Pay a Cent for Software

Freeware includes programs that are offered to the public free, although programmers will sometimes ask for voluntary donations or will limit free use to individuals or non-profit organizations.

Programmers distribute free programs for the following reasons:

> **note** The adware or spyware model for free software is not used (to my knowledge) with free security software. It would be counterintuitive, don't you think?

- It's a public service and the programmer believes there's a public need for the program (see Figure 11.1). Sometimes the programmer has idealistic or altruistic motives.

- It's a marketing ploy that helps upsell users to a paid version that has more features.

- It supports other paid interests, as is the case with free software from Microsoft or Google.

> **note** In the license for the free Spybot Search & Destroy antispyware program, author Patrick Kolla writes, "What do you get if you buy software? Lots of ones and zeros, nothing more. If they were distributed as art, I could understand paying it [*sic*]. But if the main goal of their order is to earn money—by fees or ads—I don't like it!"

- It's paid for with advertising or included adware or spyware.

- It supports a service, with which the programmer makes money.

- For self-promotion, to show off their programming prowess.

Programmers will also sometimes offer the source code free as well. The source code is the lines of programming that make up the program. This is often referred to as *open source software*.

If a program is open source, it's a good sign that nothing in it is untoward. Buried programming code in open source software that does bad things to the end user's computer would be discovered quickly by other programmers.

Advantages: It's free! It's available instantly from the Internet. It's often really great, and sometimes as good as or better than its payware equivalents.

Disadvantages: If it's not open source, you don't know if there's any dangerous code in the program. There is little support for the program from the author because he doesn't have the resources to help everyone who needs it.

Trust factor: Not trustworthy; however, if it's free and recommended by the Internet community or other reliable sources, it's pretty safe to use. If it's open source, that's even better.

11

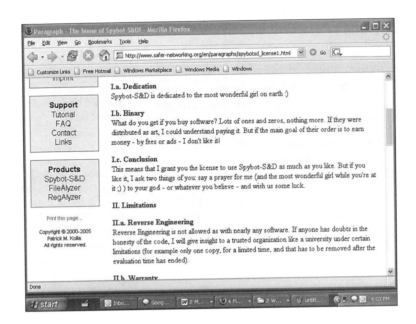

FIGURE 11.1
Patrick Kolla, author of Spybot Search & Destroy, gives away the software for a prayer and some luck sent to him and his girlfriend.

Weirdware: When It's Not Payware or Freeware

Some software lives in the netherworld between freeware and payware. Here are some types you might encounter.

Gimpware: Free Software, But Not All the Bits Work

Gimpware is a type of payware that has some of its features disabled. It's designed to allow you to use it to get a sense of whether it will be useful to you. In order to get the extra features unlocked, however, you need to pay the author and acquire a license key so you can unlock the full functionality of the program.

Some antivirus and antispyware programs scan and find infections but don't remove them unless you buy a software license, for example.

Advantages: Offers a "try before you buy" experience.

Disadvantages: Doesn't give you the full experience of all the software's features.

Trust factor: Gimpware is payware, so generally gimpware does nothing to impact the trustworthiness of the end product. It is more of a marketing tactic. Using gimpware as a full solution is not a good idea from a security perspective unless all the features you need are unlocked.

> **note** Some geeks call it crapware or bloatware.

> **note** Often you'll get trialware security software on a new computer. Getting a machine without it isn't an option because the computer maker gets paid by the trialware maker to install the software on the new machine. Dell recently started offering its customers a line of trialware-free computers.

Trialware: It's Free, Until It's Not

Trialware is payware that is free to use without any limitation for a set period of time, often 15 or 30 days, so you can try it out before you decide to purchase it (see Figure 11.2). After the trial period, the program no longer runs. Again, this is a marketing tactic.

Advantages: "Try before you buy" approach to software.

Disadvantages: Sometimes the trial period is not long enough to get a full sense of its usefulness, and if you buy a new system, it might come with so much trialware that the system is bloated out of the box.

Trust factor: Trialware tends be trustworthy and in fact can instill more trust because you see how it works before committing to paying for it.

Shareware: I Trust You to Pay Me

Shareware is usually written by a small company or individual programmer. It's distributed with the understanding that if you like it and use it, you will voluntarily pay for it after a 30-day trial period, but it doesn't become disabled when this time period expires.

Advantages: The ultimate "try before you buy" software because the trial period never ends. It's often a very affordable way to acquire excellent software. Since it usually comes from a small programming shop, the support can be excellent because the publisher is close to the product.

Disadvantages: The support may be nonexistent because the publisher is a small company or an individual. Sometimes the program is amateurish or not well designed, although I find this is the exception to the rule.

Trust factor: It's tough to feel secure when using shareware, unless it's a product that has been around for a while and has a good reputation. If you watch the Internet for feedback on shareware, you'll be able to avoid bad programs. Use shareware based on its reputation and look for reviews or commentary on the Internet before installing it.

11

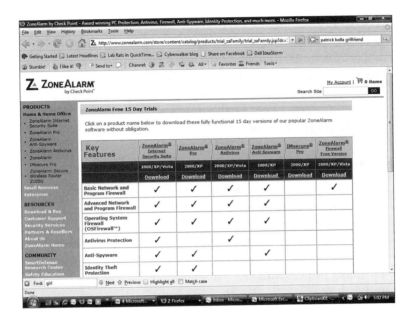

FIGURE 11.2
CheckPoint offers 15-day trials of all its software, except for ZoneAlarm Free Firewall, which it gives away for free.

What Should I Pay for My Security Toolbox?

Security problems on your computer are not your fault. So you shouldn't have to pay to protect yourself. However, sometimes the responsible parties, such as your Internet provider, the software publishers, and Microsoft, fail miserably to protect you. So you have to take it upon yourself to make sure your computer, the assets on it, and your digital life is as secure as it can be.

The programs I recommend in this book are every bit as good as the payware products marketed to you. The freebies are by no means premium products, so some conveniences are not included.

If you come across payware that you like the feel of, that you learn to trust, and that makes you feel more confident than freeware, by all means pay for the software and use it.

Sometimes it's worth buying the extra-strength, coated painkillers, right? It's better than the chalky, slow-acting, and bitter tablets. But both kinds do the job. So it is with security software. Sometimes it's worth the money to get software that's a little more palatable.

So what should you pay? Usually not more than $50 per software title. Antivirus programs run $35–$65 per year (see Figure 11.3). Antispyware products seem to float around $30 per year. You're paying annually for the ongoing signature updates.

Software firewalls and anti-spam programs are sometimes treated like services and run $30–$40 per year or thereabouts.

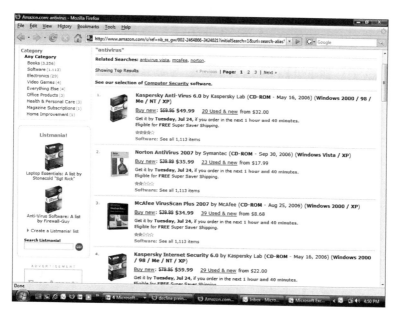

FIGURE 11.3

Big-brand antivirus payware runs around $35 to $65 on Amazon.com, which includes one year of updates and virus signatures.

BUYER BEWARE: HOW TO AVOID BAD SOFTWARE PRODUCTS

If you decide to buy software for your security needs, here are a few tips to help you buy the right program for your needs:

▪ Before buying, go to the publisher's website and look at the support area to see what problems have been posted. Also look at the support forums, if available, to see what other users are saying.

- Search for reviews of the software on the Internet and read a few. No one reviewer will have it all right. Look for a consensus.

- Use the trialware version for 30 days, if available. Most antispyware and antivirus programs have 30-day trials.

- If it's free, read the end-user license agreement. It's boring as haddock, but the publisher will sometimes reveal advertising, adware, or spyware clauses.

- New software always has problems. It usually takes a publisher three to six months to post fixes to their software after it is initially released.

- If you want to be conservative, buy only mature software that has reached version 3. Microsoft is famous for getting it right by the third time around, although I am not sure what happened with Windows XP.

- Newsgroups and user forums are also great places to get unbiased feedback on software.

Choosing the Right Security Software

Here are the features you should look for in each type of security software.

Antivirus

All good antivirus programs should come with these must-have features:

- **Virus signatures**—Downloadable digital snapshots used by the program to identify viruses available daily or multiple times a day.

- **Automatic downloads**—The program should be able to download new virus signatures once a day or more frequently as they become available.

- **Heuristics**— This is the ability for the program to learn from experience. Heuristic programming allows an antivirus program to stop a virus by detecting virus-like behavior before a specific infection is identified.

- **Automatic scans**—The ability to schedule a virus scan. Look for daily, weekly, and monthly options that allow scheduling at a specific time of day.

■ **Email protection**—Most viruses arrive and spread through email so an antivirus program should at very least scan incoming email. Some also scan outbound email, although this feature can slow a system down.

caution If you have an antivirus program that has expired but is still working, is it any good? No! An antivirus program is useless if it's not protecting your computer from new threats.

■ **Frugal with resources**—A good antivirus program should not use a lot of memory or processor power to protect a system. It should have little or no impact on system performance.

■ **Virus cleaner**—A good antivirus program should not only stop viruses, but also clean infections quickly and on demand.

■ **Redundancy**—It's nice if an antivirus program also catches some spyware or defends against other threats such as phishing emails.

Antispyware

Here are the features I recommend you look for in an antispyware program:

■ **Spyware signatures**—Downloadable digital snapshots used by the program to identify spyware adware, hijackers, and Trojan horses.

■ **Automatic downloads**—The program should download new spyware signatures once a day or more frequently as they become available.

■ **Hijacker removal**—Browser hijackers are difficult to remove, but some of the better antispyware programs deal with the nastier infections.

■ **Live protection**—This is a feature that watches for spyware infections in real time at a series of entry points on a computer. Different programs use different terms. Microsoft AntiSpyware, for example, calls it real-time protection. You might see it referred to as an immunization feature.

■ **Effective removal tools**—The program should not only be able to defend against threats, but also remove infections. Not all antispyware products are created equal in this regard.

Firewall

Here are the key features you should look for in firewall software:

- **Inbound protection**—Analysis of traffic coming from the Internet into the computer.

- **Outbound protection**—Analysis of traffic outbound from the computer to the Internet, which checks to see if a virus, spyware, or other malware is trying to communicate with the outside world.

- **Stealth mode**—The ability to make the computer invisible even if probed from the Internet.

- **Alert suppression**—Option to turn off or minimize alerts generated by attacks or probes from the outside and the ability to set alert levels for outbound traffic. These can be frequent and annoying.

- **Downloadable policies**—Filters that can be downloaded from the Internet that keep the firewall up-to-date from certain malicious websites and new threats on the Internet. Ideally these should be automatic.

- **Malware detection**—Detection and blockage of viruses, spyware, and other malware as it travels through the firewall. Some pro versions offer this.

- **Lifestyle modes**—This is an optional feature, but a nice one if you can get it. It allows you to easily set the firewall for certain specialty uses of the firewall, such as serving a website, peer-to-peer file sharing, and gaming.

- **Low maintenance**—You should be bugged by the firewall only when absolutely necessary.

- **Geek factor**—Some software firewalls are much better than others at helping novices understand what activities are being flagged and which should be allowed or denied. Some products assume that their users are all IT guys and will understand the geeky warnings. Choose one with a low geek factor.

GET IT FREE FROM YOUR ISP

As part of your security software shopping spree, check with your Internet service provider (ISP). Many offer free security suites (see Figure 11.4) that are actually made by big-brand security companies.

For example, F-Secure makes a software suite that includes an antivirus, antispyware, firewall, and other security programs that are offered free or at a low cost by many major Internet providers to their broadband customers. It's branded by the ISP, but uses F-Secure technology.

The nice thing about these suites is that you can turn some components off so you can choose to use only the applications you need in concert with ones you already have.

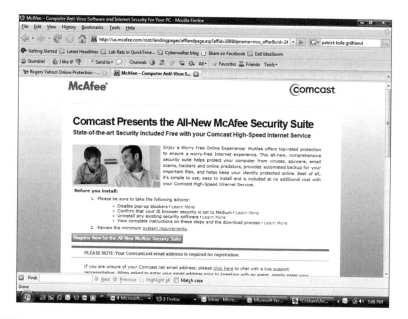

FIGURE 11.4

Comcast provides its cable Internet subscribers with a free security suite from McAfee.

Anti-Spam

Here are features you should find in good anti-spam programs:

- **High detection rates**—Good anti-spam programs should stop more than 90% of the spam headed for your inbox.

- **Few false positives**—Very few legitimate emails should be mistaken for spam.

- **Subscription management**—Emails that are from machines but are not spam, such as newsletters, should not be treated as spam.
- **Spam signature updates**—It's helpful to have an anti-spam engine that can be updated with spam signatures so the software can be alerted to new spam being delivered across the Internet.
- **Override**—An override mechanism that enables you to receive some mail that is tagged as spam but that you want to see anyway.
- **Undo**—A good anti-spam program should make it easy to restore email that has been marked as spam, but isn't. Look for a one-button option. Cloudmark Desktop, for example, has an Unblock button.
- **Anti-phishing feature**—Many anti-spam products catch phishing emails as well as spam.

HOT TREND: WIRELESS SECURITY SOFTWARE

With the popularity of Wi-Fi networks at home, there are now utilities available to make them more secure. McAfee offers WiFiScan for $49, which alerts you to intruders on your network and does a security analysis to keep your wireless network secure. Network Magic (www.networkmagic.com) offers a similar utility (priced at $29.99 to $49.99). A trialware version that retains basic functionality after seven days is also available for free.

The Absolute Minimum

- There's a lot of free security software that is as good as or better than its paid counterparts.
- You can trust freeware, if it comes recommended by users on the Internet, credible reviews, or other sources you trust (like me!). Always check with multiple sources. Seeking a consensus will protect you.
- Payware, which is commercial software you pay for, is worthwhile if it offers a better experience or features not offered in freeware.
- The best kind of freeware is open source software, where the author makes the programming code available for inspection and improvement.
- Shareware software, in which the author asks for voluntary payment, is often worthwhile; just make sure it has a good reputation before you come to rely on it.

- Gimpware or trialware are versions of payware that have been crippled or have a limited free-use period to help upsell you to a full, paid version.

- Most payware security software should cost around $35 to $75. Most products are subscription based; which means that you renew each year to continue to receive updates and signatures that identify malware.

- There are many features that an antivirus and antispyware program should have, but one critical one is daily signature updates.

- A software firewall should watch inbound and outbound data traffic. A bonus feature is detection and blockage of viruses and spyware as they cross the firewall.

- Anti-spam products should have a detection rate of more than 90% and a low rate of false positives, where legitimate email is marked as spam.

11

Tools of the Trade: Security Products You Should Own

Because home computer security is a hot topic, many companies want a piece of the action. Products have flooded the marketplace and making a choice about which one to use can be confusing. In this chapter, I've provided a roundup of some of the most common products you'll encounter, and I offer some capsule reviews.

Which Security Software Is Right for You?

Marketing is an ugly business. Its mission is to highlight the good points of a product and downplay its bad features. I always marvel at how companies can market basic products such as toilet paper or chewing gum (spanning two ends of the human spectrum!) and represent them as something more exotic than what they really are.

note Prices in this section are in U.S. dollars and were taken from common Internet software sales sites (like Amazon or Tiger Direct) or the software manufacturer's site. If the price you find is lower—lucky you! If it's higher, keep looking or consider that the manufacturer might have changed the pricing. I've done my best to use street pricing that I found when wrote this book in early 2008.

Marketers do the same with software. And since they can be really clever, it's hard not to be swayed by the influential messages they dangle in front of us simple apes. To that end, I've listed in this chapter some of the most common products that I think are worthy (with a couple of exceptions) that you'll likely encounter in your travels from tree to tree on the Internet.

Mixed in for good measure are many of the key freebies I mention in this book so that you have a single place to reference them.

Security Suites

Let's start with the security suites because that's what you'll likely encounter first from the well-marketed brands. These programs are bundles of security programs that offer antivirus, antispyware, and firewall protection in one program. Many include extra security applications such as parental controls, privacy sentries, and potato peelers. Okay, that last one's an exaggeration, but you get the idea. These programs are jammed packed with all kinds of security features, often to the detriment of your system's performance.

SECURITY SUITE SHOPPING TIPS

Shopping for an Internet security suite can be daunting, but there are some fundamentals that you should consider that will make choosing a product easy.

- **What programs are included?** At a minimum, you should be offered an antivirus product, an antispyware product and a two-way firewall. Beyond that, look carefully at what is offered. More programs require more memory and system resources, slowing your system. They also increase the likelihood that something will interfere with other programs or processes. More isn't better.

- **How many licenses?** Does the suite include a license to install on one or more computers? Many of the suites offer licenses on up to three computers.

- **What do the geeks say?** A search for reviews or posts on public Internet forums will give you a hint as to what the geeks are saying about the suite. It's a geek fetish to road-test these programs and express opinions publicly. Use Google.com to see what users and the technology media are saying about the product.

- **How much?** Do you need to spend more than $60 for a suite? No. Unless there is an obvious enticement, all of your security software (including spam, antispyware, and so on) shouldn't set you back more than $100 per year in the aggregate. If you buy a suite, aim for $40 to $60.

- **Does it work on Vista?** Make sure the suite is compatible with Windows Vista if that's what you use. Security programs can be sticky with the operating system, so make sure the publisher declares it Vista-ready before you commit.

Symantec Norton Internet Security

Norton is the granddaddy of them all. Symantec, which owns the Norton brand, is a market leader in Internet security software. As a research and development company, they have a powerful team of anti-malware people backing their software products. That's the good news.

The bad news is while their detection technologies are very good, they have buried them inside a mammoth, oppressive, and unyielding application that bogs down your computer and causes more trouble than it prevents. If the

Norton security suite were a zoo animal, you'd have a half-ton of self-righteous hairy elephant on your hands.

My colleagues and I have been bellyaching about Symantec's fat-code approach for years, but the company has been oblivious to the criticism. That is until early 2008 when they started talking about a leaner version of their security suite.

Your choice in suites include Norton Internet Security, which is a full suite, or Norton 360, which is a plus-sized security suite that includes all the NIS stuff and some data backup and recovery tools.

Go with Norton if you don't care about performance and are okay with being locked down tighter than a marshmallow in a vice. Otherwise steer clear.

Price: Norton Internet Security $59.49; Norton 360 $77.99

Info: www.norton. com

McAfee Internet Security Suite

Like Symantec, the McAfee Security suites are very well marketed. You'll either find demo copies on a new computer you buy, or you'll encounter the products in special bundled offers or other software boxes.

Once again I recommend you steer clear of this company's suites. Although the McAfee products are slightly less oppressive than the Norton suites, they still bog down the performance on an otherwise speedy, robust system.

Now a caveat here. I have a close relationship with the McAfee people and I like them and their efforts. But they are blind to the gluttonous aspect of their product and it amazes me that they are deluded into thinking it's faultless.

Like Symantec, McAfee products have world-class malware detection and removal technologies. Their user interface is also lacking. Dropping this suite on your system is like hooking up a cabin cruiser on a trailer to your Smart car (or if you don't have one of those locally, imagine one of those tiny subcompact commuter cars).

Their suites include McAfee Internet Security, a 10-part suite, or McAfee Total Protection, which has 12 components.

Once again: Steer clear. If you have to choose, go with a McAfee suite over a Norton one. That said, some people, like my dad, like the install-and-forget nature of the suite.

But trust me. You have better options. Keep reading.

> **tip** One of the bonuses you get from most suites is that the price includes licenses for three computers. This is true for the Norton, McAfee, and F-Secure products.

> **Price**: McAfee Internet Security Suite $49.99 or McAfee Total Protection $59.99

> **Info**: www.mcafee. com

F-Secure Internet Security

F-Secure Internet Security is the suite I like (see Figure 12.1). Although it's perhaps harder on system performance than other standalone products, the trade-off is worthwhile.

Most important, the impact on the system after installation is negligible. The user interface is straightforward. The signatures in the main scanner include two antivirus signatures from two separate AV teams plus an antispyware signature set. This redundancy gives you formidable protection. It also includes a firewall and a web content filter (which I turn off, but as a parent you might find it useful to protect your little clickers).

It's simple. It's easy to use and it is made by Finns. What more could you ask? Well, a lower price. Still: **Highly recommended!**

> **Price**: This suite can be priced at over US$70, but you'll see frequent special pricing that discounts it.

> **Info**: www.fsecure.com

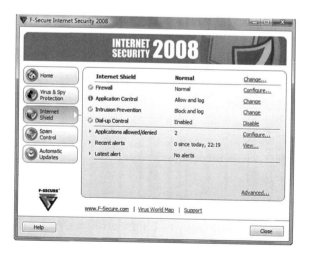

FIGURE 12.1

F-Secure makes a security suite that is one of my favorites for its simplicity and effectiveness.

CA Internet Security Suite Plus

On top of virus, spyware, firewall, and spam tools, Computer Associates have added a few new tools for their 2008 version. These include parental controls, a phishing browser toolbar, and a desktop settings migration application. Each component has its own control window, which slows the application and gives it a poorly integrated feel. On Vista, User Account Control approval is needed for every setting change, which is frustrating.

Malware scans take a healthy portion of CPU use, although RAM is negligibly impacted. While testers were running a manual virus scan, the automated virus scan started running, too, which brought the test computer to its knees. The firewall has bugs as well. It crashed the system on an attempted file transfer using an FTP server. That said, the spam filter is very good, once it is trained. This suite needs work. The upside: It is fairly easy to use compared to other suites.

Price: $69.99

Info: www.ca.com

Webroot AntiVirus with AntiSpyware & Firewall

Webroot is known for its excellent antispyware product Spy Sweeper. So I was surprised to see that they added an antivirus engine (from Sophos) and then a firewall to their offering (as a freebie download). Good thing. They needed a strong suite to compete with the bigger dogs in this market.

The product has a simple interface and a good record in terms of malware detection. One version of the product stomped on my Vista system. But Webroot quickly corrected it with a new download. It's not really forgivable, but I forgave them anyway. Good product. Good pricing. Good protection. You can't go wrong here, unless they release another sloppy version.

Bottom line here is the Webroot suite is a much better choice over the mainstream suites.

Price: $39.95

Info: www.webroot.com

ZoneAlarm Internet Security Suite

Although ZoneAlarm may be a familiar name for personal firewalls, the brand is a relative newcomer when it comes to security suites. The ZoneAlarm team has built onto its firewall control panel, integrating virus, spyware, firewall, and spam filters into one easy application (see Figure 12.2). It is well laid out and very user-friendly for the beginner. It's also packed with advanced settings to appease the ubergeeks. As for virus scanning, it's fairly demanding on the CPU and will impact system performance badly, so an overnight scan is recommended to stay productive.

The firewall is great, with three levels of protection for local network settings (LAN) and three levels of protection for internet settings (WAN). Additionally, the 14-day auto-learn feature lets the firewall learn your computing behavior for 14 days and keeps pop-up warnings to a minimum during that time. After the 14 days it switches to more aggressive firewall settings.

There is also an operating system firewall, which monitors your application use for six days, and then locks down your system asking about new applications and programs with pop-up warnings.

The spam filtering options are also comprehensive. There are many, many things to like about this suite, if you can overlook the CPU-hogging virus scanner. **Highly Recommended!**

> **Price**: $49.95
>
> **Info**: www.zonealarm.com

FIGURE 12.2

ZoneAlarm started as a firewall; now it's a nicely packaged security suite.

ESET Smart Security

ESET initially made a name for themselves in the antivirus market with geek favorite NOD32. To leverage that success, they've launched a security suite. ESET Smart Security includes virus, spyware, spam, and firewall protection in a well-designed, integrated suite. The virus and spyware scanners are combined into one application, so running a virus scan also means running a spyware scan as well. To my mind this is good. As with NOD32, the software is very resource-friendly both with CPU and RAM, when you run a malware scan. You can also launch the Smart Security control panel from Microsoft's Outlook toolbar, a nice touch. This suite is simple, streamlined, without the extra fat and bloat. It is much loved, especially by Ted Gallardo, one of my researchers. **Highly recommended!**

Price: $59.99

Info: www.eset.com

Panda Internet Security

Panda Security has done a decent job with their Internet security application. This large suite includes protection against viruses, spyware, and spam. It features a firewall, parental controls, as well as bonus applications like a system optimizer, and a backup utility. Although it can be a CPU hog when running a malware scan, there is an option to make scanning low priority so that you can run other applications while scanning for malware. It's not the most intuitive or easy-to-use suite, especially when you drill into the advanced settings and preferences. One bonus feature is password protection when you exit the suite. This helps prevent malware from disabling the suite.

On the downside, the suite does not integrate well with Microsoft Outlook. The application consistently made Outlook crash and shut down when running a virus scan from it. On the upside, there are few annoying pop-up windows. The application is good at learning your computing habits and adjusting with dumb alerts. If you are looking for a suite bundled with a lot of applications, then this one is worth considering.

Price: $69.95

Info: www.pandasecurity.com

12

Trend Micro Internet Security

Trend Micro is an up-and-coming security software company that has been growing through acquisitions in recent years. It takes security products seriously, so I think it's worth taking a look at its software. PC-cillin Anti-Virus is its flagship offering that comes in a suite of tools that includes spyware, spam, and Wi-Fi protection, as well as a firewall. As suites go, it's well rounded and relatively unobtrusive. That said, its glaring red interface gives me a headache. Its settings menus are a bit scattered, and it will take some patience to find key settings, tweak them, and master this software. The back-end virus scanning engine, however, is solid. PC-cillin is not high on my list as an antivirus product, but if you're after a well-priced and competent security suite, take a look at it.

> **Price**: $49.95
>
> **Info**: www.trendmicro.com

Antivirus Programs

As you no doubt know by now, antivirus programs rebuke viruses. Here are software packages you'll probably encounter, in no particular order.

Freeware

When it comes to free antivirus products, there's a decent selection of good ones. Here are three I like.

Alwil Software's Avast! Antivirus

Don'tbe fooled by avast!'s media player–like appearance. Under its shiny metallic skin, it is a feature-packed antivirus program. Novice users will appreciate its intuitive design. To scan your local hard drive, click on the box-like hard drive logo. Likewise, click the CD logo to select your optical drive. Then, click the Play button and avast! scans your computer for viruses. Unfortunately, avast! can only be set to perform automatic system scans when you boot up your computer. It also features email, instant messaging, and P2P scanning.

> **Price**: Free
>
> **Paid upgrade**: avast! AntiVirus Professional
>
> **Info**: www.avast. com

12

Grisoft AVG Anti-Virus Free Edition

Grisoft's AVG Free Edition is the best free antivirus software available. It features a scanner that constantly monitors your system for viruses. It also comes with an email scanner that can check your incoming and outgoing messages for viruses. The software is set to automatically perform daily updates and scheduled system scans. It's nicely laid out (see Figure 12.3), but could do with some refinements in some of the submenus; still, you can't beat its ability to defend your computer, especially given the price. **Highly recommended!**

Price: Free

Paid upgrade: AVG Professional Edition

Info: http://free.grisoft.com

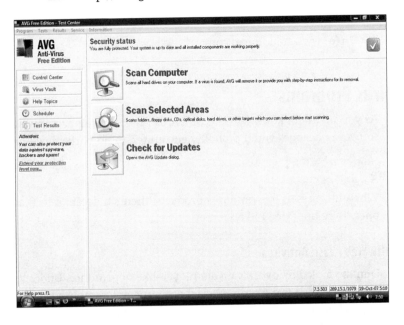

FIGURE 12.3

AVG Free Edition from Grisoft is free, fairly easy to use, and effective. As free antivirus products go, you can't beat it.

tip Grisoft also makes a paid Internet security suite for the home user, which includes an antivirus, antispyware, anti-spam, and firewall combination.

Avira AntiVir Personal Edition Classic

This antivirus program from German software developer H+BEDV Datentechnik (try saying that five times fast at Octoberfest) is another free AV product. With quirky window title names such as Luke Filewalker and menu text that doesn't make grammatical sense, AntiVir is a bit offbeat. Nonetheless, it provides simple antivirus protection to safeguard your computer with a frugal use of memory. The program can be difficult for the beginner, and note that it doesn't automatically check for updates or scan email.

> **caution** AntiVir's website is often sluggish or down, so if you can't access it, try again a little while later. It's also a problem if you need to update this application's signatures.

Price: Free

Paid upgrade: AntiVir Personal Edition Premium

Info: www.free-av.com

Paid Antivirus Programs

If you're going to pay for your antivirus program, here are two you'll definitely encounter and five more you might consider. Note that prices for antivirus products are based on an annual subscription.

> **tip** There are several good, free online virus scanners that work from the Web. Check out Trend Micro's Housecall at http://housecall.trendmicro.com and Panda Security's ActiveScan (note: use with XP; doesn't work with Vista) at www.pandasecurity.com/homeusers/solutions/activescan/. Also check out Kaspersky Lab's Online Scanner at http://usa.kaspersky.com/products_services/free-virus-scanner.php. See also F-Secure Beta Online Scan at http://support.f-secure.com/enu/home/ols.shtml and Microsoft OneCare Beta at http://onecare.live.com/site/en-us/center/howsafe.htm.
>
> You'll need to use Internet Explorer with most of these scanners as Mozilla Firefox typically isn't supported.

Symantec Norton AntiVirus

Symantec's sleek antivirus application is an easy choice for home users because it has a basic, straightforward interface and is easy for the average person to use. Its customizable menus give advanced users the opportunity to fine-tune the way Norton AntiVirus works. However, the program is a little bloated and slows your system down, especially with the email scanner on and the worm blocker, too. Put this program on a diet and it would come recommended.

Price: $39.99

Info: www.symantec. com

12

McAfee VirusScan Plus

Aimed at the beginner, McAfee's antivirus software has traditionally been easy to use and particularly competent. Not so much in 2007 as it had a false start with Windows Vista, but McAfee has since corrected the wrinkles. The program automatically checks for updates on a daily basis to keep you as protected as possible. I'm not a huge fan of this product because it can be sluggish at times, but if it comes on your machine or you are used to its interface, then it's a reasonable choice—but I wouldn't seek it out.

> **Price**: $39.99
>
> **Info**: www.mcafee.com

Eset NOD32

NOD32 is a very comprehensive antivirus product capable of detecting and removing some spyware and adware as a bonus. Unfortunately, it's somewhat difficult to use. However, it can be customized nicely and lets users control how each part of the antivirus program works. However, you'll first have to figure out the modules, each of which have been given an acronym: AMON, DMON, EMON, IMON, and NOD32 (see Figure 12.4). If you can figure it all out, it's a nice program that's very resource-friendly and super efficient when doing a full system scan. Plus it has a module to detected spyware, which it calls "potentially unwanted programs". **Highly recommended!**

> **Price**: $39
>
> **Info**: www.eset.com

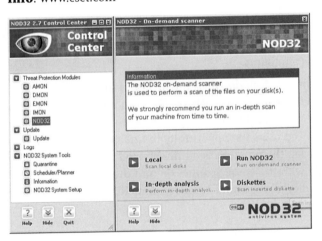

FIGURE 12.4

NOD32 is an excellent antivirus product that is lean on system resources and customizable, though not a good choice for new users.

F-Secure Anti-Virus 2008

F-Secure's antivirus product is a pricey, yet solid choice because it's easy to use, relatively light on memory, and is highly customizable for advanced users. For example, the scanning engine can be set daily, weekly, or monthly. It retrieves signature updates on demand several times a day as they become available. As paid products go, this is my first choice for new users and second choice for geeks, behind NOD32. **Highly recommended!**

Price: $65.90

Info: www.f-secure.com

Kaspersky Anti-Virus 7.0

The Moscow-based Kaspersky Lab makes a competent antivirus software package that you'll be very happy with. I like that it can be set to check for virus signatures as frequently as hourly through once a week. It's pretty much a fire-and-forget product, which is nice, although advanced users will want to explore its settings menus for gems such as the Quarantine Maximum Size setting and the option to autoscan every time the virus database is updated. This product has come a long way from its origins and from a detection perspective is as good as any of the better-known antivirus products. That said, it is by far the slowest virus scanner I've seen. In one test scan it took over five hours to scan a 20GB hard drive.

Price: $49.95

Info: www.kaspersky.com

Panda Antivirus 2008

How often do you get a panda's head sitting in your Windows system tray? That's the icon that represents Panda Security's Antivirus 2008. Warm and fuzzies aside, this antivirus product is well designed, easy to use, and frugal with system resources. I like that it does what it calls a Periodic Self Diagnosis. Every 15 minutes the product ensures your system is properly protected and will only warn you if there's a problem unless you turn on the Always Show the Result option. The program also comes with an antispyware scanner component that checks for and purges potentially malicious tracking cookies and other spyware when running a virus scan. It self-configures really well. Symantec could learn a thing or two from Panda. If you're looking for a really well-designed antivirus payware product, install this product's 30-day trial to get a feel for it. It's worth a closer look.

Price: $49.95

Info: www.pandasecurity.com

Antispyware

Antispyware software is a huge category. You'll need more than one program to catch and remove all the possible infections. My optimal configuration includes CA Anti-Spyware 2007 or Webroot's Spy Sweeper (both are payware), and two freeware products: Microsoft Windows Defender and Spybot Search & Destroy.

Freeware

Here are the key free antispyware products I have mentioned in this book. Use two or more together for optimal spyware detection.

Spybot Search & Destroy

Spybot is one of the best free antispyware applications for home users (see Figure 12.5). The program will automatically check for and fix any problems when installed, and can be set to clean and perform updates every time you start the program. The resident system blocker protects you against spyware installed through Internet Explorer. Spybot also features advanced system tools to stop unwanted programs from starting up when your computer boots up. Its myriad menus and settings can be daunting if you dig down into the program, but it's a solid application that everyone should own. **Highly recommended!**

> **Price**: Free
>
> **Paid upgrade**: None
>
> **Info**: www.safer-networking.net

Lavasoft's Ad-Aware 2007 Free

Like Spybot Ad-Aware 2007 Free is another antispyware program that's completely free. When prompted, the application scans your PC for spyware and adware. If anything is found, you're given the option to quarantine or remove the problems. Sometimes, Ad-Aware's thorough scan might indicate problems that are just normal system files. If you use Ad-Aware, be careful not to accidentally remove *wanted* files. Ad-Aware prompts you to update every two weeks so your software stays up-to-date. The paid version features pop-up

FIGURE 12.5

Spybot Search & Destroy was one of the first free antispyware products and is still one of the best.

blocking. Not my personal favorite program because in tests, its ability to catch key pieces of spyware was lacking, but lots of people would poke me in the eye for saying that. It is a much-loved program. The other irritant: its author includes disabled paid features in the user interface. This can be confusing and annoying for some end users.

Price: Free

Paid upgrade: Ad-Aware 2007 Plus & Pro

Info: www.lavasoft.com

Grisoft Anti-Spyware Free Edition

AVG Anti-Spyware Free is an antispyware application that hails from the same people who develop and program AVG Anti-Virus (Free Edition). This application scans your system for adware, dialers, keyloggers, spyware, Trojans, and worms. Automatically updates itself on a daily basis and has a live real-time protection malware scanner.

Price: Free

Paid upgrade: AVG Anti-Spyware Pro

Info: http://free.grisoft.com

12

Microsoft Windows Defender

Even though the name Microsoft isn't synonymous with computer security, the company's antispyware program is an exception. Of course it was written by someone else and acquired. But good for Microsoft for buying it and making the program free. It is excellent. The program is set to automatically scan your computer for spyware and adware daily. It also monitors Internet, system, and application activity for anything unusual, fixing problems as they arise. Because most features are automated by default, the average user shouldn't have any problems getting Microsoft Windows Defender (see Figure 12.6) up and running. My tests showed that of all the free antispyware programs, it catches the most infections. **Highly recommended!**

Price: Free

Paid upgrade: None

Info: www.microsoft.com/defender

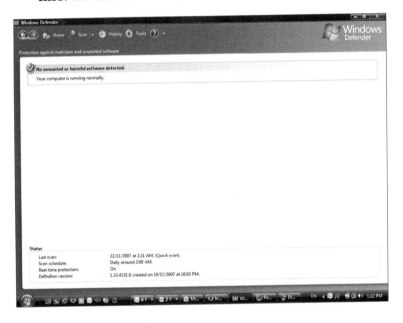

FIGURE 12.6
Microsoft makes Windows Defender free to XP users and it's included in Vista.

note Windows Defender is preinstalled in Windows Vista. To access it on Vista, simply type **defender** in the Start menu search box.

Paid Antispyware Programs

Here are some paid antispyware products I think are worthy of mention. Not all the reviews are good, but at least two come recommended.

Webroot Spy Sweeper

Spy Sweeper is a solid antispyware product that often gets rave reviews. Along with a system scanner and a resident shield that watches points of entry (see Figure 12.7), it can also block ads in web pages, prevent browser hijacks, and protect your system settings from being altered by spyware. Novice users will like the program because it is very helpful. For example, when you're looking at an option menu, text explains what different settings are for. There's also a built-in news service that keeps you informed of new malware activity. It includes a feature that allows you to disable programs from starting up when your computer loads. Plus, it makes editing your Windows startup area easy by filtering out required Windows startup components.

Price: $29.95

Info: www.webroot.com

FIGURE 12.7

Webroot's Spyware Sweeper started as a spyware scanner, but has added an antivirus and firewall component.

CA Anti-Spyware 2007

CA Anti-Spyware 2008 (it's formerly eTrust PestPatrol and still bears this brand) is one of the best antispyware products on the market. It's not perfect, but its plain user interface makes it easy to use (see Figure 12.8) and updates are fetched automatically by the software. The key to its success is that it has high spyware detection rates. In my tests it caught substantially more infections than most payware and freeware products and removed them all. **Highly recommended!**

> **Price**: $29.99
>
> **Info**: www.ca.com/consumer

FIGURE 12.8
CA Anti-Spyware 2007 is easy to use, catches and removes many infections, and is a nice complement to free antispyware programs.

PC Tools Spyware Doctor

This Australia-based antispyware program is an extremely strong contender. It features both quick and full system scans. It has good detection capabilities that outpace most of its competitors. It also automatically searches for signature updates. You can't really go wrong with this program. **Recommended!**

> **Price**: $29.95
>
> **Info**: www.pctools.com

Firewalls

Softwarefirewalls that are payware are a hard sell because a basic two-way firewall that watches inbound and outbound traffic on a computer is all you need. So the freebies cover this category quite nicely.

> **tip** If you have a home network router, you already have a firewall built in that stops dangerous inbound network traffic. Software firewalls are useful because they watch outbound traffic for malware as well.

ZoneAlarm Free

The free edition of ZoneAlarm firewall is a great choice for home computer users with some Internet experience. Although it's not as streamlined as some other firewall applications, it keeps things basic and easy to use. The paid version of ZoneAlarm automatically decides which programs can access the network. With the free version, users must permit or deny a program's access to the Internet. This might be tedious if you're unfamiliar with which programs access the Internet on a regular basis. It can also be dangerous if you unknowingly permit access to an untrustworthy program. Free is good; the Pro version, as you would expect, is better, especially since it also offers virus and spyware protection. **Highly recommended!**

> **Price**: Free

> **Paid upgrade**: ZoneAlarm Pro

> **Info**: www.zonealarm.com

Comodo Free Firewall

Comodo Personal Firewall is a powerful two-way firewall that monitors incoming and outgoing connections on your PC. When you first install it, the pop-up windows are a bother; however, after a bit of training they become less frequent. After a while you'll only see them when you install new software or upgrade older software (like your Firefox web browser) that needs to access the Internet. The main window features three levels of security that you can choose from: Allow All, Custom, and Block All (see Figure 12.9). It also features advanced settings for those who like to tweak their firewall, although a caution here—these settings can be daunting. It's hard to believe that with all these features and options, this firewall is free. Comodo is frugal with memory and processor resources so it doesn't impact system performance. It's very resource-friendly. It works with both Vista and XP.

> **Price**: Free.

> **Info**: www.personalfirewall.comodo.com

12

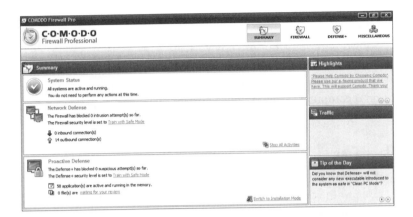

FIGURE 12.9
Comodo is a free firewall that has lots of tweaks for advanced users.

PC Tools Firewall Plus

PC Tools Firewall Plus is a very capable firewall that I like more than
ZoneAlarm Free. It is easy to use and protects your system against hackers
and worms. It includes lots of options and advanced settings choices for those
who like to tweak their firewall, but can also be left untweaked for the beginner user. Its alerts are simple to understand and respond to, and they are not
too frequent after the first few days of use.

Price: Free

Info: www.pctools.com

Anti-Spam

Other than the built-in junk mail filtering in Microsoft Outlook 2003, I have
never found a free anti-spam program worth keeping (although I do mention
one freebie here, if you are desperate), so most programs listed in this category
are payware.

McAfee Internet Security Suite (Anti-Spam)

McAfee SpamKiller (see Figure 12.10) is designed to keep junk mail out and let
legitimate email messages in. It works well with most popular email programs
(note for geeks: all POP3 clients), such as Outlook Express. When it is

installed, a toolbar is added to your email program that so that you can approve messages or flag them as spam and block them. You can add people to your friends list to ensure you receive their emails, or you can add addresses to your blocked senders list to keep spam out. It's a decent solution, but lets some spam through and sometimes blocks legitimate emails. At the time of writing, it wasn't Vista-compatible.

Price: $49.99

Info: www.mcafee.com

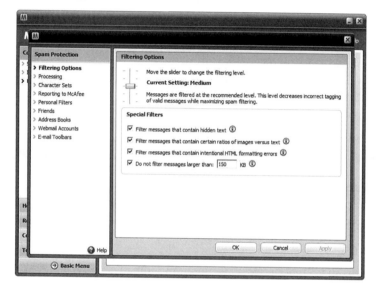

FIGURE 12.10

McAfee SpamKiller is a decent anti-spam product with five levels of automatic spam filtering.

Cloudmark Desktop

Everyone who uses Cloudmark Desktop helps guard against spam. If a commercial email slips into your inbox with this program installed, you use the program to mark it as spam and it tells the Cloudmark server. Everyone benefits. When enough people mark a piece of spam, the program starts to automatically filter inboxes for that message for all Cloudmark users. The program is a plug-in available for Outlook (see Figure 12.11) or Outlook Express. It doesn't work with Vista's Windows Mail. It has a high hit rate and rarely marks a legitimate email as spam. **Highly recommended!**

Price: $39.95 per year

Info: www.cloudmark.com

Cloudmark bar

FIGURE 12.11

Cloudmark Desktop is a spam-filtering plug-in for Outlook (shown) and Outlook Express.

Spam Arrest

This spam blocker works through an online web service rather than through an application installed directly on your computer. Your inbound email is filtered through the service and your email program in turn fetches the cleansed email from the service. Setup is difficult, and many web-based email accounts are not compatible with Spam Arrest. It works with a challenge/response system. If an email sender is not known to the system, he gets an email asking him to type in a code. When he does, the system recognizes him as a human (spam is sent blindly by automated programs, so they can't respond to individual challenges) and the sent email is passed on to the recipient. It stops all spam, but tends to block newsletter subscriptions and other legitimate automated emails. You have to manage those manually.

> **Price**: $44.95 per year
>
> **Info**: www.spamarrest.com

CA Anti-Spam 2007

This very capable anti-spam program takes a little training, but then it catches a significant amount spam. Messages are also checked for email-based phishing attacks and email scams, too. It works with Microsoft email programs only including Windows Mail, Microsoft Outlook and Outlook Express.

> **Price**: $29.99 per year

> **Info**: www.ca.com/consumer

SpamBayes

This freebie anti-spam product is worth a look if you are cheerfully cheap or tight on funds. It works with Microsoft Outlook 2000/2002/2003 (but not 2007). When it works, it is great. When messages start mysteriously being deleted (and are unrecoverable), it's not so great. Avoid it unless you really need a freebie.

> **Price**: Free

> **Info**: http://spambayes.sourceforge.net

12

Glossary

Numbers

802.11 A wireless networking standard that uses the 5GHz radio frequency range used mostly by companies but is not used much any more.

802.11a A wireless networking standard that uses the 5GHz radio frequency range used mostly by companies, but that is not use much any more.

802.11b The original and now aging wireless networking standard, which uses the 2.4GHz radio frequency range and a throughput of 11Mbps.

802.11g The most commonly used wireless networking standard, which uses the 2.4GHz radio frequency range and has a throughput of 54Mbps. Also backward compatible with 802.11b.

802.11i A security standard used with wireless networking that is also known as WPA2.

802.11n The fastest wireless networking standard to date, with a data transfer speed of up to 248Mbps.

A

ActiveX   A grouping of Microsoft technologies that allows programs to share information. However, ActiveX is most obviously encountered when using Microsoft Internet Explorer and appears as a miniprogram that downloads and executes to provide some extra function.

advance fee fraud   A scam in which the target receives an email that contains a money-laundering proposal. At some point, the target is asked to provide a fee in return for a cut on the profits of the scam. Of course, the target never sees a return.

adware   A type of spyware that snoops on computer users and then pushes unwanted advertising at them. Sometimes, simply advertiser-sponsored software.

ASCII   American Standard Code for Information Interchange. A set of codes based on the English alphabet for representing alphanumeric characters and some nonprinting characters as numbers, with each character assigned a number from 0 to 127. Computers use ASCII codes to represent plain text.

autocomplete   A software feature that makes suggestions when a user types into a web browser's address bar, a web page form, or a username or password box on a web page. An autocomplete feature also appears in Microsoft Word.

B

backup   A spare copy of a file or files that has been created in case the original data is damaged or lost.

bandwidth   An Internet connection's capacity to carry data.

bandwidth bandit   A person who accesses a network and uses its Internet connection without permission.

beets   Sugary turnip-like vegetables that are often pickled. The least favorite food of this book's author.

BHO   Browser Helper Object. An add-on program that provides extra functions for Microsoft's Internet Explorer web browser.

black hat   A hacker whose intent is malicious.

bomb   A synonym for a virus payload, the part of a computer virus that does bad things.

boot virus   A type of computer virus that hides in the boot sector of a floppy disk or hard disk. The boot sector is read as part of a disk's startup routine and this activates the virus.

bot   A program that runs automated tasks over the Internet.

botnet   A collection of infected computers (called *zombies*) that are remotely controlled to run worms or Trojan horses or other malware. A botnet can also be commanded to carry out a Distributed Denial of Service attack on a target computer to disable it.

broadband   An Internet connection that's multiple times faster than a 56Kbps dial-up modem.

browser hijacker   A program that changes the home page on a web browser, making it difficult to change it back. *See* hijacker.

Brussels sprouts   Small cabbage-like vegetables that children generally don't like. Also, one of the most comedic vegetables on the planet.

bug   A defect in the programming code or routine of a program.

C

cable modem   A device that uses cable TV lines to connect a computer to the Internet at high speed.

cache   A holding area that contains information so that it can be accessed faster than retrieving it from where it originated.

cheese   A dairy product made from fermented milk. Also, an excellent topic to make jokes about.

cookies   A tiny text file received from a remote website stored on a computer that contain data used to help identify a user to the website or useful for completing a web-based task.

cracker   What people who break into computers call themselves. Synonymous with the mass media term *hacker*.

cyber   A prefix used to indicate that something is computer- or Internet-related. Derived from the word *cybernetics*, which is the discipline that, according to wikipedia.org, studies communication and control in living beings or machines.

cyberspace   A term used to describe the nonphysical, virtual world of computers.

D

DDoS   *See* Distributed Denial of Service.

default   Settings as they were originally configured by a manufacturer or programmer.

DHCP   Dynamic Host Configuration Protocol. A protocol for assigning dynamic IP addresses to devices on a network.

dialer   A computer program that underhandedly dials a remote computer via a modem, incurring long-distance charges or toll-line fees.

dictionary spamming   A technique that combines random words and common names in an effort to come up with valid email addresses.

Digital Subscriber Line (DSL)   A broadband technology offered by telephone companies that connects a computer at high speed to the Internet.

Distributed Denial of Service (DDoS)   An electronic attack perpetrated by a person who controls legions of hijacked computers. On a single command, the computers simultaneously send packets of data across the Internet at a target computer. The attack is designed to overwhelm the target and stop it from functioning.

DNS   *See* Domain Name Server.

Domain Name Server (or System)   A computer (or series of computers) on the Internet that translates domain names (web addresses) into numerical Internet addresses called IP addresses.

drive-by download   A program that automatically downloads to a computer without the computer owner's consent or knowledge.

dropper   A file that conceals malware such as a virus or Trojan horse in an attempt to evade antivirus programs.

DSL   *See* Digital Subscriber Line.

E

email header   Address information attached to the top of an email message.

email scanner   A feature in an antivirus program that checks incoming and outgoing emails for viruses.

encryption   Scrambling of data to prevent it from being seen by unauthorized people.

End User License Agreement (EULA)   Legal text that a user has to agree to before installing a software package, usually in a scrollable box.

Ethernet   A common method of connecting computers together to form a network.

EULA   *See* End User License Agreement.

exploit   A program that takes advantage of a known security weakness in a computer.

external media   Any storage device that can contain a computer file, such as a floppy disk, DVD, or CD, that can be connected to a computer or inserted into a reader attached to a computer.

F

false negatives   Spam that is mistaken for legitimate email. Malware that is not detected.

false positives   Email messages that are mistaken as spam. Also, programming that is detected as malware, but isn't.

farming   *See* pharming.

file infector virus   A type of computer virus that attaches itself to a program file. It executes when the file is run.

filename extension   A three-character suffix that is part of a computer file name (for example, .jpg and .doc). Common to files on a PC.

firewall   A device or program that blocks outsiders from accessing a computer connected to the Internet. Some firewalls also monitor data traffic outbound from a computer or network.

firmware   Programming stored on a chip inside a device (such as a network router) that controls it.

fishing   *See* phishing.

freeware   Software offered to the public free of charge.

G-H

gimpware   Software that does not provide full features until it is paid for.

grey hat (gray hat)   A hacker who sometimes acts legally and with altruistic motives and sometimes doesn't. Think of this type of person as a thief who sometimes steals and sometimes calls you to let you know a window is open.

hack   A clever modification of hardware or software.

hacker   1. In the mass media, this is a bad person who illicitly gains access to a network or computer to which they do not have permission to connect. 2. Among programmers, a hacker is an accomplished programming guru. 3. In some circles, the term can also refer to a programmer who has no finesse. 4. In hardware, a hacker is someone who makes modifications.

hacktivism   A form of vandalism or electronic civil disobedience that serves a political agenda. Usually hacktivists have altruistic motives.

heuristics   Programming code that learns as it goes. A common feature of antivirus or antispyware programs.

HEX   Hexadecimal. A base-16 number system often used to visually represent computer bytes.

hijacker   Short for browser hijacker. A program that forces a web browser to open to a specific web page and makes it difficult to change it.

home network   A group of two or more computers within a user's home that are linked together and share resources such as an Internet connection, printer, or files.

HTML   Hypertext Markup Language. A tagging language used in web pages to format them for display on the World Wide Web.

HTTP   Hypertext transfer protocol. A mechanism or series of rules by which information is transferred across the World Wide Web.

HTTPS   A secure version of HTTP, whereby data transmitted across the Web is scrambled so that it can't be viewed by unauthorized eyes.

I-J

identity theft   The illegal use of an individual's personal or financial information to apply for credit by a criminal without the owner's permission or knowledge.

immunization   *See* live protection.

infection   The presence of a virus, a worm, spyware, or other malware on a computer.

initialization vector   The part of a security key that helps scramble information differently each time a chunk of encrypted data is transmitted.

Internet Service Provider (ISP)   A company that provides access to the Internet.

intranet   A private network that uses web technology to distribute information. Usually used to make information available inside a company among employees.

IP address   Internet Protocol address. A numerical address consisting of four sets of numbers ranging from 0 to 255 and separated by dots, which is assigned to each computer on the Internet or closed network.

IP spoofing   A bit of high-tech trickery that makes an email (or some other piece of transmitted data) look like it came from somewhere it did not. It's like sending a letter to your friend and changing the return address on the envelope to make it appear that it came from George Bush's vet or Oprah's dry cleaner.

ISP   *See* Internet Service Provider.

K-L

key logger Software or hardware that captures everything typed into a computer. This data is saved for later analysis by a third party.

LAN Local area network. A computer network that spans a relatively small area.

live protection A feature common to antispyware programs that watches for spyware infections in real time at a series of entry points on a computer. Different programs may call this feature by other names, including *real-time protection* or *immunization*.

M-N

MAC address Media Access Control address. A unique identifier given to each network device by its manufacturer. The MAC address is a series of codes separated by dashes.

MAC address filtering A router feature that allows only computers with authorized MAC addresses to connect to it wirelessly.

macro language A programming language embedded in a large program, often used to automate tasks.

macro virus A type of virus that is created in a macro language and embedded in a document. Macro viruses are the most common type of computer virus.

malware Malicious software. A generic term for software that has been written for malicious or illicit purposes, including viruses, spyware, and other damaging programming.

memory-resident virus A type of computer virus that sits in a computer's random access memory (RAM).

modem A device that connects a computer to an Internet provider or another computer over conventional telephone lines at low speeds.

motherboard The main circuit board in a computer to which the system's components, including the microprocessor and memory, are attached.

msconfig A hidden utility called, more formally, the System Configuration tool. It is used to manage a variety of settings including which programs are loaded when Windows starts.

multipartite virus A virus that attacks several parts of a computer including programs, files, and boot sectors.

NAT   *See* network address translation.

network address translation (NAT)   A technology that provides a built-in firewall feature on home network routers by hiding internal IP addresses. It is also known as natural address translation.

notification area: See system tray

O-P

open source software   A program made available for free that includes a copy of the lines of programming code that make it work.

operating system   The programming on a computer that provides a platform for all other programs and includes the basic tools to run the computer.

P2P   *See* peer to peer.

passphrase   A sentence or set of words that can be used in lieu of a password. Passphrases are often used in wireless security.

patches   Fixes or security updates issued by software makers.

payload   The part of a virus that does bad things, such as deleting files, deploying spam, or vandalizing data.

payware   Software created by a publisher that is sold commercially.

peer to peer (P2P)   A network composed of individual participants that have equal capabilities and duties.

pharming   An attack on a domain name server (DNS) that poisons it with incorrect information so that web surfers are redirected to sites posing as banking and financial sites that steal their information.

phishing   Email or web pop-ups sent by a crook that attempt to fool an individual into sending her personal and/or financial information.

plug-in   Add-on software that adds features to an existing program.

polymorphic virus   A virus that rewrites its own code to evade detection.

pop-up ad   A type of window that displays an advertisement. A pop-up ad can appear on a computer desktop or during a web-surfing session.

port scanner   Software that looks for holes in a firewall.

potentially unwanted programs (PUPs)   A term coined by security software company McAfee to describe programs, such as spyware, adware, Trojan Horses, and other malware, that can compromise your privacy and that you might not want on your computer.

PUPs   *See* potentially unwanted programs.

Q-R

real-time protection   *See* live protection.

registry   In Windows, a data storehouse of settings for the operating system and installed programs.

root kit   A programming toolkit that is used to mask a virus, spyware, or other piece of malware to prevent it from being discovered by a security program.

router   A junction box with data traffic-cop capabilities that connects computers together so that they can share files, access the Internet, and share printers.

S

salad cream   A tasty British condiment made by Heinz.

script kiddies   Electronic intruders who use freely distributed software designed by others to engage in computer vandalism, break-ins, or electronic theft.

secure web page   A web page that can only be accessed through a secure connection. All personal information entered into a secure web page is encrypted (scrambled) before it is sent across the Internet.

security key   A security code that can lock and unlock encrypted data as it moves between two devices, usually a computer and a home network router. Sometimes just referred to as a key.

security software   A program designed to protect a computer from malicious software.

service pack   A major software update issued by an operating system company like Microsoft, which repairs programming bugs and solves problems with the operating system.

Service Pack 1 (SP1)   The first major update after release of any version of Windows issued by Microsoft. SP1 was released for Vista in March 2008.

Service Pack 2 (SP2)   A major security update issued in the fall of 2004 by Microsoft for Windows XP.

Service Pack 3 (SP3)   A major update issued in May 2008 by Microsoft for Windows XP.

Service Set Identifier (SSID)   A router's name that it broadcasts via a wireless signal that can be viewed by wireless computers or devices.

share name   A name used to identify a printer or folder from another computer over a network.

shareware   Software that is created by a programmer who asks for payment on the honor system.

signature   An electronic thumbprint used by an antispyware or antivirus program to identify a threat.

Simple File Sharing   A Microsoft technology that allows you to share your files and folders with other computers on a local network.

snack   Food that is not part of a meal. Also, a reward for a job well done after following instructions correctly in this book.

snoopware   Software that watches your computer habits on behalf of someone else—usually someone you know such as a parent, employer, or spouse.

social engineering   Using trickery and charm to extract security information such as passwords from an individual.

software   A computer program.

software suite   A number of programs bundled together and sold as a package that do related tasks.

source code   The lines of programming that make up a program.

SP1   *See* Service Pack 1.

SP2   *See* Service Pack 2.

SP3   *See* Service Pack 3.

spam   Unsolicited commercial email or electronic junk mail.

spear phishing   A highly targeted phishing campaign that attempts to defraud a specific organization, company or group. A spear phishing effort could be a request for passwords or other personal or company information appears to come from your employer, a company department or specific executive.

spim   Unsolicited commercial messages that arrive via instant messenger (IM).

spoof   To fool someone electronically. For example, a spoofed email is an electronic mail message that looks like it came from someone who did not send it.

spyware   Software installed on your computer that collects information about you as you use your computer and delivers it to a third party. Spyware is often installed without your knowledge.

SSID   *See* Service Set Identifier.

SSL   Secure Sockets Layer. A data transfer method, developed by Netscape, used to move files across the Internet between two computers using a secure connection. A secure connection provides protection from hackers or snoops by scrambling data as it moves between two points.

Start button   The button in the bottom left corner of the Windows 95, 98, XP and Vista screen. When clicked it summons the Start menu. Also referred to in Windows Vista as Windows button.

Start menu   The list of programs, features, and settings that appears when you click the Start button, or in Windows Vista, the Windows button.

stateful inspection   A process by which a router checks that data arriving has been requested by a computer on its network. This is also known as stateful packet inspection.

stealth mode   A feature that makes a firewall and the computers behind it invisible to the Internet.

subnet   A subnet is a subdivision of a network, just as a neighborhood is subdivision of a town.

subnet mask   A subnet mask breaks down a network address into regions or neighborhoods acting as a filter for a router that is trying to send data. The mask says to ignore all the addresses in the world except the ones in this neighborhood, town, or state.

system tray   A collection of icons for easy access to tools, special Windows functions, and programs already running in memory. It's located on the bottom-right side of the Windows screen. Also called the notification area.

T-U-V

third party   Used to describe companies or entities independent of Microsoft that make programs that can be installed onto a Windows computer, as in third-party software.

tombstone shopping   A type of identity theft in which a thief researches deaths at a public library or by visiting a graveyard and then applies for a birth certificate in a dead person's name.

trialware   Software that is free to use for a set period of time so as to allow a user to try it before purchasing.

Trojan horse   A program posing as a harmless piece of software that can contain malware such as viruses or spyware.

UAC   *See* User Account Control.

UDP   User Datagram Protocol. A method of sending simple messages across a network connection that allows one computer to talk another to exchange information. You'll see it often referenced in a home network router setup.

USB   Universal Serial Bus. A computer port used to attach external devices such as keyboards, mice, joysticks, or digital cameras.

User Account Control (UAC)   A mechanism in Windows Vista that throws an alert and requires human intervention to proceed when an attempt is made to install software or make a system setting change in Windows. It's designed to stop malware from installing automatically or making illicit changes to Windows.

video adapter   A chipset integrated into a computer motherboard that gives it graphics display capabilities.

video card   A circuit board that plugs into a personal computer that gives it graphics display capabilities.

virus   A malicious program that replicates when deployed by a human, usually unknowingly.

virus hoax   An email, usually sent by a well-meaning friend, that contains alerts about a fictitious virus. Virus hoaxes are more of an annoyance than a real threat.

virus signature   A digital snapshot of a virus issued by a software publisher that is used by the publisher's antivirus program to detect a virus.

vishing   A criminal practice of using social engineering and a phone call (via Voice over IP) to access to fool individuals into giving away personal financial information. It is coined by combining the word "voice" and the term "phishing".

Vista   The (beleaguered) version of Windows that was released by Microsoft in January 2007 and succeeds Windows XP.

VPN   Virtual private network. A secure connection used to access a company's servers from home across the public Internet. It can also provide a secure connection between a company and a customer's or satellite office.

vulnerability scanner   A program that checks a computer for known weaknesses such as programming errors or security holes.

W-X-Y-Z

war chalking   The practice of tagging pavement near an open Wi-Fi network to alert others that wireless access is available at that location.

war driving   The practice of probing wireless networks and cataloging them for possible future use by a third party.

web browser   A program used to retrieve and display magazine-like information pages from the World Wide Web.

web server   Computers that contain websites and make them available to computers on a network such as the Internet.

website harvesting   Programs that scan the Web seeking emails for inclusion in lists that are sold to purveyors of spam.

WEP   Wired Equivalent Privacy. One of the most common security features on wireless routers. WEP is a way of scrambling information as it flies through the air between a computer and a router.

white hat   A computer hacker with altruistic motives who breaks into computers to test their security and reveal vulnerabilities to the computer's owner.

Wi-Fi   Wireless Fidelity. A wireless technology that enables a computer to connect to a network using radio waves.

Windows button   What the Start button is called in Windows Vista.

Windows XP   *See* XP.

Windows Vista   *See* Vista.

wireless hackers   People who connect to a wireless network and steal banking access information, identity, or other valuable data on a personal or corporate network.

wireless home network   A number of computers and other devices with wireless capabilities that are connected together so that they can share files, access to the Internet, and printers.

worm   A self-contained computer virus that can sometimes spread across a network without human intervention.

WPA   Wi-Fi Protected Access. A wireless network security measure that is much more secure than WEP, yet is simpler to use.

WPA2   A second generation of WPA that is considered the most secure Wi-Fi security measure available. Occasionally referred to as 802.11i.

XP   Windows XP. The operating system released by Microsoft in 2001.

zombie   A compromised computer, usually infected with malware, that can be remotely controlled across the Internet for nefarious purposes as part of a botnet.

Index

B

C

F

Q - R

V

X - Y - Z